André Béteille was a founder-m....
Sociology of the Delhi School of Economics where he was
Professor of Sociology till 1999. He has held visiting
appointments at Cambridge, the London School of Economics,
Erasmus University, Rotterdam and various other institutions
in Europe and America. He was also a Fellow at the Institute for
Advanced Study, Berlin and a Visiting Fellow at the Institute for
Advanced Study in the Humanities, Edinburgh. He was a
Jawaharlal Nehru Fellow from 1968 to 1970, and received the
Jawaharlal Nehru National Award of the Government of
Madhya Pradesh in 1994. Apart from his newspaper articles, he
has published extensively in scholarly periodicals in India and
abroad. His books include *Caste, Class and Power*, *Studies in
Agrarian Social Structure*, and *Society and Politics in India*. The
book of readings entitled *Social Inequality* edited by him and
published by Penguin Books in 1969 has been used in the
teaching of sociology worldwide.

Professor Béteille is a Corresponding Fellow of the British
Academy and a Senior Life Associate of the National Institute of
Advanced Study.

CHRONICLES OF OUR TIME

André Béteille

PENGUIN BOOKS

Penguin Books India (P) Ltd., 11 Community Centre, Panchsheel Park, New Delhi 110 017, India
Penguin Books Ltd., 27 Wrights Lane, London W8 5TZ, UK
Penguin Putnam Inc., 375 Hudson Street, New York, NY 10014, USA
Penguin Books Australia Ltd., Ringwood, Victoria, Australia
Penguin Books Canada Ltd., 10 Alcorn Avenue, Suite 300, Toronto, Ontario M4V 3B2, Canada
Penguin Books (NZ) Ltd., Cnr Rosedale & Airborne Roads, Albany, Auckland, New Zealand

First published by Penguin Books India 2000

Copyright © André Béteille 2000

10 9 8 7 6 5 4 3 2 1

Typeset in New Baskerville by Digital Technologies and Printing Solutions, New Delhi

Printed at Chaman Enterprises, New Delhi

For
P.N. Dhar
K.N. Raj
and
M.N. Srinivas

who gave shape and form to
the Delhi School of Economics
which in turn shaped countless others
among whom I was one

Contents

Acknowledgements

I am thankful to Dr Gopa Sabharwal for her help and support in the preparation of this book. She was indefatigable in retrieving, listing and cross-checking the material in it. Her practical good sense acted as an antidote to my natural apathy towards everything I have written once it has appeared in print. I also wish to thank Mr K. Balakrishnan and Ms Narayani Ganesh for retrieving two articles published in 1968 of which I had lost all trace.

The publication of this book provides an occasion for acknowledging if not redeeming my long-standing debt to that great lover of books, Mr Sham Lal. It was he who first induced me to write for the *Times of India*, fostering my early efforts with understanding and sympathy. Perhaps he does not know that I had always meant to thank him, but kept my intentions to myself for over a quarter century. I have received unfailing courtesy from successive editors of the *Times of India* among whom I would like to mention in particular the late Mr Girilal Jain and Mr Dileep Padgaonkar.

Introduction

. . . Let them be well used, for they are the abstract and brief chronicles of the time.

Hamlet II.ii.519-20

This collection brings together the articles that I have published in the editorial pages of the *Times of India* since 1968. I was, to begin with, rather diffident about putting together in a book what might be considered in more than one sense as only a set of occasional if not ephemeral pieces. But my misgivings were allayed to some extent when I found that four of these pieces had been included in the splendid collection of editorial page articles published by the *Times of India* on the occasion of its sesquicentennial. The two collections are of course very different, but they have this in common that each provides a record of changing times, the earlier one on a very wide canvas and the present one from the standpoint of one particular person.

Although I have written for newspapers for more than thirty years and have enjoyed doing so, I have been an academic and not a journalist by profession. Most of my writing has been for academic journals in the related disciplines of sociology and social anthropology, and there has been the odd book, published usually by an academic press. Given the length of time over which I have written newspaper articles, my output of such articles has been meagre: the present collection accounts for the bulk of that output, although I have written a few other articles, not reproduced here, for other newspapers such as the *Telegraph* and the *Hindustan Times*.

Leaving aside individual variations in the speed of writing, in my experience the average journalist writes much faster than the average academic. This gives the former some advantage over the latter, but there are advantages too in being able to write with deliberation and at one's own pace. Academics tend to make several drafts before they send what they write for publication, whereas journalists have far less time for revision. Since I did not have to make a living from newspaper writing, I was able to write each of my articles at my own pace which, I have to record here, some editors found unconscionably slow. I believe it is a mistake for someone who has trained himself to write in a particular rhythm to try to alter that rhythm drastically in order to meet a passing need.

Journalists have not only to write quickly, they have also to write briefly. The academic tends to spread himself out, in both time and space. The academic who writes for newspapers has to dispense with the scholarly apparatus of footnotes and of references to obscure though authoritative sources. For me the most exacting constraint in writing each of the articles presented here has been the constraint of space, and it has been an increasingly restrictive one. When I started writing for the *Times of India*, I was allowed 1500 words, which at that time seemed restrictive enough; this was brought down subsequently to 1350 words, then to 1250 words, and now it is barely 1100 words. And editors of newspapers are far more merciless in cutting down excess length than are editors of scholarly periodicals.

Why then have I submitted to these restrictions and struggled to produce the occasional editorial page article year after year for over thirty years? In my case at least, the benefits of newspaper writing have outweighed the tribulations. I believe that the strict requirement of simple and concise expression has forced me to think more clearly about complex matters than I might have done without the limitation of space that the newspaper imposes. Many of the means by which academics keep ambiguities and inconsistencies concealed from the reader are simply not available when one is writing for a newspaper.

Sociologists are notorious for being unwilling or unable to put things in a nutshell; when they do so, the language they use tends to be so arcane and recondite that few are able to understand their meaning. I am not suggesting that everyone who writes for the newspapers, whether professional journalists or professional academics, benefits from the discipline required by newspaper writing. Many in fact evade that discipline by expressing themselves quickly and briefly in a glib and vacuous prose. All I am saying is that I have myself tried hard to benefit from it.

But the main reason why I have persisted in writing for the newspapers is not that it has helped me to acquire and maintain better control over my prose. The more important objective has been to bring a sociological perspective to bear upon some of the major social and political issues of our time. This is both a challenging and a hazardous task. A great deal of academic writing remains confined to scholarly journals read by fellow academics, and that too in a particular branch of scholarship. It is only occasionally that the findings of specialized study and research are made available to a wider public not directly engaged in their production; this inevitably entails some simplification, and the borderline between simplification and distortion is easily transgressed.

Academic work is by its nature specialized work; today, nobody can hope to contribute to scholarship unless he is prepared to devote a large part of his labours to the study of specialized, not to say technical, problems. This leads sooner or later to a tunnel vision from which some relief is essential. Writing for a non-specialist readership provides that relief, and also the opportunity to see one's own work in a wider perspective.

Sociologists, particularly in India, never tire of talking about the social responsibilities of the social scientist. No doubt, the sociologist has a social responsibility that goes beyond what he owes to his career, his profession and his discipline. But there are two points to be made about this. Firstly, he cannot discharge his more general responsibility fruitfully if he neglects his more specific professional responsibility. Secondly, there can be more than one way of defining the social responsibility of the social scientist.

One view is that sociology is a policy science which has the wider obligation of contributing something to social engineering. Here the sociologist is seen as the expert who serves society by placing his technical knowledge at the disposal of planners and policy makers, in short the government. This view had wide currency in the early decades of independence, particularly in the context of rural reconstruction and community development. I was never greatly attracted by it, and my feeling now is that the expert advice given by sociologists to the government is either disregarded or put to uses other than the ones intended.

An alternative to the conception of sociology as social engineering is the conception of it as critical understanding. Here I may be permitted to quote something I had written in an article in *Seminar* magazine shortly after I had started writing for the *Times of India*:

> To engage in the task of critical understanding is not to play the part of the disinterested bystander. By analysing the forms and functions of social institutions, the sociologist can help people to gain a deeper insight into the true nature of the constraints under which they live. He can also help them to understand what choices are open to them and what price has to be paid for every choice they make. (Béteille 1972: 12)

It is through social criticism rather than social engineering that the sociologist contributes to the regeneration of society. Social criticism must be directed against the arbitrary actions of the government, and indeed of every form of established authority. But it cannot stop there, and must be directed equally against the prejudices of the people. Indian intellectuals have found easy targets for their attack in the establishment, but have on the whole dealt lightly with the evils rooted in the age-old customs by which ordinary people willingly regulate their everyday lives. I hope I have been even-handed in my exposure of the corruption of authority and of the passions of the people.

*

The essays in this collection cover a wide range of topics. But they are all written from the standpoint of a sociologist who believes that his discipline has something to contribute to the critical understanding of social institutions, social processes and social change. I have tried as far as possible to avoid being judgemental, presenting in each case what I believe to be judgements of fact on the issues being considered rather than value judgements.

I have grouped the essays into sections primarily for the ease and convenience of the reader. The sections have been thought out retrospectively; they were not in my mind when I set out to write the essays. As such, they do not constitute watertight compartments. The themes and issues discussed in one section often reappear in other sections in other forms. Within each section, the articles tend to arrange themselves chronologically, indicating some changes in the events outside as well as in my own understanding. But the work as a whole does not follow a strict chronological ordering.

The articles in the first two sections deal with ideologies, intellectuals and universities. These three closely-related topics have engaged my attention as a sociologist for more than a quarter century, and I have published longer papers on them in more specialist publications, some of which are to appear together in a forthcoming book (Béteille n.d.). I would like to stress the close interconnections among the articles in the first two sections; for instance, the article 'Feminism in Academia', which appears in the section on 'Universities', might equally well have appeared in the one on 'Ideologies and Intellectuals'.

The articles in Section III deal with the contradiction between the ideal of equality and the practice of inequality, a theme in which I have had a long-standing interest as a sociologist (Béteille 1983, 1987). Some of the articles describe inequalities of one kind or another;

others examine the implications of the legal and political commitment to equality. My own attitude towards the rhetoric of equality, which is widely expressed in public discussions in India, is one of dispassionate scepticism.

The articles in Section IV deal with tribe and caste on the one hand and with religion on the other. Caste and tribe are important features of the structure or morphology of Indian society: this morphology survives to a large extent, despite many changes in the legal, moral and political environment. Religion too continues to be an important feature of social life, and it acts often, though not in any sense inevitably, against the development of a secular legal and political order. Tribe, caste and religion are among the most important bases of the politics of identity in contemporary India.

The articles in Section V, devoted to reservations, discuss a major policy issue, and some of its diverse ramifications. They are connected with the ones on tribe and caste in the preceding section and with those on social justice in the one immediately before it. Reservations has been a contentious issue in Indian public life, particularly since 1990. In the articles in this section I have tried to explain why I do not support a comprehensive system of caste quotas in education and employment, although I am not opposed in principle to affirmative action.

The articles on power and politics comment on a variety of concrete issues ranging from agrarian politics to youth politics. They also take up the issue of empowerment on which I have written at length elsewhere (Béteille n.d.), and ask what implications the programme of empowerment might have for the distribution of authority in institutions. The section on institutions, which comes immediately after, comments on the fragility of modern institutions in contemporary India and seeks to identify some of the reasons behind it.

The concluding section is devoted to tradition and modernity. The modernization of India had a prominent place in the agenda of the governments that assumed office in the early period of independence. In course of time, modernization lost much of its shine in the eyes of a new generation of Indian intellectuals who acquired prominence after 1977. I do not believe that India can afford to dispense with modernization, and I examine some of the threats to it from traditionalist as well as post-modernist attitudes and sentiments between which the discerning reader might find some strange similarities.

REFERENCES

Béteille, André, 1972. 'The Problem', *Seminar*, September 1972: 10-14.

Béteille, André, 1987. *The Idea of Natural Inequality and Other Essays*. Delhi: Oxford University Press, 2nd edn.

Béteille, André, n.d. *Ideologies and Institutions: Some Antinomies of Society*. Delhi: Oxford University Press, forthcoming.

Béteille, André (ed), 1983. *Equality and Inequality: Theory and Practice*. Delhi: Oxford University Press.

I
Intellectuals and Ideologies

Intellectuals and Ideology

S everal of the articles in this section were published around the time when I was writing two long essays, one on ideologies and the other on intellectuals, which were published together as a pamphlet by Oxford University Press. One of the problems with which I was greatly preoccupied at that time was the relationship between sociology, my chosen discipline, and Marxism. Much as I benefited in my teaching and research from the writings of Marx, I felt that Marxism could not be an alternative to sociology and that the latter should resist being encompassed by the former. Nationalism too can have a creative influence on the sociologist, provided again it is not presented as an alternative to sociology or taken as the ultimate measure of its concepts, methods and theories.

All ideologies rest on the presumption of the unity of theory and practice. I am deeply sceptical about that presumption, believing that there is at best a loose and open connection between theory and practice, and I doubt that my objection is met by adding the phrase 'dialectical' to the 'unity of theory and practice'.

Social scientists are not captivated by ideologies to the same extent in every part of the world. In India, they are greatly captivated by ideologies such as Marxism, nationalism and now, feminism. The fascination for ideologies leads to partisanship which is in the end detrimental to the pursuit of knowledge. Partisanship is not the same thing as commitment, and in my judgement the fundamental commitment of the intellectual should be to the pursuit of knowledge, not to one or another political cause, no matter how appealing it may appear to be. Some say that the disinterested pursuit of knowledge is a luxury in a poor and backward country such as ours. I maintain on the other hand that such a pursuit is a necessity in all countries, rich and poor alike, although those engaged in it cannot expect the same kind of financial support in a poor as in a rich country.

Commitment to social causes leads the academic to neglect his craft; this is not inevitable, but it is the general experience, especially in India. The pursuit of knowledge is today a specialized pursuit; it is, to adapt a phrase from Max Weber, a 'slow boring of hard boards'. The commitment to scholarship requires stamina, and the willingness to persevere even when no immediate results are in sight. In my experience, Indian intellectuals show no lack of intelligence; what they lack is stamina. The promotion of social causes or larger political objectives easily becomes a diversion or an alibi for those intellectuals to whom the labours of scholarship appear endless and fruitless.

Intellectual Cultures (I)

Indian intellectuals may boast, if they are so inclined, of being heirs to the most elitist among the ancient intellectual traditions of the world. Learning was for the chosen few, the rest had little or no access to it. While such in fact was the practice in all pre-industrial societies, in what may be called the Brahmanical civilization this was not only the practice but the principle as well. The concentration of learning in particular castes, particular subcastes or even particular lineages and its denial in principle to the 'exterior' communities had certain effects on the content of learning. Virtuosity was promoted above everything else, and an aura of mystery was created even around self-evident truths. Everywhere the pundits try to hide their ignorance behind a show of arrogance, but here they were more successful than elsewhere.

And now we may boast, if we feel so inclined, of being, once again, the largest democracy in the world. But democracy also creates its own responsibilities, particularly in a country where for centuries millions of people have, in a manner of speaking, been kept outside of civil society. No longer is it possible for those above to claim their privileges as a matter of moral right; at the same time, moral and legal rights notwithstanding, those below find that making any real changes in their life chances is a slow and painful process. Where the gap is so large between promise and fulfilment, populism will naturally have a strong appeal.

It would appear that even today the western-educated Indian intellectual remains elitist at heart, although he has learnt to speak with a populist tongue. Elitism and populism have both been influenced, at least in the outward forms they have taken, by the Indian intellectual's exposure to the West, and, indeed, it is clear that in many cases they are two sides of the same coin. But it would be a sad lesson to draw if we were to put the blame for this solely on the West, beguiling ourselves with clichés like 'neo-colonialism', 'academic imperialism' and other such resonant phrases.

Some changes may be seen in the social background from which intellectuals are recruited; but although they now come from a wider social range than was the case in the past, a very large percentage of them in fact belongs to the few communities which traditionally enjoyed a virtual monopoly over intellectual activities. An additional factor is the dependence, direct as well as indirect, on western centres of excellence for the training of intellectuals which acts as a selective process, strongly favouring the few who come from a particular kind of privileged social background. Such people then cultivate—and jealously preserve—a style of functioning which others with a different background and training find unfamiliar and esoteric, and hence difficult to master. Elitism places a disproportionate value on the style rather than the content of intellectual activity, and makes access to privileged circles and familiarity with their exclusive styles rather than intellectual worth the test of success.

But surely the argument against elitism cannot be turned into an argument against the pursuit of excellence or the maintenance of standards. One way of subverting standards is to demand that intellectual activity be judged by its relevance rather than its quality. Intellectual activity is *always* judged by its relevance—in the long run. A well-known economist once said that in the long run we are all dead. But that precisely is the point; something of what intellectuals create should remain, even after they are dead. The preoccupation with the here and now at the cost of the long run damages every aspect of a society's life, but none more seriously than its intellectual life.

The centres for the training of intellectuals are convenient objects of populist pressures for reasons that are not difficult to understand. In a modern society educational institutions play a crucial part as avenues for social mobility by training people for the professions, the bureaucracies, both private and public, and other middle class occupations. It is somehow assumed that educational institutions, particularly at the higher levels, have unlimited capacity for expansion, and hence they ought to expand in order to accommodate every candidate for admission. This is sought to be justified by the argument that to restrict admission would be to deny a basic right to large sections of society and to condemn the under-privileged to a condition of perpetual backwardness. There is something phoney about this kind of argument because populist pressures for the expansion of primary and secondary schools have been weak, whereas those for the expansion of colleges and universities have been very strong. In other words, such populist pressures have their centres not among the consumers of primary and secondary education but among the consumers of higher education—graduates and potential graduates—who, in a society where more than half the people are illiterate, are, after all, already to some extent privileged.

The populist argument comes in very handy for those

who would like to see an expansion in higher education for reasons which have nothing to do with social justice. It keeps parliament satisfied and, at least for a time, it wins the hearts of the young. But the argument often undergoes strange transformations in being put to practice. Some of our costliest centres of learning are also the centres of the most articulate populist sentiments. The extraordinarily high cost of running such institutions is justified by providing generous scholarships and fellowships to the handful of students from the backward classes or the backward areas who are lucky enough to get into them. Everything about such institutions is elitist except the cant which is populist.

A part of the populist cant is the demand that academic institutions such as universities should be run 'democratically'. If this means that the procedures for selecting, training and evaluating people should be governed by impersonal rules without any consideration for caste, creed, community, provenance or sex, there can hardly be any reasonable objection to it. If, on the other hand, it is taken to mean that what is true or false in science and scholarship should be determined by a majority vote, then this can end only in chaos and confusion. Whether the three angles of a triangle make up two right angles or four cannot and should not be decided by the voice of the people, however much we may defer to it in other matters.

The size of an institution has some bearing on how effectively and not just how democratically it can function. Our universities have become inherently expansive, and many of them have grown beyond all reasonable proportion, generally under the pretext of accommodating democratic urges. These democratic urges have had two closely related practical consequences; the rapid increase in the size of faculty and student bodies, and the levelling of standards downwards in the case of both.

The present unhappy state of education in India (and in other developing countries) is due to the rapid expansion of higher education in response to populist pressures. Room can always be created in our universities for people to do their MA if they fail to secure employment after doing their BA. If they fail to secure appropriate employment even after doing their MA—as is increasingly the case now—they can be kept usefully occupied as research students, no matter what their ability or aptitude for research: a democratically minded government can always be milked for funds for creating more research fellowships. One might well ask why literacy has increased so very slowly in comparison with the increase of Ph.D.s in independent India: undoubtedly because those who might benefit from literacy are not democratically organized to press their claims with democratically minded leaders as the graduates and the post-graduates are.

In the meantime standards continue to decline, and those in the universities who would like to pursue academic excellence are rebuked for evading their social responsibilities. There are pressures on them to have the relevance of their work judged by popular opinion on a day-to-day basis. Science and scholarship cannot grow if they are continually beset with pressures of this kind. Advances in science and scholarship, and hence in human society, have been made in the teeth of popular prejudice, not by pandering to it. The majority is not always right in all matters; in matters of science and scholarship it is often wrong.

23 June 1977

Intellectual Cultures (II)

India's intellectual culture has been both tainted and fertilized by its close encounter with the West. The taint is there whether we like it or not, for the historical conditions under which the encounter took place revealed lack of civility on the one side and lack of dignity on the other. Nor is there any way of denying the fertilizing influence of western ideas and institutions on our intellectual life: our institutions of higher learning, our scientific laboratories and our centres of advanced research, the professional journals as well as the popular press, and, indeed, the very nature of debate and discussion in our contemporary life have been shaped by this influence.

Today the influence of the West is most manifest in science and scholarship where English is the language in use. But there is much more here than merely the use of the English language. The pursuit of modern knowledge is carried out through a variety of networks linking scholars and scientists across countries and across continents—networks that keep alive the exchange of ideas through seminars, conferences, professional associations and professional journals. Whether or not the English language is retained, or replaced or supplemented by Indian languages, the closure of these links cannot but have a marked effect on the growth of modern knowledge in India. Since the conditions of modern economic and political life make total closure impossible, what will happen is that selected scientists and scholars will have privileged access to the external world of ideas, and decide in the name of state and society how much access others should have to it.

Direct access to the external world of ideas in a country with massive illiteracy and limited facilities for education has, of course, always been a matter of privilege. Professional networks are manipulated to their own advantage by scientists and scholars of the highest calibre, not only in India but the world over. Such being the case, Indian scientists and scholars, particularly those who are young and without resources, have to pay a high price for remaining within the system. This much is certain and beyond argument. What can be argued, however, is that by choosing isolation from the larger world of ideas, they and the society of which they are a part might have to pay a much higher price in the long run.

It is not as if the impact of western ideas is felt by only those Indian intellectuals who maintain active professional links with the outside world, or even by only those who write in English. Literary writers, i.e. novelists, playwrights, critics, etc. writing in the Indian languages are also concerned about their relationship, as Indian writers, with the literary cultures of the West. Many of the new literary forms with which Indian writers experiment owe their inspiration to similar experiments in the West. Apart from the successful adaptation of forms, there are widespread charges and counter-charges of plagiarization of western works made by writers in the Indian languages against each other. There is no harm in drawing inspiration from others, but it would perhaps be against human nature for people not to feel guilty when they do this more extensively than they are ready to admit.

From their very first close encounter with western civilization, Indian intellectuals have been deeply ambivalent about their own culture. Personally, I think that this should be a source of strength, for in the long run it does not pay for intellectuals to be either too self-assured about their heritage or wholly unconcerned about it. But ambivalence can hardly be creative if it leads on the one hand to a paralysis of the will and, on the other, to intemperate outbursts of anger. If the combination of anger and impotence extends its hold over the minds of more and more intellectuals, it will be this rather than any basic incompatibility between Indian and western structures of thought as such that will present the most formidable obstacle to the growth of intellectual life in India. We will be the losers in the process, not the West, theories of academic imperialism notwithstanding.

Nationalism became an important force in India in the course of the political struggle to free the country from imperial rule. Many of the great leaders of the national movement saw the danger of carrying it to extremes. Jawaharlal Nehru, himself a great writer as well as a great leader, wrote in his *Autobiography*: 'Nationalism is essentially an anti-feeling, and it feeds and fattens on hatred and anger against other national groups, and especially against the foreign rulers of a subject country.' As an intellectual, Nehru was disturbed by the anti-intellectualism inherent in nationalism; he believed that it was a necessary but temporary phase which, he hoped, would be displaced after the attainment of political independence by a broader and more universal outlook.

But nationalism did not disappear after India became

independent. Ironically, it seems to be strengthening its hold over the very intellectuals whom men like Nehru might have trusted to safeguard the country against its evils and excesses after political independence was gained. The most articulate critics of the West are to be found today not among politicians but among western-educated intellectuals themselves. Nehru's criticism of the West was marked by its tone of civility; the criticism of the young western-educated intellectual of today is nothing if it is not harsh and grating. Perhaps the zest and passion behind the contemporary attacks on the western intellectual dominance have their sources in a different kind of experience from that which animated the spirit of criticism in an earlier generation of nationalists.

Paradoxically, it is only since Independence that Indian intellectuals have established close links with their counterparts in the West on a really large scale. Bankimchandra Chattopadhyay, one of the great writers of nineteenth century India, commented on the works of men like John Stuart Mill and Herbert Spencer who were his contemporaries, but he had no personal contact with them. This would be unthinkable today. Any Indian intellectual who makes his mark in no matter what discipline is bound to be personally acquainted with at least a few of the eminent western intellectuals in his own field. This is particularly true of the rapidly expanding tribe of academic intellectuals for whom such personal contact is facilitated by the continuing round of conferences, seminars and workshops.

Among Bankimchandra's contemporaries, or even among Nehru's, there could have been at best a few intellectuals who would have thought of leaving their country in order to make a career in the West. Quite opposite is the case today, at least so far as academic intellectuals are concerned. There are now thousands of them—physicists, chemists, biologists, psychologists, statisticians, economists, political scientists and sociologists—who have jobs in universities and research institutes in Britain and America, and there must be hundreds of thousands who have one eye on the market for such jobs. Alas, not only is this market competitive, but the competition is often brutal.

Many Indian intellectuals carry in some corner of their heart the scars from the injury they suffered at one time or another when they were students or research assistants or junior teachers in some institution in Britain or America. Western academic patrons are no more scrupulously fair to their Indian clients than patrons are to clients anywhere. Patrons often humiliate their clients, wittingly or unwittingly, and sometimes cheat them. To be aware of this and to work out a strategy to deal with it is one thing, but to construct out of this an elaborate mythology of calculated cultural domination, exploitation and oppression is another. Xenophobia may bring short term political advantages but only at the cost of long term intellectual growth.

If we are to have a healthy intellectual culture in the years to come, we must revitalize the values of humanism and universalism which were kept alive in the teeth of imperial rule by men like Nehru, Tagore—and also Gandhi. Above all, we must reintroduce civility into our intellectual debate and discussion. We seem to have a knack for picking up what is worst in western culture, and nothing can be more barbarous than the harsh and grating style which our young intellectuals bring back with them along with their disenchantment with the West. Indian intellectuals must come to terms with their twofold heritage, their own past as well as the wider world outside; they must learn to do this without posing all the time to be the victims of an imperialist conspiracy.

24 June 1977

Intellectual Self-Reliance

In 1970 an acquaintance in Calcutta, known for his antipathies to left-wing parties and intellectuals, said to me about a prominent Communist leader, then underground, 'Don't you know that he is planning secretly to go to the London School of Economics in order to fortify himself ideologically for the struggle against the bourgeoisie?' Even at that time it was evident to me that this was a piece of slander, but the statement contained an important symbolic element. All ideologues in contemporary India, including those who plead most fervently for self-reliance, are hopelessly ensnared in universal formulas discovered outside their country, almost invariably in the West.

The contradiction between the assertion of the dignity of national experience and the appeal of universal formulas runs very deep in every area of our intellectual life. We draw away from western ideas because they make us dependent, but we are drawn back to them because of their scope and amplitude. We write essays denouncing fellow intellectuals for their dependence on western ideas, and fortify our arguments with long quotations from western authorities. Our ambivalence becomes more and more disturbing every day, and with it grows our incapacity to face the truth about our predicament.

The ambivalence goes back to the nationalist movement which created a new type of intelligentsia whose heirs we find around us today. Its best expression we see in the personality of Nehru, who tried to be sincere to himself and was at the same time perplexed by the dilemma in which he was caught. About his return to India after completing his education in Harrow and Cambridge, he wrote: 'But now I returned for good and I am afraid, as I landed at Bombay, I was a bit of a prig with little to commend me.' This feeling, however, was not strong enough to prevent him from sending his only child for education to a school in Switzerland and a college in Oxford. The grandchildren were also sent to England for advanced training after freedom had been won and while a new India was being built.

The contradictions become more glaring as we see the generations which succeeded Nehru. In the twenties and thirties many young people, often from privileged homes, were fired by the ideals of nationalism while still in college. They took a stand against the entire British system, not only in its political but also in its intellectual form. In the extreme case they gave up their studies, for the British-run college was after all their most immediate experience of an alien institution. But some of them, often the most articulate ones, then found their way into a university in England where they completed their studies. No doubt the English in England were more pleasant than the English in India. But there were other advantages besides of an English education; it enlarged once's mind and prepared one better for a career, whether in government or in opposition.

The context and the possibilities changed after Independence, but the structure of our minds did not. Our policy makers and planners were simultaneously engaged in doing two things: publicly arranging for a vast expansion of higher education for people in this country, and privately arranging for their heirs to be educated abroad. I remember listening to a speech by a well-known educationist, pleading that we become completely self-reliant in our education here and now; and learning a week later that he was arranging to send his daughter for higher studies to Cambridge, having sent his son there a few years previously.

Their sons and daughters are back among us, having become in general more implacable than their fathers in their hostility to the implantation of foreign ideas. Since they have had the advantage of an education abroad, they naturally know a great deal about the weaknesses of this kind of education, and its inadequacies in coping with the problems that beset our style of society. These weaknesses and inadequacies have been exposed for a fairly long time. But all this does not prevent the very people who do the exposing from trying all over again to send their cousins for higher studies abroad.

Before Independence at least some of those who participated in the freedom movement found it genuinely difficult to pursue their education in India, and possible to do only in England. British educationists were more illiberal and inefficient in India than they were at home. And certainly, even today the Indian university is more illiberal and inefficient than the British or American university. But if this really is the truth of the matter, why should those who have themselves had the advantage of having their minds enlarged abroad foreclose this advantage against others?

The demand for foreign qualified persons has by no means declined in our national institutions of learning. Here again we witness a peculiar ambivalence, not to say hypocrisy, among those who run these institution. They make heroic claims for parity between the products of their own and foreign institutions, but while making appointments give the same added weightage to a foreign degree that was given when they were themselves appointed. The social networks through which the advantages of a foreign education are perpetuated are complex and powerful, though they are not difficult to detect or expose.

If our own products are still very inferior, then why do we make such fraudulent claims on their behalf in public? If they are just as good, or nearly as good, as the products of foreign institutions, then why do we put such a high premium on a degree from Cambridge or MIT in making our appointments? The nationalist rhetoric no doubt serves to perpetuate the interests of some, but it also creates a dense fog which reduces the chances of applying truly rational criteria in making our appointments.

Young people in our colleges and universities, however idealistic, know that a premium is attached to a degree from a foreign institution. This tends to make them combine a certain amount of cunning with their idealism. In principle and so long as they are in India, they are implacably opposed to the subversive role of foreign intellectual systems. They can give a convincing list of the ways in which western intellectuals continue to dominate our academic scene through their hired underlings in India. All the while, however, the most outspoken and articulate among them use their family and other connections to find an opening for themselves in a university in Britain or the United States. Their elders should no doubt bear the blame for most of this, but one cannot but be struck by the cold-blooded cynicism with which young people put their ideals aside once a really good chance for going abroad comes their way.

The difference between Nehru's generation and the present is that in the past a declaration of nationalist sympathies entailed some genuine risk, whereas today it is perfectly compatible with—indeed a useful aid in—making a good career. When our intellectual leaders send their children for education abroad, they must be reckoning the advantages of this for their career. When they make public declarations of their faith in national institutions, they must also be aware that this is an aid to their career. If there is some idealism in this, it is an idealism that is easy enough to combine with self-interest.

I began by considering the ambivalence in Nehru's mind regarding what we should ourselves create and what we should take from the West in the realm of ideas. In Nehru's case this ambivalence always retained a kind of civilized dignity, for nationalists of his generation could make a vocation out of their ideals. In the case of today's western-educated intelligentsia the position is rather different. They find it increasingly difficult to reconcile the demands of their ideals and their careers in an honest way. As the gap between their private deeds and their public utterances becomes wider, their voices become more strident.

As none saw better than Nehru, nationalism is a dangerous ideology for intellectuals to play with. In India we make a habit, as it were, of turning ideologies into playthings. Indians who have lived abroad for a long time often find it amusing, on returning to India, to pretend to go native all over again. They like to poke fun at others, more superficially exposed to the West and less sophisticated than they, for aping the habits and ways of their foreign patrons. So long as this serves merely to enliven social chit-chat, it remains relatively harmless. But when it is turned into an ideology, it can be picked up and put to unsuspected political uses. For nationalism has many faces, not all of which are equally uplifting.

26 June 1974

Intellectual Commitment

Only the other day the tide was in favour of committed judges, committed administrators, committed journa- lists and, in general, a committed intelligentsia; and many people took to cultivating the art of being committed. Now committed judges and administrators and, it would seem, even committed intellectuals are in somewhat bad odour. Perhaps it is opportune to ask on behalf of those who are easily baffled by the stridency of the demand to become committed how and why all this came about, and what lessons one may draw from it for the future.

The commitment of intellectuals has of course been a subject of continued discussion among intellectuals themselves, although the meaning of commitment has altered over time. Those intellectuals who regard themselves as committed like to argue that being uncommitted amounts to being unaware and ineffective. But of course commitment may be to various things. It is often forgotten by our secular-minded intellectuals that the commitment that was generally at issue until quite recent times was commitment to a church or a sect, and one should not underestimate the demand for this kind of commitment in our society even today.

But, on the surface at least, the party and the association have today displaced the church and the sect as the primary objects of commitment. When a modern intellectual talks about his commitment, one takes it for granted that he means commitment to a political programme and not a religious doctrine. Yet modern man is naïve in his understanding—or lack of understanding—of the overlap between religious and political phenomena. The fact is that there are parties and associations—of the right as well as the left—which demand the same kind of commitment from their adherents that churches and sects did in an earlier age.

Not all committed intellectuals are in fact prepared to commit themselves fully to any particular party. Indeed, the vacillations of politically-committed intellectuals, particularly those in the academic profession, often have peculiar consequences. Such academics feel free to castigate their uncommitted colleagues for sitting on the fence, yet at the same time they are themselves not always prepared to get off the fence and be bound by the discipline of a party.

But if so few intellectuals actually join political parties, why are so many of them attracted by the idea of political commitment? After all, politics too, and not just scholarship, can be a vocation. Only, one must be clear as to which of the two vocations one wishes to choose for oneself, keeping in mind the distinction between them. To put it in the simplest terms, politics as a vocation is concerned with the pursuit of power whereas scholarship is concerned with the pursuit of ideas. There is nothing inherently wrong in the pursuit of power, provided this is done within the rules of the game. What is wrong is the pursuit of power under the cover of some other end, and when academics do this, they discredit the academic profession and undermine academic institutions.

It should not be a matter of surprise that among people who join the academic profession there are those who are animated by a desire to make an impact on the larger world outside. It is common for such people to slip into the belief that the pursuit of power is a more effective, if not more easy, way of changing the world than the pursuit of the daily routine of academic life. One does not need an intellectual to assert that the world may be changed through the pursuit of power; that much should be evident to all. But how can an intellectual be committed if he cannot bring himself to believe that the world can also be changed through the pursuit of ideas?

Whether they like to admit it or not, many members of the academic profession are where they are despite their inclination: they are in universities or colleges because they have missed the bus to the secretariat. They would be much happier enjoying the power and position of the civil servant in one of the numerous branches of government. But in the modern world people do not protest too much against their karma; they learn to get round it by devising various subterfuges. Professors love to talk about their devotion to study and research, but they love even more to accumulate administrative responsibilities. The inbuilt respect for the administrator-as-man-of-action leads to a strange paradox in our academic institutions: there is hardly a university in which a professor pulls as much weight as the registrar, and there are some in which the registrar pulls more weight than the vice-chancellor.

Involvement in university administration, no matter how gratifying in itself, is hardly the same thing as making a significant impact on the outside world. For that one needs to associate oneself with government, if not directly as an administrator and policy-maker, then at least indirectly as an expert or advisor to administrations and policy-makers. The late Professor Nirmal Kumar

Bose used to say that most Indians were inwardly convinced that no significant change could be made in society independently of government initiative, and it must be admitted that intellectuals, in the guise of experts, have contributed more than their fair share to the growth of this conviction.

It should be clear that I am not talking only of the private gains made by individual scholars through their association with government. More basic than that is a certain attitude of mind and a certain scale of values which rates activities and persons in terms of how effective they are believed to be. There is, after all, no lack of well-intentioned intellectuals who would like to contribute their bit of service to government so as to make the world a better place to live in. That the actual effectiveness of the intellectual as expert or advisor in the affairs of government is negligible is another matter altogether. Bureaucracies have their own logic of functioning which sooner or later overtakes the well-intentioned intellectual, no matter how dextrous, and to think otherwise is, in general, to live in a fool's paradise.

Developments during the last few years have made it abundantly clear that radical intellectuals are not especially shy about offering themselves to the establishment in the good cause of serving society. Radical, near-radical and ex-radical intellectuals have all put their shoulders to the wheel, hoping perhaps that they might thus render the establishment a little more radical. But the main point is not whether such an intellectual is reformist or revolutionary in his orientation. The main point is what significance he assigns to the pursuit of power in his understanding of reality. If he is convinced that the world can be changed only through the struggle for power, and that the pursuit of ideas is futile unless it is made subservient to this struggle, then he ceases to be true to his vocation as a scholar.

Most people seem to realize, however vaguely and however belatedly, that intellectuals do not fare very well in the end once they hire themselves to established governments. It is surprising, on the other hand, that so many people should think, despite the evidence, that they might get a better deal from the leaders of revolutionary movements. The revolutionary leader, even more than the head of an established government, is inclined to believe that the world can be changed only through the struggle for power, and in no other way. It is impossible for the intellectual to accept this belief and to retain his self-respect.

The trouble with those who style themselves as committed intellectuals is not that they are committed, but that they are committed to too many things without being serious about their commitment to anything. A life committed to the pursuit of ideas is in many ways an arid life, for such a pursuit rarely yields quick or tangible results. In a world beset with confusion and uncertainty it is perhaps natural to look for some external signs of success; only, it may not be very appropriate to talk about commitment when this becomes the pattern. Perhaps those who would choose the vocation of scholarship need to remind themselves that the goddess of learning is a jealous goddess; she is not easily beguiled by hymns of praise, but demands unwavering dedication.

9 May 1975

Pundits and Propagandists

The vigour and enthusiasm with which our economists have marshalled their energies in order to advise the government—and incidentally to malign each other—has naturally led many to reflect on the place of intellectuals in this society. There is no doubt that among intellectuals the role of the social scientists has been greatly enlarged since Independence, and they have in some ways come to play a pre-eminent part in intellectual debates. Social scientists have, as one would expect, their own professional codes and secrets, so that from the viewpoint of the public there is a large element of mystery in what they do. To the extent that social scientists claim to work in the public interest, it is essential to reduce this element of mystery to the minimum.

I must make it clear that I believe that in a free society the social scientist, like any other citizen, has a right to define for himself his own area of responsibility. After all, not all social scientists need to be advisors to the government or leaders of revolutionary movements. One still has the freedom to opt for a more modest, a less spectacular role in life. But if one chooses a larger role one must oneself be clear about, and be able to make clear to others, the exact nature and basis of the expertise which gives one title to such a role. In a society like ours, where learning has been for millennia the cherished monopoly of a particular caste, and where the majority continue to be illiterate, people are easily baffled if not beguiled by experts with fictitious expertise.

The aim of scientific reasoning is to penetrate the confusion of observation and experience, so as to make them appear in a clearer light. It is true that this aim is not easy to realize, for scientific skills are specialized skills, and what appears simple and clear to those who have them might appear complex and obscure to those who do not. But it is also true that what we might all wish and have a right to understand is sometimes made more and not less obscure by those who we believe have the skills to make it clear. When social scientists themselves contribute to the mystification we expect them to remove, we must ask how this comes about.

As I see it, there are in India today two main sources of mystification which obscure our understanding of what is happening around us. These are technical virtuosity on the one hand, and radical rhetoric on the other. The first kind of abuse is essentially academic; it is a form of punditry of which India has a long and glorious tradition. The second is propagandist; it is essentially utopian if not millenarian in its mood.

Pundits and propagandists will of course be there in every society, but they are not likely to receive the same public esteem everywhere. When things go well in a society such people play their chosen parts, and they are not taken too seriously by the people or given very great powers by the authorities to do either good or harm. All this can alter when things cease to work smoothly, when the economic system appears to be running down or the political system seems to be falling apart. Then the authorities are much more likely to lend their ears to the pundits, and the people to the propagandists.

There has been much discussion in recent years about

planning and policy-making in this country. Poverty, economic stagnation and social inequality are all facts of our everyday experience. These are ills that disturb the conscience of most of us, if not of all. It is only natural that people should seek and offer advice on cures for these ills. Personally, I do not believe that some magical formula will ever be conjured up, whose application will enable us to remove these ills at no cost or at a very small cost. The least that we require in order to face if not to solve the problems that beset our society is a strong and determined political will. No amount of expertise or technical virtuosity can be a substitute for this. Unhappily, when the political will is lacking, many feel inclined to believe that technical virtuosity might perform the miracle.

Our planning exercises have grown more and more complex, and I understand that they are fully intelligible to only a few even among the initiated. More planning models have been generated for India than for the rest of the world—one might say, just as more metaphysical systems were created in this country than anywhere else. Why do they not deliver the goods? What goods do we really expect them to deliver? Nobody has ever seriously claimed that a good plan will by itself solve every problem. But then why do we not discuss more seriously the limitations of technical expertise, even the very best kind of it, in solving practical problems in a society like ours? When a particular exercise fails, all that we do is to blame the particular experts responsible for it. Why do we not try to define a little more clearly, not after but before the exercise, the role itself of the expert?

Let us admit that the practical value of the expertise available in even the most advanced of our social sciences is meagre. We do not know very much about the ways in which our economy works, and we know even less as to how it will respond to unforeseen pressures. Our capacities for anticipating these pressures are severely limited. The empirical basis of even our most common assumptions is vague and undefined. Because of all this we have either general theories which do little justice to the reality, or generalizations from limited experience whose theoretical validity is uncertain.

When expertise fails to deliver the goods, people turn to rhetoric. The rhetorical style of arguing about our present society and its course of future development is becoming increasingly common. What I have in mind is not so much a consistent or coherent ideology as a whole idiom of discourse which tends to permeate the thoughts, and, more particularly, the expressions of large sections of our intelligentsia. All of this is allegedly based on some objective science of society, but the scientific basis of the discourse is almost always obscured by a dense fog of rhetoric. The innocents naturally wonder if there is indeed a scientific basis, but they do not ask the question for fear of being considered timid.

Radical thought has of course been a part of the Indian intellectual scene for several decades. In recent years its appeal has increased greatly among Indians educated abroad and among western-educated Indians in general. Education in the universities of Europe and America gives such people a special sense of assurance about the scientific quality of the diagnoses they make of the ills of their society, and the remedies they recommend. They also have intellectual patrons and masters abroad who naturally commend the efforts of their disciples to change a society which will not change of its own accord.

The command and mastery of these radical intellectuals over concepts such as 'feudal', 'semi-feudal', 'capitalistic' or 'quasi-capitalistic', which they have acquired in the West where these concepts originated, give them a formidable advantage in debate and polemic. If Marx has proved something, and if what he has proved is accepted as a scientific theory in Cambridge or Columbia or Paris, is that not enough to confound the sceptics in India? Since Indian social reality has proved intractable to this kind of analysis, the reality has been largely ignored. After all, if the future triumph of a particular political programme is assured by a scientific theory, why should one bother too much about the details of the past or the present?

The characteristic posture of radical rhetoric is to condemn, denounce and ridicule existing social and economic arrangements, and such measures as may be adopted for their limited improvements in the short run. Its exponents would like to settle first and foremost what is called the question of method. Since they are assured that they themselves have an invincible method which is bound to produce the desired results, if only applied, they are inclined to dismiss others who suggest an alternative approach as either stupid or dishonest, or both. Indeed, in the eyes of such people any intellectual exercise which does not begin and end with a declaration of faith in the method of revolutionary social change is suspect, and those who undertake such an exercise are set aside as defenders of the status quo.

The most impenetrable obstacles against the free and open discussion of public issues are of course erected by those who combine technical virtuosity with radical rhetoric. Their number today is not inconsiderable and it appears to be increasing. Such people thrive on the confusion of the times and no doubt also contribute to it, wittingly or unwittingly.

22 March 1974

Self-hatred of Intellectuals

I was present recently at an academic gathering where a popular social scientist was speaking on a subject of general interest: the contradictions of Indian society. Halfway through his talk, and without much warning, he lurched into an attack on the 'intellectual class'. That class, he said, was a creature of colonial rule, without any organic relation with workers and peasants whose productive labour constituted the real basis of our sustenance. Intellectuals were, in this view, unproductive, parasitical and self-serving. There was nothing new in all this, but it was greatly appreciated by his audience which consisted entirely of intellectuals.

Now, it is all to the good that intellectuals should adopt a critical rather than a complacent attitude to the world in which they live. Nor can they fulfil their role as critics without turning the light of criticism on themselves. Many things have gone wrong in our society in private as well as public life, and intellectuals have perhaps failed to diagnose these problems and suggest remedies. Moreover, through all these failures, they themselves have not fared altogether badly, at least in material terms. So there is ample scope for self-criticism; and indeed there are intellectuals in India who are critical in a sober and constructive way. But today they seem to be outnumbered by those who alternate between being self-consciously virtuous and feeling sorry for themselves.

It is a truism that intellectuals do not perform the same kind of productive labour as peasants and workers, although some of them like to say, no matter what they feel or do, that they are of the working class. Further, intellectuals as a whole succeed in securing for themselves a better standard of life than manual workers in all societies. To be sure, they have their political troubles from time to time, usually instigated by their fellow or rival intellectuals, but in the end they generally manage to land on their feet. The record of East European countries in the last fifty years clearly shows that intellectuals have been victimized most commonly by other intellectuals, acting from a real or simulated sense of moral outrage.

Intellectuals are in every society the products of their history and circumstance, but they also shape these to a greater or lesser extent, as do other classes and strata. Their larger capacity for reflection and articulation gives them a special role in society and makes that role more visible in times of change. But the same capacity also enables them to promote their own interests more effectively, while at the same time it encourages them to offer imaginary solutions to real problems. It thus comes about that many of the disputes among intellectuals are not about real conditions and real tendencies, but about imaginary ones. There is much scope in all this for combining the pursuit of private interests with the propagation of public ideals.

Indians are heir to an intellectual tradition that is both very rich and very ancient; there are only a few parallels to it in human history. But its impressive continuity over time was associated with and partly the result of its highly exclusive character. This tradition was exclusive both in its intellectual style and in the social composition of its characteristic bearers. Perhaps the most remarkable feature of our contemporary life is its response to the dominant intellectual culture of the modern world, which is western. However much Indian intellectuals may castigate themselves, it remains a fact that they have on the whole been more positive and more successful than their counterparts in most other countries in adapting *intellectually* to the challenges of the modern world.

It is far from my intention to suggest that the intellectual adaptation to the modern world is an easy or a painless one, or one whose success is guaranteed, in India or elsewhere. At the very least, it calls not only for new ideas but also for new institutions. Indians have never been short of ideas, but they have failed signally in building and sustaining institutions through which alone their ideas can become socially effective. Despite this, their response to the intellectual challenges of the modern world has been on the whole both positive and successful. So far at least, they have neither surrendered blindly to the allure of western civilization nor, what would be even worse, turned themselves irrevocably against it out of fear of corruption, degeneration and decay.

A general condition of malaise is not unusual among intellectuals. But is there a special intensity to the malaise among intellectuals in India today? At the level of thought and expression, there is the problem of dealing intelligibly with the problems of the modern world. This can turn out to be more difficult than it seems. One of our psychologists has noted that the Indian intellectual tradition refused to dissociate history from myth. An aroma of mythology still pervades the language in which problems such as national unity, social justice and economic planning are discussed by journalists, judges and academics. That language is suited to a timeless and unconstrained world in which the reality principle does not operate and where everything is possible. The world of the modern intellectual is devoid of such enchantment; his task is, to adapt the language of a famous sociologist, 'a slow boring of hard boards'.

The inflated style habitually adopted in the public discussion of social questions leads to much mutual recrimination among Indian intellectuals. A large part of this recrimination is both pointless and harmless, except when it gets entangled in factionalism which is endemic, at least among academics. Although academic factionalism is common throughout the world, it takes a particularly disruptive form in India because of the weak institutional foundation of academic life. This enables powerful individuals to subvert, undermine or even take over institutions in order to promote their own interests and the interests of their clients, euphemistically described as 'like-minded intellectuals'.

Thus the charge made most characteristically by intellectuals against each other is that they are self-serving. Where everybody accuses everybody else of being self-serving, people come to believe that being so must be an inexorable part of their social condition. Even those who are honest and upright in their individual capacity may come to believe that they are self-serving by virtue of their class position. The cloud of rhetoric about elitism, class interest and social revolution has created a pervasive feeling among Indian intellectuals that they are at bottom a self-serving lot. Large numbers of them have been demoralized by their own rhetoric into viewing themselves as an ineffectual elite, tied to narrow class interests, with nothing to contribute to any social revolution.

But Indian intellectuals are not all self-serving, not even those who leave their country in pursuit of their vocation elsewhere. On the other hand, they are animated by a kind of self-hatred that may in the end prove more destructive than being self-serving. It will be difficult to prove that Indian intellectuals are more self-serving today than their predecessors were forty or fifty years ago; but they certainly carry the marks of self-hatred much more prominently than before. Self-hatred is not only an unamiable personality trait, it cannot possibly contribute anything positive to society.

Intellectual anxiety and malaise need not take the form of self-hatred, and can indeed have a creative potential. On the cultural plane, the Indian intellectual stands in an uneasy position between the resources of his traditional culture and the attractions of a modern outlook and orientation that first developed outside his own cultural tradition. He has all the disadvantages of the latecomer who is found wanting by others who started before him, and by whose standards his achievements appear meagre and his endeavour inauthentic. There is naturally a strong temptation to stop along the way and to look for alternatives. But the attempt to turn one's back on the intellectual resources of the modern world cannot but be retrograde, and so far at least, those who have called for its radical rejection have shown little more intellectual authenticity than those who have accepted it passively.

The tension created by the Indian intellectual's peculiar situation between two worlds will continue, and there is nothing to fear from it, unless the process is short-circuited by shutting out either the one world or the other. This tension does not by itself generate the self-hatred of which I have spoken. The real source of it lies elsewhere; it lies in a false definition of the intellectual's social commitment which, moreover, it is impossible for intellectuals in India or anywhere to fulfil. Intellectuals elsewhere have come to the slow and painful realization that neither scarcity, nor inequality, nor class interest can be abolished through a social revolution; such evils can be abolished by the power of ideas only in a world of fantasy and myth. The passage from the world of mythology to that of history is a painful one, but it also offers exciting intellectual challenges. Those challenges cannot be met by alternating between rhetoric and bombast on the one hand, and recrimination and self-hatred on the other.

20 March 1991

Two Faces of Sociology

In the short period since Independence sociology has become a part of our intellectual culture. It is no longer confined within the walls of academic institutions, but has come to provide a language of discourse for increasingly larger sections of people.

Along with its growing importance in India, sociology has also acquired a certain public image. There is a prestige rating of subjects and also an ideological rating. In terms of the second, sociology is widely viewed as a conservative if not a reactionary subject. Many have come to regard it as an alternative to Marxism, a kind of 'bourgeois' alternative which justifies, upholds and strengthens the status quo, if not by conscious design, at least as an unintended consequence. This public image of sociology is often a great discouragement to young people, and a source of vexation to students of sociology who feel, perhaps rightly, that they ought to be against the established order.

Is sociology a conservative discipline? I find it impossible to answer this question in the abstract for, like any other intellectual discipline, it may perform a conservative function in one society and a radical function in another. Western-educated intellectuals often derive their criteria of evaluation from outside, and when they find that Indian sociologists are not analysing their society in the terms employed by western sociologists for analysing theirs, they are prone to feel that sociology in this country is a rather backward subject.

The study of caste has been regarded as the hallmark of sociology and also of the conservative approach to the understanding of Indian society. I myself feel that the study of caste has been somewhat overdone by sociologists in India. But if on the other hand we find that 'committed intellectuals' use the ties of community and kinship in the pursuit of career as much as anybody else, and if sociologists can devise a method for systematically exposing this kind of thing, then I do not feel that they will be doing a very bad job.

One can take many examples where sociologists differ in their orientation and approach from those who classify themselves as radical or progressive. But it is extremely difficult to clearly identify the role of sociology in a country like India. For, in this country, people may freely express completely opposed views—in temperate or intemperate language—on virtually any subject. And this they may do from almost any position in society. Thus, one might be a senior government official and, on the side, write vitriolic articles on the public bureaucracy; one might earn a comfortable living by training business managers and make fanatical attacks on capitalism and private property; one might make quarterly trips to Europe and America and violently oppose the principle of allowing our intellectuals to be influenced by foreign ideas. This is a tolerant society, and it is particularly tolerant of intellectual confusion.

If we are to determine whether sociology is truly a conservative discipline, we must turn to a different kind of society. I think the best historical example of this kind of society is the Soviet Union under Stalin. Sociology made a promising start in Russia and the Russian

Sociological Society was established in 1916 with Pitrim Sorokin as its secretary. But it came under a ban in 1922 and remained covered in darkness for more than thirty years. It was reinstated only after Stalin's death. It is well known that throughout the Stalinist regime sociology was condemned in the Soviet Union as a bourgeois subject—decadent, immoral and subversive.

The Soviet Union became economically strong and politically one of the great powers under Stalin. I am not going to argue that the suppression of sociology hampered the material advance of the Soviet Union; in fact I am prepared to consider the argument that it helped it, although, so far as I know, no such argument has been advanced in a systematic way. The important point in the context of my argument is that sociology was suppressed when Soviet society became closed and rigid, and began to be reinstated when it became more flexible and tolerant.

What we learn from the history of a whole society is sometimes confirmed by the biography of a single individual. Stanislav Ossowski was probably the greatest sociologist of Poland, and certainly one of the greatest anywhere. Of all East European countries Poland had the longest continuous tradition of sociology, and Ossowski was the acknowledged leader of the Polish school. In 1952, when Stalinism was at its height in Poland, Ossowski's chair of sociology at the University of Warsaw was 'abolished'. He was reinstated in 1956, in the wake of the liberalization of Polish society, and almost immediately afterwards published his famous book, *Class Structure in the Social Consciousness*, a work of imagination, daring and courage: by no means the product of a conservative discipline.

Ossowski had warned that the dominance of a single

party in a socialist regime might be just as vicious as the dominance of a single class in a capitalist regime, arguing that 'it is just as much possible to use class interests as a mask for party interests as it is to disguise class interests by means of universal or national slogans in organizations whose ideology is allegedly not class-bound.'

I realize that the hard-core radical intellectuals are not likely to be impressed by these examples from the Soviet Union and Poland which they consider to be three-quarters bourgeois anyway. To meet them on their own ground one would have to talk about China. The great advantage of the Chinese example in a debate of this nature is that because we know so little about Chinese society today, any simpleton can prove to his own satisfaction that it is a paradise on earth. But any sociologist with a scruple for facts will have to note that the great difference between the Soviet Union and China today is that we know so much about the former and so little about the latter.

Yet we do have evidence of the suppression of sociology in China after 1949. A tradition of research was being built up by Chinese scholars at the Yenching-Yunnan station for sociological research in the thirties and forties. Studies were being made and published, in both English and Chinese, on the basis of empirical investigation of a wide variety of subjects including economic organization, family and kinship, and religion and ceremonial. Several of the scholars engaged in these studies went away to live in America in the mid-forties and were, perhaps rightly, forgotten by the new regime when it came to power in 1949. But some remained behind or came back after the Kuomintang regime had been crushed. Among these was Fei

Hsiaotung, the most distinguished member of the group, who had published the first full-length study in English of a Chinese village. Fei was made to repudiate his earlier work, and the whole tradition of village studies of which he was the principal exponent was destroyed.

I do not know the exact circumstances that led to the suppression of sociology in China, but what happened in Pakistan between 1964 and 1965 might throw some light on the subject. During this period the department of sociology at Dacca University came under strong attack from the guardians of the Ayub regime and barely escaped being put out of commission. What is noteworthy is that this was the only department to be picked out for such treatment. In 1964 the department was not allowed to enrol students for the new academic session, and work came to a standstill for practically a whole year. It was eventually the war with India in 1965 that helped to resolve the stalemate.

Why was an attempt made to suppress sociology in East Pakistan? The answer is, because sociology was suspected to be a subversive intellectual pursuit. It was considered subversive on the ground that sociologists were anti-Islamic and they had extra-territorial loyalties. In an Islamic society sociologists must demonstrate their faith in Islam, just as in a Marxist society they must demonstrate their faith in Marxism. In reality the sociologists in Dacca had sought to project secular values in their works.

I think the real question is not whether sociologists face up to the challenge when they find their society in a crisis. They might acquiesce as in Stalin's Russia or they might resist as in Poland or in Bangladesh. But Indian intellectuals—whether of a radical or a conservative persuasion—who live fairly comfortably in a tolerant society—rarely realize what price has to be paid for such resistance.

8 March 1973

The Attack on Marxism

There are indications in the press of a growing hostility to the body of theory and practice that is known as Marxism. Some of this no doubt is only a reaction to the excessive zeal of the official patrons of Marxism, as in West Bengal. But perhaps the current attacks are also an indication of something deeper, i.e. a large and as yet unexplored reservoir of intolerance in India of any serious critique of society. The uncritical enthusiasm for Marxism is not something to feel happy about, but a blind rejection of it will do irreparable damage not only to our critical apparatus but also to the quality of our intellectual life as a whole.

It is essential from my point of view to distinguish between Marxism as a body of thought and the practice of Marxist political parties. This is not easy to do, and indeed there are Marxists who would argue that it is neither possible nor desirable to do so. This very argument can be turned against Marxism by its adversaries who would urge that Marxists use social criticism as an instrument in the struggle for power and suppress critical enquiry as soon as they have achieved success in that struggle. It is true that some varieties of Marxism, perhaps the most successful ones in the present century, have put the pursuit of truth at the service of the pursuit of power; and it is also true that Marxists who have been successful in the struggle for power have rarely shown themselves to be amiable persons. But today the very variety of Marxist theory and practice encourages us to try to preserve what is good in the theory (of which there is much) while discarding what is bad in the practice (of which there is perhaps more).

It might appear that there has been during the last ten or fifteen years a spread of Marxist ideas in intellectual circles in India. But what has spread is in effect a kind of Marxist rhetoric rather than Marxist analysis in any serious sense. Marxism invaded teenage culture in the more privileged academic institutions, and it received a certain amount of official patronage in states where Marxist governments were in power—and sporadically in New Delhi as well. But to me it appears that the vitality of Marxism as a system of ideas has been weakened rather than strengthened by the eagerness of its proponents to find places for themselves in the intellectual establishment.

The intellectual postures of the last thirty years have taken much for granted by way of tolerance in the Indian people. There are two things to which we have till now pointed with pride: non-violence on the one hand and ideological tolerance on the other. We have said to ourselves and to others that, whatever our failings might be as a people, we are always ready to appreciate if not to accommodate divergent points of view, and that we have a particular regard for the sanctity of life. Our claims to being a non-violent people carry little conviction today, and our belief in our own intellectual tolerance may turn out to be equally ill-founded.

There is greater need for clear thinking in India today than there has ever been, and we must draw upon all the available intellectual resources to fill this need. Marxism occupies a central place among the intellectual resources of the modern world, and we can neglect or reject it only at our own cost. Nothing would be more ill-conceived than to try to put a ban on Marxist writings on the ground that Marxist parties have in some places tried to put a ban on the writings of others whose works we also admire.

Marxism has established itself in the modern world as an essential part of its intellectual culture and its sensibility. It has been used and it continues to be used as an instrument in the struggle for power, but it is much more than just that. Marxism has been described as the Latin of the twentieth century, and the only thing that was wrong with Latin in the Middle Ages was the excess of authority it enjoyed from its association with the Pope. It is doubtful that even among Communists today Marxism enjoys the kind of authority it did while Stalin lived. As Marxism has grown in richness and variety, divisions among Marxists have also grown, and today there is less to fear from the tolerance of Marxism than from its suppression.

As an apparatus for the critical analysis of man and society Marxism still remains in many respects unrivalled. The fact that orthodox Marxists have applied this apparatus to only some societies while refusing to apply it to others indicates a failure more of orthodoxy than of Marxism. Indeed the great strength of Marxism as a critical apparatus is that it can help us to penetrate the surface of every type of society, although it is true that Marx himself applied it mainly to the understanding of capitalist society in the nineteenth century. It should not in principle be impossible to separate the method of Marxism from its dogmas, although it is true that orthodox Marxists do their best to resist this separation.

A scientific as against a metaphysical perspective on society requires us to see the disjunction between principle and practice that is a feature of all human societies. Marxism has developed a method for revealing this disjunction, not an infallible or a perfect method, but one that is infinitely more powerful than what is available to the resources of common sense. Marx had argued that the ideas of people, including the intelligentsia, cannot be accepted at face value; they must be related to a structure of interests which does not stand automatically revealed but must be sought beneath the surface of everyday life. This insight is still valid and offers vast possibilities for a clearer understanding of the problems with which we are beset today.

Marxism focuses our attention on the great significance of material conditions for human life, including those aspects of life and thought whose connexion with material conditions is by no means easily apparent. In the West new interpretations of Marxism have emerged which assign increasing importance to what has come to be known as the superstructure; that probably is a necessary corrective and in keeping with the improvements in material life that have come about in the West since Marx's time. But in India, where poverty and scarcity are all-pervasive, it is necessary to keep the material conditions of life closely in sight in every kind of social analysis. One does not have to be a determinist in the sense in which so many Marxists have been; but to ignore the methods developed by them for revealing the great significance of material factors in social life would be to put blinkers on one's eyes.

As a method of social analysis what is distinctive of Marxism is the way in which it brings out the relationship between structure, contradiction and change. Every society has a structure; this structure may not be visible to the naked eye, but its nature is revealed by analysis according to certain methods. Every structure contains certain contradictions; these again may not appear on the surface, but can be shown to exist by means of a deeper analysis. The contradictions inherent in the structure of a society generate changes that are in some sense inescapable. Thus, what Marxism emphasizes is the essential impermanence of the forms of social life, and this is not something that people always find easy to accept.

We are now passing through a phase in which the disorder of social life is reflected in irrational beliefs of every kind: whatever happens there is always some secret conspiracy, a hidden hand or some evil personality behind it. The habit of clearly and rationally considering the social conditions that underlie personal misfortune takes a long time to become established among people. Such a habit, and the intellectual discipline associated with it, has not acquired a secure foothold in our society even among the intelligentsia. Our own intellectual tradition lends itself easily to fatalism: either a fatalistic acceptance of the existing order of things or a fatalistic withdrawal from the concerns of this world. Nothing could be a better corrective to this kind of fatalism than Marxism in its critical and rational form.

It is true that Marxism has not only a critical and rational form, but also a dogmatic and sectarian one. To oppose Marxism for being dogmatic is one thing, and to wish to suppress it for being critical is quite another. Those who seek to oppose Marxism for being dogmatic ought to show concern for preserving what is critical in it. Marxism has become part of the intellectual heritage of modern man, a heritage on which all have a claim, irrespective of nationality and party affiliation. Those who value the spirit of critical enquiry and the scientific approach to the understanding of society will gain nothing by the suppression of Marxism.

13 June 1981

Nationalism as Ideology

Fifty years ago, when India became independent, ideological categories had a pleasing simplicity which they have now largely lost. Reading through the debates in the Constituent Assembly, one is struck by the general enthusiasm for nationalism and the general antipathy towards communalism and imperialism. It is hard to imagine anyone in that august Assembly supporting communalism or opposing nationalism. Today liberal intellectuals have become more sympathetic about what is due to the community and less categorical about what may be claimed for the nation. The idea that all social attachments, large and small, can be easily harmonized carries less conviction than it did before.

As an ideology, nationalism can easily run to excess and acquire a doctrinaire and intransigent form. But doctrinaire nationalism is not the same thing as a sense of attachment to the nation. Many persons carry an attachment or even a loyalty to their nation without being nationalists in the ideological sense of the term.

Who then is a nationalist? A nationalist, in the ideological sense, is someone who seeks to subordinate every attachment and every loyalty to attachment and loyalty to the nation, for himself and for all others. Mere attachment to one's nation does not make a person a nationalist, just as mere attachment to his community does not make one a communalist. There is something single-minded about the nationalist as there is about adherents of ideologies in general. Ordinary persons do not adhere to ideologies consistently, but they may be swayed by those who do.

It is a truism that every individual has many attachments—to things, places and persons, and his life is to a greater or lesser extent shaped by these various attachments. On the social plane, there are attachments to groups, classes and categories of many different kinds. These include family, lineage, clan, caste, tribe and other communities of birth such as those based on language and religion. Communities of birth are particularly important in India, but they do not by any means exhaust all the social attachments in and through which the individual fulfils himself in life.

No doubt the nationalist recognizes that the individual has multiple social attachments, but he assigns a pre-eminent moral value to one and only one among them. Ordinarily, he has nothing against attachment to family, kin, community, locality or profession. But he believes that a strong attachment to the nation is a precondition for the healthy development of all other attachments. If any of those other attachments weakens, or appears to weaken, one's attachment to the nation, then it is condemned by the nationalist as unhealthy.

What is distinctive of the nationalist is his belief in a hierarchy, and not just a plurality, of social attachments. This sense of a hierarchy of social attachments can take an extreme form when there is a real or imaginary threat to the social order. It led even the benign and well-meaning Kaka Kalelkar to declare in 1955 that 'nothing should be allowed to stand between the individual at one end and the nation as a whole at the other to the detriment of the freedom of the individual and the solidarity of the nation'. This denial of legitimacy to a plurality of attachments does not go well with the spirit of democracy. It is also at odds with the structure of Indian society with its intricate balance of classes and communities. (I must make it clear that I am speaking here of attachment to the nation which is not the same thing as obligation to the state; the former, unlike the latter, cannot be defined in clear and precise jural terms.)

What does it mean to opt for a plurality rather than a hierarchy of social attachments? Surely, it cannot mean that attachment to the nation should come last instead of coming first. If one grants a creative role to family and community in shaping the moral personality of the individual, how can one deny a similar role to nationality? It would hardly be reasonable to repudiate loyalty to the nation solely on the ground that its demands may take oppressive or coercive forms. Every kind of social attachment, including attachment to family and community, can lead to coercive demands. There must be many Indians who find the nation a more worthy object of their attachment than village, sect or caste.

Nationalism has undoubtedly lost some of its shine among liberal intellectuals in the years since Independence. One can find various reasons for this. Firstly, nation and state are easily confused in men's minds, and in the last fifty years the state has shown itself to be both impotent and oppressive. It has been callous and even brutal in its treatment of disadvantaged classes and communities. These failures of the nation-state have led many well-meaning persons to shift their sympathies from the nation as a whole to the communities which are its component parts.

The politics of caste and community, which was viewed

with extreme disfavour in the wake of Independence, has been given a new lease of life in the name of social justice. As liberal intellectuals turn their sympathies away from the nation as a whole, the places vacated by them are filled by nationalists who are less humane, less compassionate and more intransigent than those of fifty years ago. Thoughtless attacks on the nation-state by the self-consciously virtuous make matters worse and not better. The nation-state may not be as dispensable as some of our well-travelled intellectuals seem to believe.

The ideological climate has altered in the world's major metropolitan centres where the nation-state is now rumoured to be on its way out. Liberal political opinion in the West seems to be concerned less with the fate of the nation in Asia and Africa than with minority rights and human rights. Indian intellectuals who move in and out of the metropolitan centres can be easily put out of countenance if they try to speak up for the nation as against the exploited, the oppressed and the unempowered whose numbers are legion in their own country. But the rumours of the impending obsolescence of the nation-state are grossly exaggerated and have to be taken with more than a pinch of salt. So far as the advanced countries of the West are concerned, national sentiment is strong and healthy, and will outlive changes in intellectual fashions.

1 September 1999

A Tribute to Edward Shils

The death of Edward Shils on 23 January 1995 at the age of eighty-four marks the end of an era in the development of sociology. He contributed immensely to the development of the discipline, through his collaborative work with Talcott Parsons; by translating and editing the works of the great European sociologists, notably Max Weber and Karl Mannheim; and through his voluminous independent publications. His intellectual influence extended to many areas beyond academic sociology. He had a restless, active, even aggressive intelligence, and he continued to write and speak tirelessly till almost the very end. He was a regular visitor to India in the fifties and sixties and contributed to the work of the Education Commission of 1964-66 chaired by the late Professor D.S. Kothari. He had a special attachment to the journal *Minerva*, devoted to science, learning and policy, and his last letter to me of 4 August 1994 was to ask for support in its continued publication.

When I first met Edward Shils in 1959, I was a very new entrant to the profession in which he already had a great reputation. This was at a conference in India where I believe he annoyed some of the senior scholars with his overbearing ways but instantly attracted the younger participants to himself. For my part, I was overwhelmed by his sharp intelligence and his sheer intellectual energy. Being very young, I naturally wanted to make a good impression. I asked him whether he had read a certain book, recently published. He quickly said 'No', and went on with what he was saying. I waited for a pause, and asked the same question about another book. Again he said 'No', and a little more curtly. When I asked him the third time, he stopped in his track, held me by the arm and said, 'Look here, young man, nowadays I don't read books, I write them.' I have on occasion used that line with eager young scholars.

The remark about not reading books was meant to silence me and, naturally, I was not taken in by it. Shils read voraciously, and not merely in sociology or social theory but in a very wide range of fields. He also had an enormous capacity to carry what he read in his memory. One could always rely on him in a seminar or a discussion to supply a fund of useful and detailed bibliographical references. Legend has it that the pupils of Marcel Mauss, the great French ethnologist, used to say 'Mauss sait tout' (Mauss knows everything). Edward Shils was the only sociologist of my acquaintance about whom I could say something similar.

Shils wrote on the grand themes of sociology: status, power, intellectuals, ideologies, institutions and tradition. He was caught between his great admiration of the civilization of Europe and his deep attachment to America where he grew up and lived most of his life. For many years he alternated between the Committee on Social Thought in the University of Chicago and Peterhouse at Cambridge. He reflected on the nature and significance of public institutions in America, particularly the institutions of science and scholarship, and brooded over the threats they faced from within and without. But he returned again and again to the traditions of

European thought and culture for illuminating the working of modern institutions.

Although a comparatist in principle, Shils did not write much on non-western civilizations. His work on the Indian intellectual was not very well received by Indian social scientists, some of whom felt slighted by his observations. But I believe that he had a deeper sense than most sociologists of the agony of the Indian intellectual torn between the attachment to a great cultural tradition and the need to make a home in the modern world. He was fascinated by the vitality of Indian intellectual life, particularly in Calcutta where he seems to have made friends easily. But, with some exceptions, he did not find the writings of Indian social scientists very profound and was attracted more by poets such as Sudhindranath Datta and, of course, Nirad C. Chaudhuri, whom he pressed continually to write a sequel to his great *Autobiography*.

Shils's own approach to sociology was humanistic and literary rather than scientific. He appreciated the need for making the discipline systematic and rigorous through the use of carefully collected or selected empirical material, but did not himself undertake the kind of survey research with which American sociology is often identified. He was inclined to be a little disdainful of much of what passed for 'research methodology' in American sociology, but he did not approve of the kind of intemperate attacks made on it by C. Wright Mills and others.

In his writing, Shils paid great attention to style. Although he was immensely learned, he did not clutter his writing with bibliographical references and other external markers of learning. He ruffled many feathers by his brutal treatment of shoddy writing. I was once warned by a distinguished sociologist of science in Germany not to send a paper to *Minerva* on the ground that the editor, Edward Shils, habitually rewrote the papers submitted to it for publication. In the event I did send the paper and was not a little surprised by his gentle and sensitive treatment of it. On a later occasion, while persuading me to revise a Note for publication in *Minerva*, he wrote, 'Unlike your British and especially your American fellow-participants in the symposium, your contribution is written in English and not in academic slang'. He hated academic slang but, alas, had little success in eliminating it from sociology.

Even more than academic slang, Shils hated political correctness, especially when it was used as an alibi for shoddy scholarship. He stood firmly for liberal values and was not intimidated by the prospect of being labelled a conservative. He earned the gratitude of many Americans by his bold and moving attack on McCarthyism in *The Torment of Secrecy*, published in 1956. There he showed how extremisms of the left and the right feed on each other and undermine the dignity of civil society and its institutions. 'Political genius,' he wrote, 'consists in seeing the moment when heroism and the quest for perfection are called for; political madness consists in demanding them at all times.'

Shils agonized over the role of intellectuals and the institutions of science and scholarship. He had a lifelong interest in universities and chose 'The Universities and Government in the United States' as the subject of his Jefferson lectures in 1979. There he pleaded strongly for respect for the autonomy of the universities within their own sphere of competence, choosing as his text the words of the Gospel, 'Render therefore unto Caesar the things which are Caesar's; and unto God the things that are

God's'. The plea to the government not to encroach thoughtlessly into the sphere appropriate to the universities was matched by the warning to the universities not to seek recklessly to enlarge that sphere.

For those who entered the profession of sociology in the fifties and sixties, the names of Parsons and Shils were often paired together. Among academic sociologists, Parsons enjoyed the greater reputation, and perhaps deservedly so. But Shils had one advantage, apart from his luminous prose, over Parsons. He had a better sense of the historical character of civilizations and a stronger impulse to speak in the cause of institutions. If I have in recent years written and spoken repeatedly about institutions, part of the inspiration for it comes from my long association with Edward Shils.

21 February 1995

Universities

As indicated earlier, the essays in this section are closely linked with the ones in the preceding section. When I began my career in the Delhi School of Economics in 1959, the university was the pre-eminent site of intellectual activity in India as in most countries in the world. This was not always the case, and a great deal of highly productive intellectual activity took place outside the universities before the nineteenth century. It is not at all certain that the universities will continue to maintain their pre-eminence in the pursuit of science and scholarship in the twenty-first century.

The first modern universities were set up in India in the middle of the nineteenth century, and there was a great expansion in their number and size after Independence. They have had to struggle with both internal and external problems, and many have now begun to feel that the universities are faced with a deepening crisis. Apart from the question of funding, a major problem in most Indian universities has been that of maintaining some measure of institutional order and stability. Indeed, the problems faced by the Indian university are not very different from those faced by all modern institutions in contemporary India, which are discussed again in Section VII. They appear more acute because universities are among the most open and exposed of all public institutions.

There are many threats to the university as an institution. Some come from external agencies that have no respect for and little understanding of what the university stands for or what it can be reasonably expected to do. But there are equally severe threats from within: from populist academic politicians and from irresponsible, not to say corrupt, academic administrators. A university would be worth very little if it did not enjoy autonomy as an institution: autonomy in the pursuit of knowledge as well as some autonomy in the disposal of funds. Both academic politicians and academic administrators appear much more concerned about the latter than about the former.

Those who look at the universities from within—professors, deans and vice-chancellors—complain about the shortage of funds; those who look at them from outside—the bureaucrats in the ministries and the UGC—complain about the wastage of funds. There is both shortage and wastage of funds, and they are in some sense two sides of the same coin. It is common knowledge that some university professors are supernumerary professors in more than one sense of the term, and in several provincial universities, they are like the absentee landlords under the Permanent Settlement, treating university salaries as a form of rental income. Senior academics not only show a lack of intellectual stamina, but when they become vice-chancellors, they show an even greater lack of political will.

Improving Higher Education (I)

It is now a commonplace that there has been a massive expansion in higher education in India since Independence. A large number of new universities have been set up, and a much larger number of new colleges; old universities and colleges have sometimes become unrecognizable because of the large and rapid increase in the number of students and teachers.

Our colleges and universities have been beset with a number of financial, administrative and other problems. These problems are neither new nor unique to the Indian system of higher education. They derive many of their distinctive features from the massive expansion of the system over a relatively short span of time. Leaving aside the other problems, there has been much concern in recent years over the quality of education made available by our colleges and universities. It does not require much skill or enterprise to show that the quality of our higher education—at both undergraduate and postgraduate levels—leaves a great deal to be desired.

The quality of college education depends on many factors, but of central importance is the qualification of the teachers who impart it. It is obvious that many of our colleges are staffed by ill-qualified teachers, many of them recruited willy-nilly, at least partly as a result of the sudden expansion of college education.

It is in this context quite understandable that

educational policy makers in general and the University Grants Commission in particular should try to devise measures for improving the quality of university and college teachers. The unfortunate thing is that the academic community itself should have treated the matter with complaisance for so long, leaving it to the UGC to demand better qualified teachers to match the higher scales of pay it is now prepared to offer.

But what is to be done in order to improve the quality of university and college teachers? The problem is by no means as simple as it might appear on first sight. One solution which is bound to recommend itself to many, given our love for degrees, is to require a person to have a third degree in addition to the two he has needed until now to become a college teacher.

From a certain point of view one can easily understand the anxiety that a plain MA degree may not be enough to qualify a person to be a college or university teacher. Perhaps some added qualification is needed to fit oneself for the role. After all, it is now widely accepted that a mere BA—or even a mere MA—is not enough to qualify a person to be a high school teacher. One needs additional training, leading to a BT or a BEd. to qualify for the role. If one needs some kind of additional qualification to be a high school teacher, surely a case may be made for the same for the college teacher.

What kind of additional qualification, beyond the necessary first two degrees, should one require for college and university teachers? The agreement seems to be quite general that the additional qualification should be a research degree. The research degree so far considered as a desirable qualification for teachers at the post-graduate level has been the Ph.D. Opinion within the UGC appeared to favour the Ph.D. as a condition of eligibility for the new scales of pay.

Despite the formal distinction maintained between central and other universities, it is a generally accepted principle that there should not be too much disparity between teachers in different universities, either in their scales of pay or in their qualifications. Now it is not going to be easy to ensure that college and university teachers throughout the country get Ph.D. degrees within a limited period of time. Even if we consider only the college teachers in a single, relatively well-endowed university, like the University of Delhi, the problem still appears to be a large one. Some sections of the academic community are understandably anxious that the universities might fail to maintain the standards of their Ph.D. degrees if they are suddenly confronted with a problem on such a large scale. As it is, the academic community and the public at large are worried about the falling standards of the BA and MA degrees. Those who are responsible for post-graduate teaching know all too well that it is vastly more difficult to maintain standards at the Ph.D. level than at the BA and MA levels.

It is not easy to predict the proportions of college and university teachers who will have Ph.D. degrees at the end of the next five-year or the next ten-year period. The proportions are not likely to rise very sharply if existing standards are to be maintained, and, naturally, there will be variations between colleges and universities, and also between the different disciplines. But if one cannot make provisions for a Ph.D. degree for all, on even for all new recruits, one can think of some other degree which, like the Ph.D., could also be a research degree. Here perhaps lies the significance of the recent emphasis placed by the UGC on the MPhil. degree.

rThe idea of the MPhil. is a relatively new one in the

context of the Indian university system and, although a few universities have already started MPhil. programmes, we do not as yet have a very clear picture of its actual working. On the face of it, it offers a number of obvious advantages. Firstly, a time limit can be set for it as in the case of the BA or MA, and unlike as in the Ph.D. which tends to drag on for an indefinite period. Secondly, course work can be introduced, so that both training and evaluation become more standardized than in the Ph.D. as at present.

From this point of view the MPhil. may be seen as a stage preparatory to the Ph.D., or as a terminal degree. So far the Ph.D. has generally not involved any course work, requiring from the candidate only a dissertation, guided by an individual supervisor. The idea behind the MPhil. is to get the research student to do a certain amount of course work, so that, whether he goes on to do the Ph.D. degree or not, he will have done something more than merely writing a dissertation. If the MPhil. is to be normally of one year's duration, and if the candidate has to spend a part of this time in course work, then obviously the time he will have for writing his dissertation will be short, and the dissertation will consequently be limited in scope.

It is not fully clear as yet what the relationship will be at the MPhil. level between course work and dissertation. At least as far as the social sciences are concerned, the course work is likely to revolve around what has come to be broadly described as Research Methodology. Courses in Research Methodology undoubtedly serve a useful purpose, but this purpose is largely lost unless they are closely linked with the actual work of research. To take one example: in most such courses in the social sciences much emphasis is placed on training students in the techniques of survey research. Now, if the student is required to do a short dissertation for the MPhil. based on the analysis of secondary materials, and if he does not go on to do a Ph.D., this training will have served only a very limited purpose.

This raises a much more general question: is a training in research in general and Research Methodology in particular the best way of ensuring that teachers become better qualified for teaching undergraduate students, most of whom will be preparing for pass degrees? Or do we need a somewhat different kind of training, at an advanced level, to enable college teachers, dealing mainly with undergraduate students, to do their work more efficiently?

A training in research, including Research Methodology, may be better than no training at all. But surely, this is the time to think of the best kind of training for improving the quality and performance of our college teachers. Research leads to specialization which all too often means narrow specialization. Much more important in the making of a good teacher at the undergraduate level is a command of the general principles of a subject and familiarity with a wide range of topics within it. It is not clear that the purpose of training such people is best served by organizing their training within the constraints of a research degree.

15 July 1976

Improving Higher Education (II)

The emphasis on research in our higher education is likely to continue whether or not our university and college teachers are all required to have Ph.D. degrees in the short or long run. No system of higher education can survive, far less advance, without proper attention to research. Further, one cannot do research merely by inspiration, one has to learn how to do it; and one cannot learn it all by oneself, initially at least—one has to be taught.

There is a presumption of creativity in research. The research worker is expected to present not only new data, but also now interpretations; he is expected to make some addition, however limited, to the existing body of knowledge. Thus, it will be seen that the problem of training people to do research is in some significant ways different from the problem of teaching students at other levels. This, of course, is not to deny that every discipline has accumulated a body of standardized methods and techniques which the research student can be taught, whether or not he then succeeds in applying them creatively to his chosen problem of investigation.

In the past the training of research students in university departments had something of the character of the training of medieval craftsmen. Each professor took on a few research students who learnt their craft as best they could through personal association. The learning process was informal, and much depended on temperament, character and ability—in short, on the personal equation between the supervisor and his research student. This in fact is how research is still done at the Ph.D. level in most university departments in India.

The defects of the system as described above are obvious. It leaves too many things to personal inclinations, particularly those of the research supervisor. The exposure of research students to their supervisor varies enormously; some have close and frequent contacts, others few and limited. There is much wastage in this kind of system, and the dropout rate is generally very high. At the same time, those who survive are likely to acquire much valuable experience by slowly coming to grips with an intellectual problem, either largely on their own or under close supervision. The successful student is judged by his dissertation which embodies the results of his work, spread over a period of three to five years, and sometimes more.

There are two ways in which some amount of standardization in training may be introduced for research students. A variable amount of course work may be made an integral part of the Ph.D. programme itself, as has indeed been the case in American universities for some time. Alternatively, a new degree, such as the MPhil., may be instituted between the MA and the Ph.D. levels to take care of such training in the methods of research as may be considered essential or desirable. The first alternative will have the advantage of flexibility, the second will probably ensure tangible, though limited results for larger numbers.

Part of the anxiety over the MPhil. may reflect nothing more than a fear of the unknown. But leaving this aside, there are still a few points to ponder on. The two most obvious among these relate to the amount and nature of course work which is to be made compulsory at this level. There will naturally be much variation in both as between different subjects, and my observations will be confined to the social sciences.

It is difficult to visualize exactly the shape that the MPhil. programme will take, but those who are admitted to it will have come after taking an MA degree, in the large majority of cases in the same subject. The MA in Indian universities, unlike in many universities abroad, is a taught degree, based entirely on courses administered through classroom lectures. Thus, a person who registers for an MPhil. in Economics or Political Science or Sociology will have spent two years previously, taking a large number of courses in that subject, and usually only in that subject. Not only that, he will have spent another three years before that in taking lecture courses in the same subject at the Honours level.

It may not be altogether fair to blame students if they feel somewhat exhausted by the course work involved in attending classroom lectures for five successive years in one and the same subject. Those who are at all serious about their academic intentions usually want to get started on a different kind of work, whether or not they are fully equipped to take off on their own. If we are to sustain the interest of the serious-minded students through their first phase of research, something more than the usual stereotyped lecture courses will have to be thought of for them; here lies the advantage of flexibility in designing a programme for training research students.

Courses at the MPhil. level cannot be too general. The real problem will lie in relating these courses to the specific topics of research which naturally will vary from one student to another. At the MA level itself there is a certain amount of specialization. This specialization should enable the prospective research student to choose the broad area in which he will work, if not the specific topic, by the time he completes his MA. If such a student is to benefit from course work after registering for research, he must be able to choose from among a fairly wide range of courses which have to be not only advanced but also specialized.

The only courses which at this level can meet the requirements of all students alike will be courses in Research Methodology. Such courses have acquired a certain vogue in the social sciences, although they appear to be more popular in some disciplines than in others. In some cases, as in Sociology, it is already an established practice to have at least one course in Research Methodology at the MA level itself. It may be noted that at this level courses in Research Methodology have become rather more popular in relatively new disciplines like Sociology than in more established ones like Economics, and the natural sciences seem to have managed without them.

Where courses in Research Methodology already exist at the MA level, care will have to be taken to ensure against repeating the same course material for MPhil. students. The natural tendency will be to teach Research Methodology at a more advanced level here. But the danger of being too far · advanced in Research Methodology is that the student may lack the resources to make use of his training in his own individual research. The social sciences have for some time been burdened with people trained in the most advanced methods and techniques of research, but frustrated by their inability to put their training to use for lack of resources.

The training of research students is not an easy job. In

the past training suffered from a lack of uniform procedures. In the changed context of today the most important thing is to ensure that it does not become top-heavy. However successfully the student clears his courses in Research Methodology, his ability as a research worker must in the end be judged by his success in applying this training to his chosen subject of research, or, in short, by the quality of his research dissertation.

One comes across a not uncommon feeling among prospective research students in the social sciences: that there must exist somewhere some super-quality course in Research Methodology, whose mastery will at once illuminate all the dark corners into which the research worker has to look for the day-to-day solution of his problems. Research students have to be told that no such course exists or can exist. Research is, in an important sense, a plunge into the unknown. Too much emphasis on course work, particularly in Research Methodology, can easily make the student shy of taking this plunge, and lead to the proliferation of dull, routine and stereotyped dissertations.

16 July 1976

Supernumeraries All!

About fifteen years ago I lived for some time in a village in Tamil Nadu. Being a university teacher from Delhi, I enjoyed a certain position there, since most of the villagers were either peasants or petty landowners with little formal education. However, there was one fairly well-to-do pleader from a nearby town who came regularly to visit his in-laws in the village, and he never tired of trying to put me in my place. He would point to his wife's brother, who had no particular occupation, and say that the boy's father had wanted him to be a teacher since, being a sensible man, he had realized that the boy would not be much good for anything else in life. He would then go on to tell a story about Jawaharlal Nehru. According to his story, after Jawaharlal had returned from England, Motilal, who was worried about a future for his only son, once consulted Mahatma Gandhi who then said, 'Well, if the young man does not seem to be much good at anything, why not settle him in a job as a teacher?'

I doubt if the story about Motilal and the Mahatma is true, but the sentiment expressed by my antagonist, the pleader, is, undoubtedly, very widely shared. 'If you can, do; if you can't, teach.' The irony is that the sentiment is not uncommon among teachers themselves, even though they may fail or refuse to recognize it as a part of their mental make-up. The contrastive evaluations which many professors make of their employment by the government and by the university brings this out fairly well. Many would appear to think that when they work in a university they serve a small purpose, but when they work in the government, they serve the nation.

All professors, at least in Delhi, are presumed to be scholars of eminence, but there are different kinds of professors. Recently a new category has been added, for which the term 'Supernumerary Professor' has been found. The circumstances under which this new category came into being are not very clear, but presumably its creation had the blessings not only of a government armed with emergency powers but also of independent-minded university bodies. Not that academic opinion is unanimous on the advantages of having this new category of professors. Of the two universities in Delhi, one agreed to have Supernumerary Professors, the other, presumably, did not.

What kind of personage is the Supernumerary Professor? The word 'supernumerary', unlike the words 'distinguished', 'emeritus' or even 'honorary', has a disagreeable sound. It signifies something extra, something over and above what is necessary, hence, something not really necessary. Now, why should sober, hard-working scholars wish to have such a label attached to them? An additional sense of 'supernumerary', given by Chambers, is of 'one who appears on the stage without a speaking part'. Ordinary professors must surely ask whether their supernumerary colleagues really mean to appear on the campus 'without a speaking part'. What kind of part, then, has been created for them and by whom?

In a civilized society every person should be free to decide what kind of career he wishes to pursue, and every professor to decide at any point in his career whether he wishes to serve in a university or in the government. Now, it is important to keep the distinction between the two kinds of institutions clear, for when it is obscured, this is almost always at the cost of the university, not of the government.

There is of course no reason why a person, once he has been appointed a professor in a university, should be required to remain in that position for the rest of his life. He might wish to vacate his position in the university in order to take up a position in government or in industry, or even to become a full-time journalist. Conversely, people from these other walks of life might occasionally be attracted to take up a teaching position in a university. It would be absurd to object in principle to all interchange of personnel between the universities and the government. But the terms of such interchange must be fair; they should not violate the interest or the dignity of any of the institutions involved in the interchange. Institutions, like individuals, need to protect not just their interest but also their dignity; otherwise they cannot prosper.

A professor might wish to work outside his university for a short or a long period of time. In the former case he would naturally not like to sever his links with his university for all time. Universities ought to be liberal in such matters, but no university can function properly if it allows its professors to come and go according to their will and pleasure, or even according to the interests of some agency external to the university. Now, if it cannot do so in all cases, should it do so in some cases, favouring a few select persons? This perhaps is one of the main points at issue in the distinction recently instituted between professors in general and Supernumerary

Professors.

In recent years professors have involved themselves increasingly in the activities of the government. There are now divisions, commissions, committees and bodies of various kinds in which many of them would like to find a place and to keep it as long as they can. Such involvement brings them honours of a certain kind, but it cannot be denied that it leads to some neglect of their duties to their students. The problem arises because even when they are wholly immersed in extra-academic activities outside the university, they are reluctant to vacate their positions within the university. A professor, according to common usage, has a chair, and who has heard of a person giving up his chair when he can hold on to it?

One then takes a lien on one's position in the university and tries to keep it as long as one can—for a year or two years, but sometimes for as long as three, four or even five years. Now, when a person goes from the university to a really important position in government, he does not generally come back to his old position in the university; even when he does, he rarely settles back into it. He might at the most mark his time in the university for a short while before moving on to another important position outside it. The absentee professor is a well-known figure, particularly in the larger metropolitan universities. It is too early to say as yet, but perhaps the Supernumerary Professor is only the big brother of the absentee professor.

When a professor returns to his chair in the university after extended periods of absence in unrelated spheres of activity, no questions are of course raised about his competence to take up the work which he had left off. But it might well be asked if a person who taught and did research in Elizabethan drama, let us say, or, urban demography, can continue at the old level of competence after an interlude of five or more years spent in the pursuit of wholly different aims. In this age of specialized competence, how does a professor maintain his specialized competence as a teacher and as a research worker?

From the way in which academic policy makers sometimes behave it might appear as if the idea of specialized competence is a myth created by academic people to be used or discarded by them according to the convenience of the moment. This kind of mental climate leads readily to the view that when the government requires the services of professors, they should serve the government, and when their services are no longer required by the government, they can go back to the universities: since the government serves the nation's purpose which is large whereas the university serves its own purpose which is small. It will be a pity if such feelings take root within our universities, for they will merely confirm a common prejudice. The common prejudice is this, that all professors, and not merely a select few, are supernumeraries, more or less.

7 April 1977

The University Today

Academics who had until recently walked in step with the prevailing regime and had rebuked their colleagues for remaining aloof and uncommitted are now clamouring for university autonomy. Let us hope that those who had then stood for autonomy will not now demand from academics a closer involvement with the new regime. For if we plead for involvement when our friends are in power and for autonomy when they are out of power, how can we expect anyone to take the academic profession seriously?

University autonomy is in any case something fragile and precarious. If the coercive apparatus of the state decides to destroy it—as it has done in some countries—there is very little that the academic community by itself can do to save it. But university autonomy may also be eroded from within. What the university community must ask itself is how much of its autonomy it is prepared to barter in return for other advantages of a more tangible kind. In this light the most important question that faces us today—and not just in the universities—is how institutions come to be eroded from within.

University autonomy is a more urgent need for the scholar today than it ever was before, because it is much more difficult now than in earlier times for him to function outside the university or some similar institution. It has often been said that in the eighteenth and nineteenth centuries the best scholars in the West had made their contributions to knowledge not from within the universities but from outside. A scholar, whether in the moral or in the natural sciences, with even moderate private means could do his work on his own quite effectively. The tremendous expansion of specialized knowledge has made this difficult if not impossible in the second half of the twentieth century. One does not know of many physicists, economists or even historians, whether in India or elsewhere, who are doing significant work on their own in isolation from universities and other institutions of higher learning. Therefore, much more is at stake in maintaining university autonomy now than in the past.

Academics, perhaps not wholly unlike other professional people, tend all too often to attribute their misfortunes to the machinations of unscrupulous politicians. The real problem of course is that the two categories of people are not mutually exclusive, and academics themselves often play the very same games which they blame the politicians for playing. Thus it would be less than fair to say that the government always intervenes in university affairs on its own. Sometimes university people themselves invite such intervention.

Why should university people invite government intervention in their affairs? There are several reasons behind this, but one of the more obvious ones is the desire on the part of some of them to build empires for themselves. Needless to say that people who occupy academic positions do not always perform academic functions or pursue academic interests, even when they have high academic qualifications. In India one is familiar with the example of the scholar who begins his career with great promise of academic distinction, and then midway through it finds himself on the path of empire building. Indeed, very few academic people of eminence end their careers as academics; when they do so they tend to be regarded as failures.

What exactly is involved in building an empire in an academic institution? Many things are involved, but over and above everything else is patronage. Patronage is a complex phenomenon, but this much should be evident, that the demands of patronage and those of academic excellence do not coincide. Given the luxuriant growth of patronage within academic institutions, it is astonishing that academic people should think, as so many seem to do, that politics is a game which only those labelled as politicians play.

One cannot build an empire or even dispense patronage in the university on nothing. For this one requires resources which are not all generated within the university. Universities are in any case dependent on external agencies for material resources, but when give and take within the university becomes based on patronage, then patronage begins to govern also the relationship between the external agencies and the university. In other words, the chain of patronage has many links which run up and down, and the more these links ramify, the more precarious does university autonomy become. Clearly, there can be no easy formula to help academics choose between patronage and autonomy, but there is a point beyond which the choice cannot be evaded.

Higher education has expanded enormously in India over the last thirty years. Any reasonable assessment of this expansion will show how readily academics have been prepared to sacrifice the principle of autonomy when the demands of patronage required them to do so. It would be wrong to put all the blame for this on a few prominent architects of academic empires, for patronage is not an isolated act but a system and, as such, it cannot flourish unless many if not most people have a stake in it.

The building of institutions is not an easy task. The task is one of securing their foundations on a firm basis, and not merely of expanding their scale of operation. Many people, both within and outside academic circles, have viewed with alarm the rapid growth of universities during the last three decades. No doubt there have been pressures of various kinds, but the lure of patronage has also been a motive force. University people have on the whole not resisted the temptation to expand, perhaps hoping all the time that the cost to their autonomy and integrity might not be too high.

It would be a mistake to believe that empire builders, whether in the universities or outside, do things only for themselves. They also pursue larger aims, and if this pursuit is so often self-defeating, one must try to find out why. When expansion becomes a major objective in a university, entrepreneurial skills come to be highly prized among academics. The successful academic entrepreneur is the one who can procure large grants for his university, his colleagues and his students. When government is the main source of funds it is easier to manoeuvre for grants by bringing the university or department into alignment with the prevailing plans and policies of the government. One knows all too well the eminent professor who serves on many committees and says that he cannot otherwise get grants for his students and younger colleagues. Grants are of course needed for research, but are they always needed on the scale on which they are sought? A short-sighted government will be inclined to demand quick and tangible results in return for the funds it gives. Academic entrepreneurs are generally ready to promise these results without always realizing what this means for the autonomy and integrity of their institutions.

There is thus a premium placed, both within and outside the universities, on those academics who are willing and able to deliver the goods. But deliver what goods, and to whom? It is here that academics tend to falter, for even among those of them who have the best of intentions there is much confusion and uncertainty about the criteria for assessing their own achievement and worth. Quite understandably, it is only in rare cases that they have the confidence to leave it to the people or to posterity to judge their contribution. For the rest, the choice is between self-assessment, i.e. assessment by the academics community itself, and official recognition, usually in the form of increased patronage, and many seem to set more store by the latter rather than the former.

The lack of faith in self-assessment goes with the feeling that the disinterested pursuit of knowledge may not in itself be a very worthwhile thing, and that one must do something in addition in order to prove oneself worthy. Academics have become shy to assert the view that the pursuit of ideas can be an end in itself. Admittedly this cannot be the only end for all people in any society. But there must be in every healthy society a place where at least some people can make this their predominant end, and if the university cannot be such a place, what else can it be? The plea for university autonomy will not mean very much unless academic people themselves are inwardly convinced that the academic life is in itself a good life.

23 April 1977

Crisis in the Universities

The current strike by teachers in the University of Delhi is leading the university to a crisis from which it is not likely to recover without serious and perhaps permanent damage to the quality of its academic life. As recently as ten or fifteen years ago the university provided an orderly framework for regular and continuous academic work: classes were held, courses were covered and examinations conducted according to schedule. At that time there were other universities, particularly in the eastern region, including the University of Calcutta, the oldest in the country, where academic life was disrupted and threatened with destruction by strikes and agitations on the one side, and vacillation and bad faith on the other. We may now be facing in Delhi the same general dislocation that in the seventies swept through so many universities in West Bengal, Bihar and elsewhere.

The current strike threatens to assume or even surpass the scale of the one that took place in the University of Delhi in 1982-83. It is the material success achieved by the earlier strike that makes the present one appear ominous. A strike by university teachers cannot be judged solely by its material success of failure. Far more important in the long run are its moral and psychological effects. The typical pattern of such strikes is to create an initial state of exhilaration which is then followed almost inevitably by a state of profound demoralization. This is what happened in the universities of Calcutta, Jadavpur and Patna, and this is what in all likelihood will happen in Delhi.

No matter how powerful or militant teachers' union may be, the ordinary university teacher is not an industrial worker and he does not ordinarily see himself as one. He not only cherishes the amenities of middle-class life but has also a middle-class sense of self-esteem. Long periods of absence from work eats into the self-esteem of teachers, no matter what material benefits they may secure by their collective action. The unions have paid too much attention to the amenities of teachers and too little to their self-esteem.

What needs to be stressed is that in the case of university teachers a strike is separated by only a thin line from plain absenteeism. This fact is well appreciated by the unions which often time a strike in such a way that it can be prefixed or suffixed to a vacation, thus extending the latter from, say, a fortnight to months. A strike does not merely disrupt the academic calendar, it encourages absenteeism even after the settlement. When teachers have been absent from work for two or three months at a time on account of a strike, they feel less inhibited about being absent for a day or a week even when there is no strike.

The everyday work of a college or university teacher is such that it does not lend itself easily to policing or surveillance as in the case of many other kinds of work. Any attempt to impose on university teachers work schedules appropriate to a factory or an office is bound to be counter-productive. If they are to be effective in what they do, they must have far more control over their own rhythm of activities than office or factory workers can be allowed to have. The only guarantee of regular and dependable service in their case is the internal censor of each individual teacher. It is this internal censor that is damaged and sometimes destroyed by frequent and prolonged strikes.

Prolonged absenteeism has not as yet taken the same toll on the teachers of Delhi University as it has in some other universities. In the state of Bihar it is not always easy to know when a university is in session and when it is on vacation. Even when the university is in session, the student can never be sure that a particular class will be taken by a particular teacher according to the time table announced. The teacher may be indisposed, or have other business to attend to, or be absent without leave for unknown reasons. It is all a matter of chance whether the courses will be covered, and the best bet for students, therefore, is to ask for the examinations to be postponed. Examinations have sometimes taken place two or three years after they were due.

As I have said, things have not come to this pass in Delhi, but the teachers of Delhi University, including those who are on strike, cannot escape the foreboding that they might. This foreboding cannot do much good to their self-esteem, no matter how secure the guarantee of merit-promotion may be. Teaching and other normal activities slackened down when the colleges reopened after the long strike of 1982-83. They have not yet picked up to the level at which they operated before September 1982. That strike did not seriously disrupt the academic calendar in the sense that teaching and examining were both completed within the academic year, but the system as a whole moved down to a lower gear.

Teachers in the colleges freely admit that, even when there is no strike, classes are not always held according to schedule, and that absenteeism is now widespread and thinly disguised. To be sure, this is not equally true of all colleges, and there are some in which the academic routine is observed in both letter and spirit. But perhaps in the majority of colleges taking classes is becoming increasingly a matter of personal convenience. Not only has the teacher's internal censor weakened but the sanctions of the community have lost their force. The teaching community no longer has the will to voice any complaint against individual teachers who habitually neglect their work.

When some teachers neglect their work with impunity, others feel encouraged to do the same. Absenteeism acquires a chronic form, and spreads easily from teachers to their students. Nobody should labour under the illusion that prolonged and frequent strikes by teachers will leave unaltered the relationship between students and teachers. In the first round of a strike or in the initial phase of teacher absenteeism, students might feel a sense of relief that there will be no classes for some time and that the examinations may be postponed. But this euphoria cannot last for ever. University students have as keen a sense of their material interests as their teachers. Confronted by chronic irregularity in the teaching schedule, they become cynical, surly and disrespectful towards their teachers.

In a free society university teachers may wish to defy the vice-chancellor or the ministry of education, but they cannot escape their responsibility to their students and to the public. The public views a strike by university teachers in a very different light from a strike by industrial workers. The respect traditionally accorded to teachers in this society has few parallels in the world. Teachers have been venerated not only as men of learning but also as men who have sacrificed material well-being in the pursuit of an ideal. Therefore, when they go on strike, the public is at first inclined to believe that their cause must be just.

University teachers have now become unionized and their leaders are able to take a strong stand against the authorities. It is easy for these leaders to feel that they owe their strength to the solid support of organized numbers. But this is an illusion. A hundred teachers may be able to browbeat a college principal or a university vice-chancellor, but university teachers are a mere handful in a very large society. What strength they have in their dealings with the authorities they owe not to their numbers but to the esteem and sympathy of the public.

Public sympathy for university teachers is not an inexhaustible commodity. There are signs that it is already running out. Middle-class parents in a city like Delhi are very career conscious, not only for themselves but also for their children. A prolonged strike by teachers holds the threat of the loss of a year for students, a prospect their parents may view with more anxiety than their teachers. When public sympathy runs out, teachers may find that the government has become cool and indifferent to their demands. Their leaders may continue to shake their fists at the vice-chancellor, but that will not cut much ice outside the university. Those in authority will then feel free to ignore the unions.

21 January 1986

Universities and Government

The relationship between universities and the government is a very important subject which has been discussed with much heat and passion during the last few months. It is natural that such a subject should arouse strong feelings when the relationship is faced with a crisis as it was during the prolonged strike by college and university teachers in August and September 1987. However, the subject is important enough to call for discussion in a dispassionate manner and when the relationship is not under strain. Only in this way can we prepare ourselves, intellectually if not politically, to face the next crisis when it comes.

As I see it, there is no escape from a close financial relationship between universities and the government, at least in the Indian case. Universities are not financially self-sufficient and they have to depend for funds on the government, which brings the two into a close relationship. They may of course seek funds from private industry or business or from religious organizations, in which case they will exchange one kind of dependence for another. There are private universities in other countries and in the past European universities, including the best ones, have been tightly controlled by the church. However much university teachers might chafe at the control exercised over them by the government, it is doubtful if many of them would like, as an alternative, to be controlled by either captains of industry or heads of religious bodies.

It is too late in the day to expect those who hold the purse strings to continue making increasing allocations to the universities without seeking to exercise any control. However, the nature and extent of the control to be exercised by the government over the universities should not be beyond debate. But a serious debate will be difficult so long as we remain ensnared by the rhetoric of absolute autonomy.

It is argued that universities should be governed by academic and not bureaucratic principles. This is a reasonable argument but in making it we must not forget that some part of academic life, perhaps a large part of it, is governed by neither academic nor bureaucratic principles, but by patrimonial considerations or by personal ties of patronage governed by considerations of community, caste and kinship. This is too large a subject to discuss here, but it should not be brushed under the carpet. All I can say at this point is that it is a mistake to believe that the cure for academic patrimonialism is a bigger dose of bureaucracy. Academic bureaucracies are only half-baked bureaucracies, and at least in India they have shown an unfailing tendency to acquire a patrimonial character.

If I were to distinguish sharply between the two, I would say that bureaucracy rests on a foundation of impersonal rules and standardized procedures whereas the essence of scholarship is the exercise of personal judgement and discernment. It goes without saying that the expectation in both cases is that one will act 'without fear or favour'. Bureaucracy works under compulsion to reduce the space for individual discretion as far as possible, and new rules and procedures are continuously devised to that effect. This is generally a good thing in many spheres of public life, but not necessarily in the academic sphere. In the field of scholarship the displacement of personal judgement by routine procedures leads to the point of diminishing returns far more quickly than in general administration.

The freedom to exercise academic judgement can be easily misused to accommodate undeserving dependents: kinsmen, caste-folk and lame ducks of one sort or another. It cannot be said that our universities have a very clean record in this regard. I would go even further and argue that no university in the world, not even the best, has an absolutely clean record. Hence, as universities have grown, they have had to devise a variety of standardized rules and procedures for their own internal governance. I believe that it is a needless provocation, and in the end also a fruitless one, for the government to seek to extend its powers to make rules on behalf of the universities in order to secure a convenient uniformity.

During the last few years the ministry of education and the University Grants Commission have made a number of moves to streamline the organization of universities with a view to maintaining standards. They have given evidence of a growing lack of their confidence in the capacity of the universities to reform themselves. These facts have to be acknowledged before we can proceed to consider whether the moves have been justified or are likely to bear fruit.

I shall give three examples of intervention at the all-India level which I consider to be unfruitful as well as contrary to the norms of academic life. All of these aim at standardization and show a mistrust of the academic judgement of the men on the job. My first example relates to the institution of national tests by the University Grants Commission for the selection of research scholars; these tests put a premium on trivial mental skills which have little or nothing to do with the aptitude for research. The second is of the creation of Research Scientists in three grades, corresponding to those of lecturer, reader and professor, and their direct recruitment by the University Grants Commission for placement in the various universities; this amounts to the creation of a parallel cadre of academic staff for the universities in whose selection the universities concerned will have little or no say. The third and to my mind the most offensive example is of the national tests being contemplated for all aspirants to faculty appointments in the universities. These are all misguided moves because, in spite of all the risks involved, the selection of scholars can only be made by their peers through the exercise of academic judgement based on close professional interaction. There simply cannot be any counterpart of the Union Public Service Commission in the world of science and scholarship.

Having said all this, I will have to add that the pressure for standardization and mechanical uniformity comes not only from the bureaucracy outside but equally, if not more strongly, from the trade unions within the universities. Unions of college and university teachers have become extremely powerful, and their demands have sometimes a decisive influence on university affairs. As teachers have organized themselves into mass movements, men of real academic distinction have withdrawn into the background, although a few of them have acted as very able lieutenants of leaders enjoying a more solid popular support. Leaders of unions tend to present the demands of teachers in the language of collective bargaining where what counts are large categories rather than individual distinctions.

The cultivation of excellence and the exercise of individual judgement in identifying and promoting talent, which are essential to the vitality of academic institutions, are both viewed with mistrust by mass movements and trade unions. Firstly, trade unions have a negative attitude towards distinctions and disparities which they associate with elitism and privilege. Secondly, where they admit the need for disparities, they insist that these be based on objective as against subjective criteria. Experience has shown that the only objective criteria they really trust as being foolproof are age and length of service. To these one may add the number and class of degrees (MPhil. preferred to MA, Ph.D. preferred to MA plus MPhil.; First Class degrees preferred to Second Class ones), and, a little grudgingly perhaps, the number of publications, preferably arranged according to their length.

What has struck me most about the leaders of teachers' unions is their bureaucratic outlook, their preoccupation with objective criteria, their obsession with foolproof procedures. Nothing brings out the bureaucratic outlook more clearly than the insistence on 'time-bound promotion', or the demand that promotion should be guaranteed after ten years with Ph.D. and after fifteen years without Ph.D. That demand is the assertion of a bureaucratic and not an academic value. I am convinced that such demands touch a sympathetic chord in the bureaucrat. It is true that there was much acrimony and some show of injured innocence on both sides during the bargaining over the new scales of pay. The unions wanted the promotions to come quickly and smoothly whereas the bureaucrats felt that the teachers ought to sweat a little longer for their promotions. But that indicates a difference of interests, not one of ideas or values.

University teachers have to decide what kind of identity they wish to create for themselves. They do not have unlimited choice in the matter, but they do have some choice. In the past academics have viewed themselves as 'independent professionals', somewhat like doctors or lawyers. The professions, including medicine and law, have become increasingly bureaucratized everywhere. To the extent that scientists, scholars, doctors—and even lawyers—work in large organizations, and have to adapt themselves to some of the requirements of such organizations. This does not mean that they have to surrender everything of value to their professional work and identity. But if they wish to secure every advantage that the civil servant enjoys, they cannot at the same time expect to retain all the privileges enjoyed by the independent professional.

18 January 1988

Academic Autonomy

The subject of academic autonomy may be discussed in more than one way. There is firstly the autonomy of the academic *institution*—the university or college—in relation to the government or other organs of society. Closely related to this is the autonomy of the academic *profession*, involving a particular kind of work viewed as a service by society as a whole. In the latter case the problems are similar to those of the legal and medical professions, although lawyers, doctors and academics function in institutional settings that differ considerably from each other.

There are self-employed doctors and lawyers, but hardly any self-employed academics. Doctors certainly recognize that when they give up their private practice to work in a public hospital, they give up a part of their autonomy in return for other considerations, including those of security. Perhaps there is a lesson to be learnt from this about professional life in general: it may not be possible beyond a point to maximize both professional autonomy and occupational security at the same time.

It may be argued that doctors and lawyers who value their independence above everything else should work as self-employed professionals. At the same time, even when they seek employment in public institutions, they should not be made to surrender their autonomy as professionals, because that would harm those whom they serve and not just themselves. The demand for professional autonomy is based on something more than trade union rights of the ordinary sort. It is justified in so far as there is a link between the strength of professional autonomy and the quality of professional service. I am not sure how widely this link is recognized in our society, or how far doctors, lawyers and other professionals employed in public institutions carry conviction when they claim that they want more autonomy for themselves in order to be able to serve others better.

It cannot be too strongly emphasized that the strength of academic autonomy will depend ultimately on the value assigned by society as a whole to independence in academic life. This value is formally acknowledged by making academic institutions self-governing. In India universities are not departments of government, they are governed by their own Acts, statutes and ordinances. It is not always realized that at least formally Indian universities enjoy greater institutional autonomy than universities in many other countries, including some European countries with strong academic traditions.

Even in the best of times universities have not enjoyed complete autonomy anywhere. Because the institutional autonomy of the university can never be complete, it can never be fully secure. In Europe the principal threat to university autonomy in the past was the church, now it is the state. The long arm of the government has reached into the inner recesses of universities in one European country after another, and I have heard academics in Belgium, Holland and England say that their governments are determined to destroy their universities. Without yielding to hysteria, one has to take note of the changes taking place in the relations between universities and government throughout the world today.

In India the government is making its presence increasingly felt in the universities even though it has not shut down university departments as in Holland or told university professors to take early retirement as in England. The main instrument of intervention, whether it is applied directly by government or through the University Grants Commission, is the financial sanction; if universities were not perpetually in need of more money, the intervention would probably be less odious. The justification most commonly given for intervention in the affairs of the universities is that they are not able on their own to either maintain standards or control corruption.

Indian universities would be able to protect their autonomy better if they were less open to charges of corruption and inefficiency. No public institution can insist on enlarged rights of self-governance against universal suspicion of corruption and inefficiency. The university's right of self-governance is damaged most when the strongest charges against the authorities of the university come not from outside but from university teachers themselves. A growing number of young and talented teachers have convinced themselves that professors, heads of departments and deans, not to speak of the vice-chancellor and the pro-vice-chancellor, are corrupt as well as inept. A very common argument in support of time-bound promotions is that academic selection committees cannot be trusted to either recognize or reward merit. When academic selection committees cannot be trusted by new entrants to the profession, what happens to academic self-governance and university autonomy?

While it is undeniable that corruption and inefficiency are widespread in self-governing institutions, it would be foolish to tar all universities or all sections of any university with the same brush. In talking about corruption and inefficiency, we must never forget that universities are perhaps the most exposed among institutions, and therefore their faults are always exposed to the public gaze. And if it be argued that these particular faults in our universities must be corrected by tightening governmental control over them, who is to say that our governmental bureaucracy is lily-white in its purity? It will be very hard indeed to prove that our better universities—like the University of Delhi or Jawaharlal Nehru University—are more corrupt or more inefficient than the University Grants Commission.

Denigration of their own profession has become a way of life with our academics, and it sits ill with their plea for greater academic autonomy. The attack from within on the university's organs of governance has acquired a new character with the development of an active, vigorous and militant trade union movement among college and university teachers. Whereas in the past the vice-chancellor, the academic council and the executive council were criticized privately and discreetly, the onslaught against them is now direct and open. The indefinite strike provides an occasion to otherwise sedate men and women to express themselves without let or hindrance against the constituted authorities of the university.

Where a union of college and university teachers is particularly strong or self-confident, it might seek to negotiate directly with the education secretary or even the education minister, over the heads of the vice-chancellor and the executive council. An irresponsible government might even encourage this as a way of setting one part of the university against the other. The union defines the university in the image of a capitalist enterprise and others, willy-nilly, come to acknowledge this definition. To the extent that teachers play their part in accordance with such a definition, the case for autonomy and self-governance becomes weakened.

It can of course be argued by the union leadership that the constituted authorities of the university are so inept that they are forced to bypass them and enter into direct negotiations with the government. This way well turn out to be true in the future, although I do not believe it to be true today. But when it does turn out to be true, if it does, the universities will hardly be in a position to ask for greater powers of self-governance. No vice-chancellor should be above criticism, but university teachers must recognize the damage done to the case for autonomy when they allow their unions to undermine the dignity of the vice-chancellor's office.

Unionization has not only led to increasing confrontation between the elected leadership and the constituted authorities of the university, it has also provided a foothold to political parties within the university. Our political parties being what they are, it would be a surprise for them to miss an opportunity, while in opposition, to embarass the constituted authorities. Moreover, some parties are committed to the view that in a class-divided society every institution conceals a division of interests as in a capitalist enterprise.

University teachers have the freedom to join political parties of their choice. This is a part of their professional autonomy, and it is a good thing that they enjoy the freedom, provided they respect their non-partisan colleagues and provided they do not always put loyalty to their party above loyalty to their university. We must surely acknowledge that if interference by civil servants in the affairs of the university is a violation of university autonomy, so too is intervention by leaders of political parties. Throughout the strike of August-September 1987 major decisions concerning the resumption of normal academic work were taken not in the universities but in the offices of political parties. The record of these parties does not inspire much confidence in their commitment to the principle of academic autonomy. And it is one thing for academics to be unwilling victims of bureaucratic highhandedness, but quite another for them to court party leaders and seek direction from them in the conduct of their own affairs.

6 February 1988

Feminism in Academia

F ew developments in recent yours have generated as much enthusiasm in the Indian academic world as the arrival and growth of women's studies. New areas of enquiry have been opened up in literary studies, in philosophy, sociology, psychology, history, political science and other disciplines in the humanities and the social sciences. Established concepts and methods of enquiry are being put to question, and what were once accepted as facts now no longer appear as such.

What gives vitality to women's studies is that it is not just a branch of scholarship but part of a larger social movement. The ablest exponents of the subject see themselves as contributing simultaneously to a new type of theory and a new social practice. The movement of which women's studies is a part is an international movement. One of the reasons behind the rapid growth of the subject in India is the presence of extensive networks among women active in the cause of gender studies and gender justice. No purely academic discipline can grow very rapidly within the universities without promotion from outside.

Not all those who are engaged in women's studies—whether in universities or outside—are women, although a remarkably large number of them are. Not all women engaged in women's studies are feminists, although many of them are—or become—feminists, of whom there is a great variety. Like all such movements, feminism has its sectarians and its militants. The culture of the Indian university is still largely a bourgeois culture, and militant feminists introduce a sense of excitement and adventure into it. More and more women are now becoming university students and teachers, and the radical critique of patriarchy strikes a sympathetic chord in even the most placid among them.

Scholars working in the humanities and the social sciences do not always seek to relate their study and research directly or consciously to practical action. Historians examining the movement of commodities in the sixteenth century, anthropologists studying the types of lineage structure or students of literature doing research on medieval religious poetry do not usually see their work as contributing to the politics of the day. Yet, few of them can honestly say that they have never experienced the urge to play some part in the political struggles of the wider world. Most scholars resist the urge but some yield to it, so that the idea of the unity of theory and practice maintains a certain appeal in even the calmest of academic backwaters.

The space within the academic world dominated by ideas about the unity of theory and practice was occupied for some time by Marxism. That space is now being increasingly taken over by feminism. It is well to remember that Marxism was not always welcome within the universities, but it made rapid inroads into European, American and then Indian universities in the fifties, sixties and seventies. It even secured, however briefly, a position of intellectual dominance in some centres of scholarship. The decline of Marxism has been as dramatic as its ascendance, and few now have the intellectual energy even to attack it, not to speak of defending it. If a need still exists within academia to assert the unity of theory and practice, the idea of gender justice seems to satisfy that need better today than that of the class struggle.

The issue of gender justice has far-reaching moral and political implications. When it takes a hold over the minds of scholars, it directs their study and research along particular channels. Every scholarly discipline— social history, cultural anthropology, literary criticism—is also a craft, and every craft has its own conventional demands. Feminism tends to make light of those demands as being artificially constraining in the context of its larger moral and political concerns. It is characteristic of feminism, like Marxism before it, to ignore the established boundaries between academic disciplines and to call for a global view of problems and issues.

It is difficult to judge to what extent developments within women's studies have actually altered scholarly practice in the different academic disciplines. They are as yet new developments, and a clearer focus will no doubt emerge with the passage of time. For the present, their contribution has been more to question and challenge conventional wisdom than to present well-tested new propositions.

The change noted above in the intellectual climate of the Indian university is taking place at a time of a significant change in the demographic composition of students and teachers, particularly in the humanities and the social sciences. Here, one will encounter a great deal of variation, with universities in metropolitan centres such as Bombay and Delhi showing most clearly the tendencies being discussed. Women students are making their presence increasingly felt in them, and in the best departments in the humanities and the social sciences, they not only outnumber the men but often outshine them. The situation may still be somewhat different in the provincial universities, but a feminine, if not feminist, presence is now quite conspicuous in departments of language and literature, anthropology, sociology, history and political science in the two premier universities in Delhi.

For a long time, even in those departments where the students were mainly women, the teachers were mostly men. This is now changing rapidly, and by the end of the present century the sex composition of college and university teachers, at least in Delhi, will be markedly different from what it was fifty years earlier. It would be safe to say that the overwhelming majority of the best lecturers appointed in the undergraduate colleges in Delhi in recent years in subjects such as English, history and political science have been women. These who sit on academic selection committees in the humanities and the social sciences frequently remark on the superior quality of the women candidates in comparison to the men.

Men of superior ability no longer find employment as college or university lecturers as attractive or challenging as before, and they will find it even less so in the future. For one thing, the facilities available in colleges and universities are deteriorating rapidly and are likely to deteriorate further. For another, academic salaries are likely to decline sharply in comparison to the salaries in administration and management. The middle-class Indian family will change far enough to accept the need for two incomes, but not so far as to treat the wife's rather than the husband's income as the first income. The man of the house will seek to maximize income and status, and the woman to optimize the use of time. College and university employment will still remain attractive, but for women much more than men.

What seems clear is that as we enter the twenty-first century, university departments in the humanities and the social sciences will look increasingly different from what they did at the time of Independence. There will almost certainly be a more active concern with gender issues, and there will be more women in them, as both students and teachers. Women's studies programmes the world over have shown a certain exclusionary tendency, and men either stay away or are kept away from them. It is true that gender studies can in principle relate to men as well as women, but in fact the term continues to be mainly an euphemism for women's studies. Unless the scope of these studies is widened to accommodate divergent viewpoints as well as persons of both sexes, they will diminish the vitality as well as the credibility of the institutions within which they have lodged themselves.

27 December 1994

III
Equality and Justice

The articles in this section deal with the facts of inequality as well as the ideal of equality. Traditional Indian society was characterized by the most extreme and the most pervasive forms of inequality, and their marks are readily visible in contemporary India. At the same time, we now have a Constitution that has the most comprehensive guarantees of equality. This contradiction between ideal and practice is a very striking feature of our social and political life, in which the rhetoric of equality co-exists with the most invidious practice of inequality in both private and public.

Inequality is not merely a matter of income distribution or of the distribution of land and other forms of wealth. It is also, and in some ways even more fundamentally, a matter of status and of power. We are a peculiarly status conscious people and we frequently, and sometimes gratuitously, oppress those who are weaker than ourselves. We do all this while passionately proclaiming our love of equality; and I am not speaking only about politicians, but also about professors, judges, lawyers, doctors, civil servants and many others.

I do not profess to be an egalitarian since I do not believe that every form of inequality is to be condemned, or that equality has to be secured in every case and at any price. There is a world of difference between equality of opportunity and the equal distribution of benefits and burdens. There is also a difference between formal and substantive equality of opportunity. Formal equality of opportunity requires us to disregard distinctions based on caste, community and gender, but we have reintroduced those distinctions in order to secure substantive equality of opportunity. It is doubtful that substantive equality of opportunity can be secured by our legal system, or by any legal system. The Indian road to equality has been full of snares and pitfalls.

I have urged the need to make a distinction between equality and universality. Universality is the principle which seeks to secure certain basic necessities, such as primary education and primary health care, for all citizens, irrespective of merit and irrespective of caste, community or gender. It is concerned with basic necessities and not with everything that human beings at any point of time may desire. It can and does accommodate a great deal of inequality in the distribution of those things that may be considered desirable but are not essential for human existence in a given society at a given stage of its development.

The Concern for Status

Indian society is beyond question marked by a high degree of concern for status. One might say that Indians, including those who are modern and western-educated, are among the most status-conscious people in the world. The place where we live, the way in which we speak, the people with whom we associate, the family into which we marry, the school to which we send our children—these are all chosen with an almost obsessive concern for the status they are likely to confer or sustain.

We are often told that Indian society is changing in many ways and, indeed, signs of change are present in almost every sphere of our contemporary life. The British introduced many new institutions and others have been added since Independence. The political system is new, many sectors in our economy are new, and the very idea of planned social change is new. Yet some of our most basic values have shown a most remarkable resistance to change. I shall argue that the concern for status and hierarchy reveals a fundamental continuity between the past and the present in Indian society.

How does one account for this concern for status and hierarchy in Indian social life? The most readily available explanation is that it grows out of certain basic material conditions. Where the economy is backward and disparities in income and wealth are large, it is natural that status and hierarchy should be major concerns. There is, however, more to it than just this. The concern for status, the value placed on hierarchy as a thing in itself, seems up to a point to vary independently of economic factors. I would go even further and argue that it is this value which often acts as an obstacle to a greater equalization of the material conditions of life.

In one important respect, traditional Indian society was perhaps unique. The caste system on which it was based not only divided the population into high and low, but also provided a powerful ideological justification for this elaborate system of inequality. Perhaps it went further than any other system in the extent to which it sanctioned inequality, although it must be remembered that the modern preoccupation with social equality is a relatively recent feature of human history. The contemporary significance of caste is to be sought not so much in any set of actual divisions in the population as in the extent to which the social value placed on status and hierarchy continues to hold its ground.

There is no need to dwell on the rigidities of status gradations in traditional Indian society. Some of these rigidities in their specifically traditional form have become attenuated although others continue to exist. The traditional conceptions of status were for the most part grounded in religion, particularly in the notions of purity and pollution. It would be hard to deny that ritual concerns in general and the concern with purity and pollution in particular have declined at least among certain sections of Indian society. It would however be wrong to conclude that preoccupation with status has on this account become less keen. On the contrary, many new conceptions of status are emerging which appear to be no less invidious than those of the past.

The notions of purity and pollution have become weakest in the upper layers of urban society and it is here that we encounter the new kind of hierarchy in its fullest elaboration. The new hierarchies give an important place to certain elements in the western style of life and are based on income, occupation and education. Their most characteristic expressions are to be found among civil servants and military officers, among business executives and in professions such as law, medicine and engineering.

One conspicuous feature of the new hierarchy (as of the old) is the way in which people at different levels in it are segregated in different residential areas. This is most clearly in evidence among government officials in New Delhi, but the principle has a much wider application. Differences in speech are also conspicuous between people at different levels of the hierarchy: those above speak English more extensively and more fluently than those below, both at home and outside. Differences in speech are closely related to differences in type of education and the educational system has contributed much to the creation and maintenance of new forms of inequality in India. These differences—in speech and education—go hand in hand with many others in culture and style of life.

Those who live in Delhi cannot avoid encounters with government servants either in their capacity as officials or in ordinary social life. A consideration of the nature, types and activities of government servants can tell us much about the working of contemporary Indian society. Government servants are of three major kinds: gazetted officers, non-gazetted officers and menial staff. Coming back to Delhi after a ten-month stay in a south Indian village, I could not help being struck by the detailed similarity between this pattern of division and the division of the village into Brahmins, non-Brahmins and Harijans. For, in both cases the divisions are not only clear and unmistakable, but they reach into almost every sphere of social life. Gazetted officers, particularly those of the ICS and the IAS, occupy a unique position in Indian society. IAS officers are selected and trained so as to be both versatile and indispensible. Because of their unique position they have to be protected from their public by an army of junior officers, clerks and other underlings. Yet virtually every important document requires at some stage the signature of a gazetted officer. It does not seem to matter that he cannot reasonably be expected to vouch for what he is signing; the document cannot acquire its due importance unless it is signed by a gazetted officer.

That, then, is one side of the coin, the urge to involve men of status in every conceivable activity in order to create an atmosphere of importance for what is being done. The other is the impulse to avoid every kind of work whose performance may be construed as being beneath one's station. V.S. Naipaul has described how a clerk at the Bombay customs, when confronted by a fainting lady, made a long search for a chaprasi who could get her a glass of water instead of fetching the water himself. This kind of concern for status might be amusing if it did not lead to such colossal waste and inefficiency in public life. Things do not get done or are done too late because people of the appropriate status are not available; those who are available are either too far above or too far below, although in every other way they may be perfectly capable of doing what is required.

The concern for status is present in private as well as in public life. A certain amount of hierarchy is after all inevitable in the official world; it is there in every society and is in fact a basic requirement of any complex organization. But the remarkable thing about Indian society is the extent to which these distinctions permeate almost every sphere of private life. People belonging to the different divisions do not meet on equal terms, if at all they meet each other socially; they do not interdine except on formal occasions where again distances are carefully maintained; and the question of intermarriage seems hardly to arise. The social world in modern India thus appears to be fragmented and broken up in much the same way as it was in the past, although some change has undoubtedly come about in the cultural idiom through which distances are now maintained.

The Indian preoccupation with status was given a new dimension by contact with the British. The British in India attempted to maintain a certain distance between themselves and the native population, partly on account of race but also on political and cultural grounds. Indians who received western education in this country and abroad and entered the higher services and professions acquired some of the prestige of their British masters. This was reinforced by the adoption of western styles of life by many. It is remarkable how rapidly certain sections of western-educated Indians took over some of the habits, attitudes and values of the English. And British society itself placed a higher value on status than perhaps any other society in the West.

Thus the status distinctions that we observe derive

partly from a particular kind of exposure to western culture. It can be argued that western-educated Indians took over the status concerns of the English because it was here that they found something truly consistent with the values of their own society. Viewing Indian society in this way may serve to provide a new perspective on caste and a better understanding of its real significance in contemporary life. For caste is not merely an arrangement of specific groups such as Brahmins, Baniyas, Kayasths, Jats, Ahirs and Chamars. It is also a system of values, a mode of ordering social relations between people in different spheres of life. The values most systematically elaborated in traditional India were those concerned with status and hierarchy. Can we say that these values are now on their decline?

25 September 1968

Social Inequality in India

I s there greater social equality in India today than there was twenty-three years ago? This is such a large question that few sociologists would even attempt to approach it directly. So, if I seek to explore some aspects of it, I do so in awareness of the difficulties and dangers inherent in the task.

What I would like to do here is to examine the question from two particular angles. The first relates to the change from a closed to a relatively open system of social inequality or stratification. The second concerns the extent to which, irrespective of changes in actual conditions, the existence of a hierarchy is ceasing to be regarded as just, proper or legitimate. In what follows I shall confine my observations to rural society since the problem is so large that it would be otherwise difficult to deal with it meaningfully.

I will need to begin by explaining a few terms. Indian society might be described as having had, traditionally, a closed system of stratification. In such a system not only is the society divided into groups which are ranged as high and low, but all the advantages—of wealth, privilege and power—tend to be combined at the top and the disadvantages at the bottom. In an open system of stratification, towards which some societies appear to be moving, the advantages of wealth need not be combined with those of status, and the latter might exist independently of the advantages of power.

How different modes of social inequality in India were combined in the past can be best illustrated by examining the traditional association between the caste system and the system of agrarian relations. Both systems were elaborately hierarchical and there was a large measure of correspondence between the two. At the top were the large landowners who belonged usually to the highest Brahmin and Rajput castes. Just below them came a variety of non-cultivating tenure holders, also belonging to the upper castes. Then came the cultivating owners, belonging usually to the peasant castes and located at the middle levels of the hierarchy. At the bottom of the heap were the sharecroppers and agricultural labourers who either belonged to the lowest among the 'clean' castes or were Harijans and, in some places, Adivasis.

There were of course, many variations on this broad pattern. In some areas the hierarchy was less elaborate than in others. What is interesting is that the caste hierarchy was particularly elaborate in those areas, such as Malabar, where the agrarian hierarchy was also elaborate. Conversely, in areas like Uttar Pradesh and Haryana, both hierarchies were relatively simple.

Everywhere power was concentrated in the hands of the landowning upper castes. At the higher territorial levels these would be Brahmin and Rajput (or high status Muslim) landlords and tenure holders. At the village level these were often cultivating landowners belonging to the peasant castes. The Harijan sharecroppers and landless labourers, who belonged to the bottom of the caste and class hierarchies, were almost everywhere denied access to positions of power and authority.

There are signs that the close associations which prevailed in the past between caste, class and power, are being loosened in contemporary Indian society. While it is easy to illustrate this kind of change, it is difficult to say how widespread or far reaching it has been. The little evidence that we have would seem to suggest that so far at least such change has been of limited significance and that it has made its impact felt more at the upper than at the lower levels of the hierarchy.

The relationship between caste and landownership is changing and this change is visible, though not always clearly, at the upper levels of the hierarchy. The agrarian hierarchy itself has become less elaborate than it was. In most parts of the country the large zamindars, taluqdars and jagirdars have ceased to exist, although in some areas they seem to be reappearing in a new guise. Landowners now probably belong to a wider range of castes than they did before and in some areas the gap between tenant cultivators and owner cultivators seems to be lessening.

Several factors have been responsible for these changes. The land reforms have had some levelling effect, although their exact significance is difficult to assess. In Rajasthan, for example, many large jagirdars have been reduced in wealth and power, and tenant cultivators have often acquired ownership rights and sometimes augmented their holdings. The fact that land has come into the market also means that it is now possible for members of non-landowning castes to buy land. In practice, of course, most of the buying and selling is confined to people who already own some land. But today it is at least possible in principle for tenants to acquire land by purchase, whereas in the past virtually the only effective way of doing so was by inheritance.

I must emphasize that these changes—such as they are—are confined largely to the upper levels of the hierarchy. The bulk of the sharecroppers and agricultural labourers remain where they were and neither land reforms nor market forces have made any significant change in their social composition. The correspondence between the lowest positions in the caste structure and in the agrarian hierarchy continues to be marked. Adivasis, Harijans and castes which were just above the line of pollution supply the overwhelming majority of sharecroppers and agricultural labourers. And it is far more difficult for a Harijan labourer to become a tenant cultivator than for a Jat tenant to become an owner cultivator.

In the political sphere also some changes have taken place, and here again these seem to have made a greater difference to people at the middle as opposed to the lower levels of the hierarchy. The control exercised over the political system in pre-Independence India by upper castes such as Brahmins, Rajputs and Kayasths is well known. It is also well known how in many areas these castes were at first challenged and subsequently overshadowed by peasant castes such as Jats, Marathas, Reddis and Vellalas. Today particularly at the village, taluka and district levels, power resides in the hands of well-to-do people who often belong to the numerically preponderant peasant castes. Without denying the importance of this change, it should be pointed out that it has hardly affected the actual conditions of the vast majority of sharecroppers and agricultural labourers who belong to the lowest castes.

We could perhaps sum up the changes described above by saying that the social pyramid has been flattened somewhat, but less by the bottom being raised than by a slight lowering at the top. As we move downward from the middle of the hierarchy, the opportunities for effective upward mobility become progressively reduced. To take a crucial example, very few avenues are actually available for upward mobility to the vast majority of Harijan landless labourers.

We encounter a different set of changes when we consider, instead of actually existing inequalities, the attitudes which people have towards them. It has been argued that what was unique about traditional Indian society was not the fact of inequality as such, but the elaborate ideology developed to justify it. It is in this sense that the theory and practice of caste were of such profound significance to the working of traditional Indian society. What we have to ask ourselves now is how far the old ideology in which inequality was considered acceptable if not legitimate is being replaced by a different kind of ideology.

The normative order prescribed in the Constitution is of course radically different from what was prescribed in the classical Hindu texts. This might be of little comfort to those who seek to defend democratic values by appealing to tradition, but no amount of sophistry can disprove this simple truth. It is, however, one thing to create a normative order by acts of legislation; we have to examine how far this has led to a real change of values at the different levels of Indian society.

The most conspicuous change in the normative order is to be seen in the attitude adopted in the Constitution towards caste in general and the practice of untouchability in particular. The legal and ritual sanctions which supported caste have been withdrawn, but what difference has this made to the attitudes of people towards the high- and the low-born? There is little doubt that these attitudes have changed, but it is not easy either to measure the extent of these changes or to identify the specific economic, political and cultural factors which have brought them about. All that we can say perhaps is that the new normative order provides a favorable environment in which such changes can establish themselves when they do come about through various causes.

The practice of untouchability certainly continues as is evident from the annual reports of the commissioner for scheduled castes and scheduled tribes, but there are two notable changes. Untouchability is practised less extensively than before and, what is more important, it is practised less openly. The attitude towards untouchability is clearly changed by higher education and among urban middle class people it is common to find a somewhat ambivalent attitude towards those Harijans with whom they have direct relations, mainly as their employers. While most such people would prefer to exclude Harijans from their kitchen, many of them feel embarrassed to openly admit this for fear that their orthodoxy might be disapproved by their more modernized friends.

It is true that caste was the most concrete expression of hierarchy in the traditional set-up, but even if people are changing their attitudes about caste, does this mean that they are beginning to feel differently about inequality in general? This is a difficult question, and all the evidence is by no means clearly on one side. In the higher services people are known to have an almost obsessive preoccupation with elaborate gradations of status based on income, occupation and education. On the other hand, in industry in general attitudes towards manual work are changing, and manual workers are less unequal in relation to clerks than they were even twenty-five years ago.

In agriculture, which is our main concern here, large

disparities continue to exist between the landowners and the landless, and among the different grades of landowners. Are people inclined to accept these disparities in the same way in which they did in the past or has there been any basic change of attitude in this regard?

Hierarchy is an important feature of the relationship between landowner and tenant (or farm labourer) in all agrarian societies. In Bengal, for instance, the landowner, even when he was a peasant proprietor, was called *manib,* meaning master, and the labourer was his *munish,* or man. Notions of masterdom and servitude provided the general context of agrarian relations in most parts of the country, certainly throughout the period of British rule and probably in earlier periods as well. The penetration of market forces into the village introduced a new element in this context, but did not change it substantially. The land reforms did not initially have any direct effect on the relations between landowners on the one hand and sharecroppers and agricultural labourers on the other. What does seem to have some effect are the political movements organized to make the reforms effective, and the new political environment in general.

The land reforms altered the *legality* of large holdings but it is doubtful that they had any immediate effect on their *legitimacy.* Several years after the enactment of the laws on ceilings, landowners in most parts of the country continued in possession of large holdings and this was not socially disapproved in the villages. Today this is no longer true everywhere. Where large landowners continue to exploit their tenants or farm labourers, they do so more by stratagem than by the exercise of legitimate authority. In states like West Bengal and Kerala the relations between large landowners and the landless have undergone so much change during the last two or three years that one might argue that in these places the boot is now on the other foot. Some might feel that the price which is being paid for these changes is far in excess of the benefits they will bring, but that would open out an altogether different problem for discussion.

24 July 1970

The Indian Road to Equality

The unanimous and enthusiastic endorsement by Parliament on 11 August 1982 of the report of the Backward Classes Commission constitutes an important landmark in the history of contemporary India. If Parliament has acted in full awareness of the likely consequences of its action, we are perhaps entering a new phase in the reconstitution of Indian society. This reconstitution may be no less far-reaching in its scope than the one attempted by the new Constitution which Indians fashioned for themselves on achieving independence.

What was acclaimed by all parties in Parliament was the spirit of equality embodied in the commission's report. The Constitution too is marked by its emphasis on equality, and in that sense our present Parliament can claim to be carrying forward the task begun by the Constituent Assembly. But there the similarity ends. The aim of the Constituent Assembly was to bring about a casteless and a classless society. The aim of the commission under Mr B.P. Mandal was, presumably, to exorcize the disparities of class by placing caste at the centre of Indian society.

It will be a mistake to miss the moral impulse behind the acclaim with which the report was greeted in Parliament. Indians are too ready to mistrust their politicians and to attribute the worst motives to their every action. It is not true that support for job reservation, which is the principal recommendation of the commission, is motivated solely by the calculation to gain something for oneself or one's nephew or one's own community. Job reservation is coming to be viewed sympathetically by more and more people who have nothing to gain personally from it. The moral impulse behind it is the commitment to equality. Indians today seem to be ready to do anything in the cause of equality, even to rehabilitate the caste system, and this is the case with all political parties and with intellectuals as well as politicians.

Equality and distributive justice are universal concerns in the modern world, and it has been said that these concerns were activated among Indians by their exposure to the world outside, particularly the western world. The Indian Constitution has relied heavily on other Constitutions, particularly in the various guarantees of equality written into it. What seems to be unique therefore is not the Indian concern for equality, but the means being increasingly recommended for the attainment of equality in India. The rehabilitation of caste may not be the intention of those who recommend job reservation, but it will certainly be a consequence of their recommendations if these are seriously acted upon.

Mr Mandal's commission was not the first to be set up in independent India for recommending measures for the betterment of backward classes other than the scheduled castes and scheduled tribes. The first backward classes commission was set up in 1953 under Kaka Kalelkar and it submitted its report in 1955. Nothing much came of that report which was equivocal in its attitude to caste, unlike the present report which is clear in recommending caste as the basic unit in all considerations of distributive justice. It is not surprising that some members of Parliament wanted that, in addition to the castes and communities listed in the report, religious minorities should also be brought within the scope of its recommendations.

In the Constituent Assembly, Dr Ambedkar had argued for adopting the individual as the unit in the new scheme of things: compensatory measures for the scheduled castes and scheduled tribes were regarded as exceptional and transitory. At about the same time, Dr Radhakrishnan's commission on university education had asserted: 'The fundamental right is the right of the individual, not of the community.' In boldly asserting the claims of caste, Mr Mandal's commission has brought back an alternative conception of Indian society whose appeal may go far deeper than the appeal of the conception on which the Constitution is based. Indian intellectuals do not like talking about caste, but that does not mean that they are not moved by its appeal.

The first backward classes commission had come too soon after the Constituent Assembly to be able to advocate the cause of caste and community without any reserve. The commission as a whole was in favour of extensive reservations on the basis of caste. But its chairman, Kaka Kalelkar, could not in the end bring himself to endorse a recommendation which he felt would be bound to lead to a rehabilitation of caste. In his covering letter to the President, he pointed out that in a democracy official recognition could be given to only the individual and the nation, and added that he was 'definitely against reservation in government services for any community'.

The recommendations of the first backward classes commission were thus infructuous, but reservation in the service on the basis of caste and community has continued to flourish, particularly in the states of south India. The Supreme Court, after resisting caste quotas for some time, has taken a more latitudinarian stance in recent years. Various commissions have been set up in the states to recommend measures for the betterment of the weaker sections, and these have almost invariably recommended the reservation of more jobs for more castes. The Karnataka backward classes commission under L.G. Havanur has sought to provide the most comprehensive rationale for caste quotas in every sector of employment, arguing that, far from being unconstitutional, the official recognition of caste is in fact required by the Constitution itself.

To the framers of the Constitution equality meant above all equality of opportunity, which takes only individuals into account without any consideration for caste or community. As against this is the idea of the equal distribution of all benefits, particularly the benefits of education and employment, among the castes and communities into which society is divided. The two conceptions are different, and in their application mutually incompatible. It is difficult to predict how far equality between castes will in fact be achieved by the kind of redistribution recommended by the commission. But any attempt at a redistribution which seeks to satisfy the claims of castes is bound to strengthen rather than weaken the hold of caste over public life.

Why have Indians become more sympathetic to the claims of caste between the commissions of Kaka Kalelkar and Mr Mandal? Firstly, people are left with fewer illusions today than they probably had thirty year ago as to how far equality of opportunity can carry them in this society. Politicians, civil servants, engineers, doctors, lawyers, professors, journalists have all come to believe that, whatever the case may be elsewhere, in India competition is neither free nor fair. If you tell them that reservation penalizes merit and ability, they will tell you that merit and ability are in any case penalized in this society. Reservation tries at least to make some reparation for the injuries suffered by disprivileged groups in the past.

There is also the argument that equality is a universal value, but that we must find an Indian way to make it work in this society. Indians have become increasingly conscious of the need to find 'alternatives' in every sphere. If very little progress has been made so far in the attainment of equality, this may be because the methods adopted, being primality western in inspiration, are not well suited to the Indian social environment. For better or for worse, this environment has always favoured the community over the individual, and it may be possible in India to combine the preference for the community with the commitment to equality. The West may go its own way, but we in India will have both equality and caste.

It is said that extensive reservation will lead to a decline in the efficiency of our public institutions. There are other, more important, consequences to be considered. Reservation on the scale being proposed will alter the character of these institutions and not merely reduce their efficiency. The object of reservation is to provide equitable representation in them to all castes and communities. But not every institution performs representative functions or is designed to perform them. A bank or a hospital or a research laboratory has a very different job to do from a political party or a district council. It may be legitimate for a member to represent the interests of his caste or community in a legislative assembly. Can we legitimize the representation of caste interests in institutions such as the universities without changing their character altogether? The maintenance of efficiency is, in my judgement, less important than the protection of the very norms by which alone such institutions can be governed.

28 August 1982

Indian Society Today

Many years ago Jawaharlal Nehru wrote about Indian society that the group was of paramount importance whereas the individual had only a secondary place in it. He had in mind the three basic institutions of traditional Indian society, the village community, caste and the joint family. He himself believed that caste and community should not be allowed to intrude unduly into the domain of public life in a democratic society. Communalism and casteism were regarded by him and his whole generation as unmixed evils which ought to be weeded out from public life.

The question whether the individual or the group should be treated as basic came up for discussion in the Constituent Assembly. Dr Ambedkar argued forcefully in favour of the individual and observed, 'I am glad that the draft Constitution has discarded the village and adopted the individual as its unit.' To be sure, he advocated special measures for the benefit of Harijans and Adivasis. However, these measures, though widely endorsed, were also regarded as exceptional in two important respects: they were to apply to limited sections of the population and they were to be time-bound. Dr Ambedkar himself took pains to point out that the special measures should not be allowed to 'eat up' the general provision of equality of opportunity for all individual citizens.

The Constituent Assembly met under the shadow of

the Partition of India and the fratricidal divisions that accompanied it. Those who met in it believed sincerely, if a little naïvely, that communalism and casteism were plainly and simply creatures of the imperial policy of divide and rule. They felt that, even if they made very generous provisions for the Harijans and Adivasis, they could still build up a structure of equal opportunities for individuals as a bulwark against casteism.

In the years immediately following Independence, the Indian intelligentsia, at least outside peninsular India, was on the whole reluctant to concede that caste might play a continuing role in public life. Evidence of the continuing role of caste in politics began to accumulate from several parts of the country during and after the elections of 1957. It took some time for the weight of this evidence to make itself felt, and in any case the evidence was not all of the same kind. The pressure of caste did not remain confined to electoral politics but began to influence government policy in regard to distributive justice, haltingly at first, but with increasing vigour after 1977.

Caste and community are now factors in public policy in a manner and to an extent not anticipated by the makers of the Constitution. Quotas in education and employment can no longer be treated as exceptional, either in regard to the number of groups whose claims are admitted or in regard to the time span over which such claims may be expected to prevail. A major factor, in my view, has been the change in the attitude of the higher judiciary, which may be seen by comparing Justice Gajendragadkar's arguments in Balaji's case (1962) with those of Justice Krishna Iyer in the case of N.M. Thomas (1976).

No doubt the judges decide in the interest of what they

consider to be equality and social justice, and one prominent advocate of a comprehensive system of quotas has argued that there must first be equality among castes before there can be equality among individuals. As against this it may be argued that, while the gains to equality from such a system of quotas are at best doubtful, its immediate effect is to strengthen the identities of caste and community and to slow down the growth of individual initiative.

It is believed that in traditional India caste and community provided security to all individual members of society and that society in turn discouraged individual initiative and enterprise. Perhaps the system of quotas, which has spread itself so widely across the public domain in the last couple of decades, corresponds to a sense of social justice that lies very deep in the Indian consciousness. But does the general acquiescence in a comprehensive system of quotas for castes and communities indicate that the structure of the old society, which the Constitution sought to dismantle, will recover the entire ground it appeared to have lost? Such a conclusion will be premature and probably wide of the mark.

Indians may yearn for the security assured by quotas, but many of them have also acquired a taste for the sweets of success in competition. One has only to see what goes on in the schools in our metropolitan cities to appreciate this. Middle-class Indians not only strive to secure whatever benefits their community has at its disposal—and where necessary to enlarge those benefits by collective action—they also seek to get ahead as individuals. And it may not be altogether unusual for the same person to try for both.

While our legislators and judges might be attentive to

the claims of groups in their concern for social justice, the prime minister is keen to carry the country forward into the twenty-first century. That means putting the accent on technology, management, dynamism, efficiency and achievement. These are the virtues of a competitive society—competitive capitalism, if one prefers the phrase—which appeal to many Indians of the younger generation besides the prime minister. Competitive capitalism has also its own sense of justice, but that is a very different kind of justice from the one which appeals to the majority of our legislators and judges; hence when one points to the virtues of capitalism, one points to efficiency rather than justice.

The spirit of competitive individualism is now in full cry in some of the countries regarded until the other day as models of socialism. In India it has to contend with the demand for parity or balance between castes and communities in the public domain. That demand, as I have suggested, corresponds to a sense of social justice that is widely shared by people in many walks of life. It is articulated by politicians of all complexions, and the government itself has created an elaborate apparatus to give satisfaction to it. It is difficult to see how that apparatus can be dismantled in the foreseeable future. But what cannot be dismantled may be bypassed, and that would be in keeping with the Indian way of dealing with conflicting demands.

Wherever a government is involved directly in distribution—whether in employment or in education—that distribution will be governed by considerations of social justice in which the claims of castes and communities feature prominently. This is not to say that all such claims will be received with equal enthusiasm by every government, but few will have the energy to resist the claims, and most will find it easier to acquiesce in them. It would be shallow to attribute all of this to the cynicism and opportunism of politicians. A deeper cause lies in the unwritten sense of justice carried by most Indians according to which groups, and not just individuals, have legitimate claims on the government. That sense of justice seems to tell them that if such claims could have been admitted in a hierarchical society, there is no reason to deny them in an egalitarian one.

It is not as if Indians are unable to recognize today that individuals have claims as well. But the majority of them feel perhaps that individuals should be encouraged to look after themselves without grudging too openly what the government decides to set apart for groups. They have in fact shown considerable private initiative and enterprise in opening up new fields outside of government control, and forging ahead in these fields. Methods and styles of management, publicity and advertisement are rapidly changing so as to keep pace with the advances in the rest of the world. The rewards of success are very high here, and they go to individuals without much attention being paid to caste or community.

There are indications that the best products of our colleges and universities are turning more eagerly to careers in management than in the civil services. Even the Indian Administrative Service has lost the social cachet it enjoyed in the years immediately following Independence; it has become crowded in by too many new entrants who settle too easily into careers in which real challenges and legitimate opportunities have become steadily restricted. Below that level, in the states the machinery of government has become a vast and unwieldy apparatus where administrative procedures are hamstrung by caste quotas on the one hand and political patronage on the other. These are safe places where nobody loses his position or misses his promotion and where there are caste quotas not only for appointments but also for promotions. But they are not places where the race is to the swiftest or where efficiency brings one any special advantage.

It does not appear that the present government is keen to discourage the growth of a sector, outside its immediate control, in which efficiency, competition and individual initiative will be allowed free play, unimpeded by those considerations of distributive justice from which it is unable to free the public sector under its own control. The former is as yet a relatively small sector, but India is a large country where it may not be too difficult to find space for its further growth and development. The orientations of the people who operate in these spaces will be very different from those whose primary concerns are with distributive justice and the balance of power between groups. No developing society can sustain itself solely on distributive justice; it also requires a work ethic. It is as yet too early to say how far such an ethic will grow in the new spaces being opened up in Indian society. But the really important question is whether such an ethic, if and when it grows, will succeed in infusing a new meaning into our conception of social justice which appears bland and colourless, and a little sickly in its prevalent form.

29 March 1988

Access to Medical Education

The organization of medical education has recently received wide public attention. Some feel that medical education is so vitally important for society as a whole that it should be made available on easy terms to all who wish to secure it. Others maintain that it is so very expensive that there should be a charge for it, at least on those who can afford to pay. Clearly, the state cannot remain indifferent to the amount and quality of the medical education available in the country. At the same time, it would be a mistake to treat the availability of medical education as a matter of right; it should be treated as a matter of policy and not of right.

It would of course be disingenuous to pretend that medical education can in fact be made available to all those who wish to benefit from it, or even to all those who are technically qualified for it. Availability on such a large scale cannot be ensured in any country today, and the question hardly arises in a poor country like India. We should hesitate to talk about a right to something, and especially a fundamental right to it, when we know that access to it is in fact severely restricted by material constraints. It may be reasonable to talk about a right to literacy, but to talk about expanding the scope of our fundamental rights to include access to medical education is to invite confusion.

Broadly the same issue has been addressed by the

distinguished jurist Ronald Dworkin in the context of access to legal education in the United States. Dworkin was arguing against the claims made by Marco DeFunis who did been denied a place in a law school in the interest of the school's affirmative action programme. He argued that no right had been violated, because DeFunis did not have a right in the first instance. 'DeFunis does not have a right to equal treatment in the assignment of law school places; he does not have a right to a place because others are given places. Individuals may have a right to equal treatment in elementary education, because someone who is denied elementary education is unlikely to lead a useful life. But legal education is not so vital that everyone has an equal right to it.'

We can of course argue that what applies in the United States does not apply to us, that we should aim higher because we can achieve more. But then it will be pointed out that we have failed rather dismally in providing even the minimal amenities of life, including the benefit of literacy, to large sections of our population. Some might go a step further and suggest that we wax eloquent about the fundamental right to medical education—and to other such things—not despite our failure to provide universal elementary education, but because of it. And of course, access to medical education touches middle-class interests far more deeply than the interests of other sections of society.

Is it reasonable to expect the state to bear all the responsibility for providing medical education where it has failed so conspicuously in the matter of elementary education? The cost of medical education is very high, and the fees charged from students in state-funded medical colleges are very low. A substantial proportion of medical students come from middle-class if not well-to-do homes, and they can be expected to earn well after they qualify as doctors. Surely, it will not be unreasonable to require them to bear some of the cost of their own education. This calls for some serious policy initiative, but that initiative is liable to be choked if we carry the discussion straight on to the plane of fundamental rights.

The case for private initiative in the organization of medical education should be considered carefully and dispassionately. Some are inclined to argue that the costs and benefits of medical education can be balanced better by leaving at least a part of it to private initiative, particularly in view of the limited resources of the state. We could then have, in addition to the state-funded medical colleges, privately-funded ones which will recover their costs by charging high fees. If people have the money to pay, why should we grudge them the benefits of the education they are able to secure for themselves and their children? After all, private universities in the United States, such as Harvard and Chicago, have excellent medical schools that charge very high fees from their students.

While it may be in principle perfectly all right to charge high fees from those who can afford to pay, much will depend on the terms and conditions under which the payment is extracted. The point about the fees being demanded by private medical colleges in India is not simply that they are high but that they are extortionate. It is this issue, rather than the issue of fundamental rights, that calls for a sober assessment from the practical point of view.

It will be futile to try to decide from first principles whether private or public institutions are better suited to providing a good medical education. The comparison between private medical colleges in India and medical schools in the United States can be misleading. Harvard and Chicago do not have to compromise on professional or academic standards in making admissions to their medical schools: they charge very high fees and also select the very best students. It would be foolish to presume that the two things can be simultaneously ensured through the magical operation of the market principle. That principle has in fact shown itself in its worst colours in the field of medical education in this country. Whatever the case may be in America, private medical colleges in India attract students who are below rather than above the average; students turn to these institutions not because of their high professional or academic standing but because they have failed to secure admission elsewhere. It is this that provides the opening for extortion.

It is alleged that a student has to pay between four and five lakh rupees for the full course of education in a private medical college. This is an enormously large sum of money by middle-class Indian standards. Is an institution which charges such a large sum of money from a student entirely free to turn him away at the end of the course without giving him the degree which he had hoped to secure in return for his investment? We must remember that these colleges are unable to attract students of the best quality. Dealing as they do in such large sums of money, the authorities must find it very hard to maintain a strict control over standards of academic performance.

The organization of medical education raises a number of issues of policy. But the state alone cannot ensure that medical education maintains high standards and at the same time remains widely available. The natural tendency of the state, at least in India, is to subordinate professional considerations to bureaucratic (or political) ones, while the natural tendency of the market is to subordinate them to commercial ones. The main responsibility for protecting medical education from political as well as commercial debasement must rest with the medical profession. If the profession abdicates its responsibility, there is very little that either the state or the market can do to maintain its vitality. In Germany medical education is largely the responsibility of public institutions whereas in the United States it is also the responsibility of private institutions; what the two countries have in common is an active and responsible medical profession that is able to protect itself from subversion by narrow political and commercial interests.

Much has gone wrong with the organization of medical education in India, and there is real cause for public anxiety on that score. There should be extensive discussion of the subject so that the faults in the system get identified and corrected. No improvement can be effected without raising public awareness, and public awareness cannot be raised either by sweeping inconvenient facts under the carpet or by adopting postures from a high plane of principle.

Outside observers are often struck by the extensive use of the language of rights in our contemporary public life and it appears striking also in the light of our traditional legal culture. It has often been noted that the law of the *Dharmashastra* was structured in terms of duties rather than rights. Now it is true that a legal order that stresses duties at the expense of rights does not appear very attractive in the light of modern democratic conceptions. The current preoccupation, not to say obsession, with rights may be an unrecognized or unconscious reaction against the traditional order which took so little account of rights. But then one has to reach for a balanced perspective, for very little can be gained by swinging violently from one extreme to the other. The emergence of a balanced perspective requires at the very least that the highest judicial authorities should exercise some restraint while making public pronouncements on rights. Appealing to fundamental rights in season and out of season may not be the best way of showing that we take our rights seriously.

1 September 1992

Judicial Activism

How actively should the courts intervene in the internal arrangements of institutions, and indicate, propose or demand changes in them in the larger public interest? This question has acquired some urgency in view of the precarious condition of many of our public institutions, such as universities, hospitals, municipalities, and so on, and the widespread disenchantment with them. Indifference to their condition hurts the public interest; but excess of zeal in directing changes in them from outside might hurt it no less.

The kind of civil society envisaged in our Constitution requires a variety of public institutions to mediate between citizens and the state. It is hard even to think of just 950 million Indians and then India, with nothing to connect individual Indians with each other and with the wider society. Kinship, caste and community have mediated between individual and society in the past and continue to do so in the present. But they are not enough. We need, in addition, open and secular institutions more in tune with our present economic and political objectives. It was hoped at the time of Independence that such institutions would take root and grow as a part of the modernization of Indian society.

It goes without saying that public institutions cannot place themselves beyond public scrutiny. They are designed to serve the public, and their maintenance is typically at public expense. Their existence is justified by the range of important functions with which they are entrusted. These involve activities of a specialized and sometimes technical nature in such very diverse fields as health, nutrition, education, research, communication, the environment, and so on. The point to note is that each type of institution has its own division of tasks and its own rules of procedure for selecting, promoting and evaluating the work of its members, determined largely by the specific nature of its functions. A certain measure of autonomy and self-governance, again depending on the function of the institution, is essential to its health and well-being.

The courts themselves are among the most important institutions of society. Some would say that today they are the only dependable institutions, and it is rightly believed that at least the higher courts have so far withstood well the many threats to their integrity from within and outside. Our judges do not need convincing that the autonomy of the court in its own sphere of action is an essential prerequisite of its health and well-being. But even that institutional autonomy cannot be taken for granted. After all, there are ministers, opposition leaders and other powerful agents who might sincerely believe that they know better than any salaried functionary how the affairs of society should be conducted in every sphere.

Judges are well aware that the elected representatives of the people, no matter how well-meaning, do not know everything that needs to be known about the working of such a large, complex and differentiated society as ours. Democracy means not simply the rule of numbers, but also the rule of law. Legislators often have only a rudimentary knowledge of the complex machinery of the law, and our judges serve us well by upholding the sanctity of the law and the autonomy of judicial institutions. But in a democracy, it is not enough to be jealous of the autonomy of one's own institution; one must have some regard also for the autonomy of other institutions.

No matter how high they stand in the public eye today, judges are not the only persons responsible for the well-being of society. Scientists, teachers, writers, journalists, doctors and many others also have important contributions to make to society in their respective spheres. The nature and conditions of medical work in a hospital, scientific work in a national laboratory or teaching and research in a university are different from those of judicial work in a court of law. That is what differentiation and specialization mean in a modern society. Now judges, to whom all this ought to be plain, sometimes show a surprising lack of regard for the particular conditions of work in the different types of institutions when making statements about them from the bench. Today such statements are issued forth more freely and actively than was the case forty years ago.

Judicial activism often stems from the best of motives, the desire to set things right in corrupt and decaying public institutions. Now it is true that forty years ago our public institutions appeared to be in better health, and hence judicial restraint could be more easily observed. But it can also be argued that in a democracy, judicial restraint is a virtue not only in good times but also in bad times.

A clear indication of the movement from a restrained to an activist mode may be found in the slow but distinct shift in the quality of judicial prose. A few years ago, while making a close study of the judgments delivered by our higher courts on a subject of some interest to me, I was startled to discover that the prose style of our judges is not much better than that of our professors, and that is saying a great deal. It tends to be prolix, repetitious and diffuse; it can at the same time be vacuous and incoherent; and it is not always free from grammatical errors of the ordinary kind. We are very far indeed from the measured prose and the balanced style of Vivian Bose and M.C. Chagla. The uncomfortable feeling one gets is that today even important judgments are dictated, with little time left for eliminating repetitions, errors and inconsistencies.

A multitude of complaints against public institutions, both serious and frivolous, pour in from every quarter, and the courts seem hungry for more and more. This must make judicial work very exasperating, and it is beginning to show in the harsh and sweeping pronouncements about the internal arrangements of institutions. These institutions have, in their turn, now learnt to be on their guard against possible strictures from the courts. As a university professor, I can speak from personal experience of academic selection committees. It is true that such committees do not always act in good faith, but even when they do, they are too worried about what the courts might say to be able to exercise their academic judgement freely and fearlessly.

The courts do not always have the capacity to determine what the exercise of academic judgement entails. They are increasingly inclined to assume that there has been foul play, and to intervene on that assumption. The result is that the good candidate is often passed over for the safe candidate, meaning the one who appears on paper to be the best qualified and whose selection does not call for any application of mind. Such examples may be found from almost every public institution entrusted with specialized and technical functions. The courts must certainly exercise vigilance in the public interest; but they will not serve society well if they choke off all initiative in its major institutions by maintaining a habitually intimidating stance.

11 December 1995

A Right for Every Season

Fifty years after Independence, India's record as shown by some of the basic social indicators of development is dismally poor. The spotlight is now on failures on the front of elementary education, and there has been much public recrimination. Educationists have blamed the politicians, and politicians have blamed each other. There is something odd about all this. Every time the advocates of universal elementary education seem to argue as if it is the first time that its great significance for the health and well-being of the nation has been discovered.

It has rarely been doubted that the spread of education is a good thing for both individual and collective well-being. At least the makers of the Constitution were free from such doubt. Article 45 in the Directive Principles of State Policy urged the state to provide 'within a period of ten years from the commencement of this Constitution for free and compulsory education for all children until they complete the age of fourteen years'. The Constitution has been in force for nearly fifty years, yet elementary education is even now far from being universal.

Would it have been better if elementary education had been made a fundamental right instead of being made a matter of state policy? There would no doubt be some difference. There would be a greater sense of urgency, at least in some quarters, though perhaps not in all. There would also be greater pressure on the courts to enforce the right created by the law. Some judges would welcome this as an opportunity to enhance social well-being, but others would probably be alarmed by the prospect of the courts having to cope with unresolved and perhaps unresolvable litigation. Judges now appear to be less alarmed by the arrears of pending cases than they might have been a few decades ago.

It is simply not true that the people of India or even the ruling classes are opposed to all change. There is widespread desire for change and betterment among all sections of society, all communities and all professions. Everybody wants to get to the end of the rainbow, but not many worry about how to get there. Economists seek to create their utopias through planning, politicians through legislation, and social activists through empowerment. They can all give detailed and eloquent accounts of what the utopia will be like once it has been created. But they find it tiresome to dwell too closely on the obstacles that lie on the way. Perhaps in our social environment these obstacles are so pervasive and so oppressive that the mind turns naturally away from them. In the event, people tend to alternate between being utopian and being fatalistic, or fluctuate between a moralizing and a cynical perception of the world.

India has a complex, divided and hierarchical society in which life chances are very unevenly distributed among individuals and groups. Although there are many currents of change, they do not all flow in the same direction or work towards the same end. Societies are governed by their own laws of change; they do not change simply because change seems desirable; and they cannot be changed according to the mere will and pleasure of individuals. This is not to argue against conscious or directed change, without which no society can move forward in the modern world. It is only to draw attention to the obvious fact that human intervention in social processes and institutions has unintended consequences. By their nature, these consequences—of economic planning, of social legislation or of political mobilization—can never be fully foreseen. But more thought can be given to them than is usually done by the advocates of a radical break with the past.

The first two to three decades following Independence were marked by an enormous enthusiasm for the transformation of society through economic planning. If economics was the imperial science anywhere, it was in India in the fifties and sixties. In Delhi, the economists maintained a high profile, and they were to be seen everywhere: in the universities, in research institutes and in the government. They were brilliant, articulate and highly skilled technically, but they also overestimated their own capacities as brilliant intellectuals sometimes do when they are gripped by a social mission. Some of the best among them became victims of their own fantasies about the transformative powers of econometric models.

Planning models are still important and useful, but the days of their glory are over. Now the spotlight is on 'rights' rather than 'models', and judges, advocates and jurists are joined by social scientists and social activists who all demand the creation and expansion of rights: the right to education, the right to health care and the right to work. But the belief in the transformative power of rights may turn out to be no less delusive than the belief in the potency of planning models.

When people do not have the schools and the school

teachers to give them a decent education—or, for that matter, any kind of education—it will be a small consolation for them to have the right to education. The government can no doubt take satisfaction from giving people at least something: the right, if not the real thing. It is a little like the French queen Marie-Antoinette's observation on a clamouring Paris mob. When told that the mob was clamouring for bread, she is reported to have said: 'They don't have bread? Well, let them eat cake.'

Responsible judges and jurists should surely tell our legislators and our public that rights must not be created unless they can be enforced. It is not enough to create rights that can be enforced only in some cases or even in many cases. Conditions must exist for their enforceability in most if not in all cases. Let it not be said about the Indian legal system that it has the most rights and the fewest sanctions. Nothing can be more corrosive of the laws and the Constitution than to take rights lightly.

Political theorists since the time of de Tocqueville have known that what contributes even more than the laws of a nation to the working of democracy are its customs. It is vastly easier to replace old laws by new ones than to replace malign customs by benign ones. Good laws certainly help to change customs, but the creation of laws that cannot be enforced, that are disparaged and disregarded, does more harm than good to society.

28 January 1999

Equality and Universality

In the decades that followed Independence, there was great public enthusiasm for equality. Most articulate members of society showed themselves to be supporters of equality, and anyone who raised a sceptical voice was viewed with mistrust as being a supporter not only of inequality but of its worst excesses. Yet if people examined their own lives, they would recognize that inequality is not only tolerable but in some cases also desirable.

The enthusiasm for equality went with the conviction that the state could progressively reduce and perhaps eventually eliminate inequality through legislation and economic planning. Legislation and planning are both important as ways of bringing about change, but in the last forty years they have suffered some loss of credibility by promising too much and delivering too little. Those who begin with utopian ideas about the triumph of equality risk accepting existing inequalities fatalistically in the end. To raise a sceptical voice about the limits to which equality can advance is not to treat every existing form of inequality as either tolerable or irremovable.

Today the enthusiasm for socialism and for a 'socialist transformation' is on the wane, and there is in its place a new wave of enthusiasm for the market. This is reflected in a noticeable shift in economic policy and the generally favourable public response to it. But there is a difference between the two kinds of enthusiasm. The proponents of socialism had a clear view of the good society, and, no matter what others might think of it, they were generally able to expound it with great force and eloquence. Their intellectual adversaries may feel passionately about the virtues of the market, but they rarely have a clear view of the good society, and some of them are even opposed to any attempt to impose a single view of it.

The idea of equality is of course central to the socialist vision of the good society. That idea does not generate the same strong feeling among those who advocate a leading role for the market. Advocates of the market principle should not be viewed as supporters of inequality, since they are opposed to discrimination on grounds of race, caste and gender; but they are certainly more tolerant than socialists of inequalities of income and wealth, or of any form of inequality that is an outcome of open and free competition.

When an economy so large and complex as ours changes course, there are bound to be major social consequences, foreseen as well as unforeseen. There will perhaps be less talk about equality now, and that may not be a bad thing, for it may be good to be concerned about equality but not always to be obsessed about it. All things considered, the public rhetoric on equality did not bring about any great change in the actual distribution of income, although it did alter people's perception of the traditional social hieararchy. It is not at all unlikely that a more competitive economy will lead in the long run to a further decline in the significance of caste and gender, the two most important bases of the traditional hierarchy, although such an economy is also likely to increase at least some forms of inequality.

In the context of the changes that are likely to ensue, it

is essential to keep in sight the distinction between equality and universality. A modern society can afford to have reservations about the claims of equality; it cannot afford to ignore the claims of universality. Where equality and inequality are concerned, it is impossible in such a society to disregard differences of ability and performance, and the need to relate them to income, esteem and authority. By contrast, the principle of universality demands access to certain basic things irrespective of ability or performance. Drinking water, food, shelter, and also elementary education and primary health care should be universally available to all, and in their case questions of ability, merit or dessert simply do not arise, or at least should not arise.

The commitment to universality as a social principle is a modern one. In its early expression it was closely associated, not to say confused, with the principle of equality, but the two are not the same. Only a limited number of things, not everything, can be made universally available to all. Beyond that, the regime of scarcity determines that certain things will be available to some and not to others, and that some will frequently have a larger share than others of the same thing. This leads to many different kinds of inequality even where the claims of universality are acknowledged and protected.

The economic reforms now being introduced are bound to lead to some increase of inequality in at least some important sectors of society. But that does not mean that those reforms will necessarily jeopardize the claims of universality, or worsen the conditions of the most disadvantaged members of society. It is a plain superstition that every increase of inequality, in no matter which stratum or class, always worsens and never betters the conditions of those who are worst-off. For my part, I am perfectly happy to accept some increase of inequality among the middle classes, provided it leads to even a slight improvement in the conditions of the most disadvantaged stratum of society.

It would be surprising if those who are making the new economic policy were unaware of the fact that it is likely to lead to some increase of inequality. Signs of this increase are already in evidence, and they will become increasingly manifest where they will be most visible to the media, in the corporate private sector, among professionals such as doctors, architects and accountants, and, in course of time, perhaps also in the public sector. But this does not mean that agricultural labourers, migrant workers and others in casual employment will necessarily be worse-off as a result. Those at the helm of economic affairs should be forthright in admitting that their policy might increase inequality among the middle classes, and explain, if they can, how it might benefit rather than harm the worst-off members of society. It is the latter point that needs to be openly and seriously addressed, for there may be reason to hope that the poor and the downtrodden could in the end be better served by a dynamic economy than by one that is hamstrung by controls and regulations imposed in the name of equality.

Much of the advocacy of equality and social justice has been for the benefit of the educated and the salaried middle classes. It is often propelled by white-collar trade unionism, and it is occasionally self-serving. There is no reason to believe that a continuous levelling of income, esteem and authority among doctors, scientists and academics will benefit either directly or indirectly the really disadvantaged members of society. The relentless drive for levelling in the name of equality by organized middle-class interests calls to mind the words of Justice

Holmes who said, 'I have no respect for the passion for equality which seems to me merely idealizing envy.' The real thrust in social policy should be to make basic rights and facilities universally accessible to all, and its aim and purpose should not diverted by the obsession with salary differentials between secretaries, under secretaries and section officers, or the extent to which one caste as against another is over- or under-represented among doctors, engineers or pilots.

8 March 1995

Tribe, Caste and Religion

The articles in this section deal with the division of Indian society on the basis of tribe, caste and religion. The nature and significance of these divisions is changing, and I raise questions about the implications of these changes for social analysis and social policy.

The first question we must ask is whether there is one unique way in which Indian society has to be conceived and represented. The divisions of caste and community are indeed important, but so also are those based on wealth, occupation and education. Which kind of division becomes salient depends to some extent on the political process to which official policy contributes a significant element. During the period of colonial rule the view became established that India was essentially a society of castes and communities, a land of 'the most inviolable organization by birth'.

During the struggle for independence, the leaders of the nationalist movement contested the view that India was and would remain at its core a society of castes and communities. In the early years of independence, the political executive on the whole took a negative view of the role of caste in public life, and the courts too viewed caste classifications for official purposes with disfavour. But with the passage of time, political pressures began to mount for giving official recognition to caste classifications. It was argued that discrimination on the basis of caste and community was a significant part of the Indian social reality, and that such discrimination could not be eliminated without giving official recognition to the divisions on which it was based. The question thus is not whether the divisions of caste and tribe exist but whether they should be given official recognition in the hope that discrimination will thereby be reduced or eliminated.

Religion is, like tribe and caste, a very important basis of social identity. In the politics of identity, the divisions of religion—and to some extent also those of language—tend to operate in the same way as those of tribe and caste. But religion is not just a matter of social identity, it is also a matter of faith. India is a land of different religious faiths which manifest themselves in different modes of worship. But although religious beliefs and practices are of great importance in the lives of most Indians, India is a secular state and has a secular legal order. There are different conceptions of secularism, some more accommodative of religion that others. An unaccommodating conception of secularism will have very little future in India. At the same time, India can hardly move forward into the future if it fails to accommodate secular ideas and secular institutions.

Language, Religion and Caste

Language, religion and caste are increasingly seen to act in similar ways in the context of contemporary Indian politics. As a result, some sociologists and political scientists now speak of all three as forms of the same kind of social identity for which they use the more general concept of ethnic identity.

There is some basis for this perception in the structure of Indian society where the same term, jati (or jat) is used to cover a range of identities of various degrees of inclusiveness. While conducting a survey in Giridih town and its neighbouring villages in Bihar in 1958, I came across a variety of names in the columns asking for the respondent's caste. In addition to names of castes in the ordinary sense of the term, the entries included 'Oriya', 'Marwari', 'Muslim' and 'Jain'. Of these four, the first two refer to language (and region) and the two others to religion.

This broad equation of categories was given a new twist by the dialectics of 'nationalist' and 'communalist' politics in the decades preceding Independence. In north India generally, the term 'communal' referred to division by religion, particularly the division into Hindus and Muslims. In the south, the same term, as for instance in the phrase 'Communal GO', referred characteristically to division by caste, particularly the division between Brahmins and non-Brahmins. The confusion was worse confounded by the fact that the British not only lumped all kind of groups together, but freely used the term 'classes' to refer to them collectively. It is from this that we derive the practice of referring to the schedule castes, the scheduled tribes, the Anglo-Indians, and so on as 'certain classes' in Part XVI of our Constitution.

The identities of language, religion and caste have been used so persistently for the mobilization of political support in the last forty years that they have now come to be regarded as unalterable features of our political landscape. Their continued, if not increasing, importance in Indian politics has been a source of some disappointment to both liberal and radical intellectuals. Liberal intellectuals had hoped that democratic politics would teach citizens to choose rationally between alternative candidates according to the merits of their programmes, policies and personal qualities of leadership. Radicals had hoped that politics would serve to override all particularistic differences to unite people into classes whose combined actions would transform society as a whole. The remarkable persistence of ethnic identities appears to have confounded the hope of creating a more liberal and equal society through politics, at least for the time being.

Despite their obvious similarities, there are also important differences between language and religion on the one hand, and caste on the other as bases of social identity. Caste is a specific feature of South Asian societies, whereas language and religion are universal features of all human societies. It is possible, though now not very easy, to conceive of Indian society without caste; it is impossible to conceive of a human society without language, and nearly impossible to conceive of one without religion.

It is a truism that human beings need a language, not just language as such but a specific language, to communicate with each other, creating and sharing a common life thereby. A shared life without a common language is barely possible. Thus language and territory tend to go together to a large extent in our country where several states carry names that refer also to languages, for example, Gujarat, Assam, Tamil Nadu and Punjab. But of course those who speak the same language may live in different territories, for instance, Tamil speakers in Tamil Nadu and Sri Lanka; and persons who inhabit the same place may speak different languages, as in any large Indian city. This always creates the possibility of linguistic difference becoming a significant political factor. The sense of community provided by a shared language is so strong that it survives, as American examples show, even when its members do not speak the language any more but carry only a memory of it.

Religion, like language, also binds people together through shared beliefs and practices, and perhaps even more deeply through shared symbols that are repeatedly evoked on occasions such as birth, marriage and death, and the calendric festivals. Many individuals are able to do without religious doctrine; but few can do without the religious symbols that mark the turning points in one's life and in the life of the community. Here again, as with language, the memory of shared experience may be kept alive by symbols when very little in fact survives of shared practice.

Maintaining a social identity through a shared

memory is never the same thing as its maintenance through the sharing of lived experience; and language is part of the lived experience of every individual, and religion of almost every individual. The same can scarcely be said about caste. It is for this reason that attempts to treat caste identities and caste differences on the same plane as the identities and differences due to language and religion may be misleading beyond a point, no matter how common the practice may be of treating them alike in the politics of the day.

The hold of caste over a person's social practice is more variable than that of religion and much more so than that of language. The rules relating to interdining, sharing food, accepting water and so on, which were central to caste practice in the past, have become greatly attenuated, particularly among urban, educated, professional Indians. To be sure, when an educated Indian declares that he takes no account of caste, his words should not be taken at face value. He will take caste into account at the time of his marriage and also while arranging the marriages of his children, particularly his daughters. But there are now many urban, educated Indians, particularly in the higher occupational strata, who do not consciously take much account of caste in their own social practice outside of marriage, although it may still act on that practice without their being fully conscious of its role.

Politics has now brought caste back into the minds of many persons who may have thought a generation ago that it was on its way out. I have known many intellectuals who take little account of caste in their own social practice, including the practice of marriage, to argue forcefully that caste must be of paramount importance in

Indian society because it is of paramount important in contemporary Indian politics. This is a tendentious argument that diverts attention away from the changes taking place in many of the social aspects of caste. A society has many faces, and they do not all change together at the same pace or even in the same way.

The long-term trend in the present century has been towards the weakening, though by no means the disappearance, of caste consciousness in the minds of people. It is politics that is now reversing this trend. If the experience of ethnic politics in the United States is anything to go by, then politics can keep alive the memory of caste in the minds of people long after it has ceased to be a significant part of their social practice.

23 February 1994

The People of India

Who are the people of India? In an obvious sense, the people of India are those who think of themselves as such, although they do not all think of themselves in the same way everywhere or at all times. How people think of themselves depends in part on the ways in which they are classified and represented by themselves and others. These classifications and representations are everywhere influenced, directly and indirectly, by state action, and in India such state action has played a particularly important part in shaping collective identities—both common and separate identities—in the last hundred years.

The colonial government embarked on a comprehensive project of ethnographic mapping towards the end of the nineteenth century. This was organized and supervised by a succession of highly able ICS ethnographers whose aims were both scholarly and practical. What emerged from their labours was a picture of Indian society whose basic and irreducible units were a multitude of castes and tribes. This representation of Indian society systematically subordinated the individual to the group. To use a popular expression, the colonial construction of Indian society was a society of castes and communities and not of individuals. Like all such constructions, it reflected the existing reality and also served to give it a new shape.

It is possible to say with the advantage of hindsight that Ibbetson, Risley, Thurston and others could not have anticipated all the social and political consequences that were to flow from their efforts to identify, classify and rank the various tribes and castes of India. They were, by the standards of colonial administrators or even administrators in general, well-intentioned and moved by a genuine desire to understand the society that had come under their rule. But it did not take them long to realize that their labours had opened up a Pandora's box of social divisions; and if they encouraged and used those divisions in the interest of what they considered good governance, we should not judge them too harshly.

It was natural for the ICS ethnographers to be attracted by the unfamiliar and the exotic, and it is not difficult to recapture the excitement of their discovery in the nineteenth century of a whole new world of tribes, castes, subcastes, clans and sects. They described them in the voluminous reports of the decenniel censuses, and there were separate accounts of them, usually in several volumes, for the different regions of the country. In the meantime, each caste or even subcaste was becoming increasingly differentiated in terms of income, occupation, education and a variety of factors. But the treatment of them in official publications as the basic and irreducible units of Indian society contributed, at least in part, to what has been called the 'substantialization of caste'.

The ethnographic mapping of India in terms of its tribes and castes continued till almost the time of

Independence. The ICS ethnographers obviously considered it a necessary and useful task. Nationalist intellectuals, on the other hand, viewed it with misgiving since they thought that it gave a distorted perspective on Indian society and fostered divisiveness. It is impossible to draw a fair and objective balance sheet of the gains and losses that resulted from this large ethnographic enterprise. It brought together much new information and created a new awareness of the multiplicity of the people of India; and who is to say that the pursuit of knowledge must stop wherever there is a fear that its results may be politically divisive? At the same time, it cannot be overlooked that the colonial government put the demographic and ethnographic knowledge at its disposal to some queer political uses.

The new government of independent India began with a different view about the people of India from that of its predecessor. Is it in the process of changing that view and bringing it more in line with the one that prevailed before Independence? This question naturally arises when we consider the massive People of India project undertaken by the Anthropological Survey of India on behalf of the government. The title of the project echoes the work of Sir Herbert Risley, and the very conception of the people of India as essentially a congeries of castes and communities seems to be the same in the present project as in the earlier colonial one.

The new People of India project was designed on an ambitious scale to cover every type of community through the length and breadth of the country. The investigations were completed over a period of seven years from 1985 to 1992 at a total cost of Rs 69,157,234. A few volumes have already come out, and a total of seventy-two volumes will be published over the next few years. A project on such an ambitious scale would probably have been beyond the resources of a colonial state.

An initial list of 6,748 communities was prepared and of them 4,635 have been investigated and described. The director of the project has skirted around the issue of nomenclature, proposing the term samudaya in place of jati, but they are in all essential respects the same kinds of communities that received the attention of the earlier ethnographers who would have been more forthright and just called them tribes and castes.

Now that we will have all this information, it will be put to various uses by various persons. Facts are always valuable, although we should avoid the mistake of thinking that they speak for themselves. No less important is the framework of ideas which regulates the selection and arrangement of facts; and it is here that there will be disappointment and misgivings about the new project. Has nothing changed since Risley and his associates decided to represent the people of India as a congeries of tribes and castes? In the decades since Independence there have been five-year plans and economic liberalization; agrarian reform and industrial development; adult franchise and Panchayati Raj; and a host of legal and constitutional changes. If through all these changes the people of India have continued to remain in the same mould in which they were caught by the ethnographers of the nineteenth century, this must surely make us pause and ponder.

No doubt there will be disagreement on how the people of India should be represented at any given historical juncture. Some will say that Indian society has changed very little and that it continues to be at bottom a society of castes and communities. Others will place more emphasis on the divisions in society based on wealth, income, occupation, education, and so on. It is not necessary or even desirable that there should be complete agreement on this. What is disturbing, however, is that the government should set its seal on a particular representation of the people of India, and that too in terms of categories on which it appears to have turned its back at the time of Independence. Whatever else may come out of the People of India project, it will certainly contribute further to the substantialization of caste. If Indians are persuaded to believe that their society is nothing but a society of castes and communities, then in the end that is the kind of society it will be.

10 May 1994

Head Count of Harijans

A little over fifty years ago, when a joint committee was deliberating on the seats to be reserved for the depressed classes in accordance with the Poona pact between Gandhi and Ambedkar, representatives from both Bengal and the Punjab raised objections to the terms of the pact on the ground that there was no depressed classes problem in their provinces. Twenty-five members of the Bengal Legislative Council had earlier stated in a telegram to the prime minister in London: 'No depressed classes problem in Bengal as elsewhere in India, as found on careful examination by Lothian Committee.' Bhai Parmanand from Punjab had deposed in his evidence that, 'It is in the report of the Simon Commission and the Government of India report also that the distinction between caste Hindus and the depressed classes does not exist in the Punjab.'

These categorical assertions, made with the political objective of shifting the burden of the Poona pact on to other shoulders, must be taken with a large pinch of salt. The practice of untouchability and the division into caste Hindus and the depressed classes, now designated as scheduled castes, were features of every part of the country and are to be found in every major part of it to this day. The traditional structure of the Indian village not merely tolerated but required the presence of untouchables for both economic and ritual reasons.

There had to be in every group of villages, if not in every village, labourers to do the hard physical work in the fields as well as scavengers, flayers and tanners to insulate the community from pollution. It would be very difficult to sustain the argument that Punjab was at any time a total exception to the general pattern; and Bengal certainly was not.

At the same time, it is also true that the preoccupation with purity and pollution was not equally marked in every part of the country. This means that the distinction between caste Hindus and the scheduled castes, though found everywhere, varies greatly in significance from one part of India to another. The representatives from Bengal and Punjab were no doubt making exaggerated claims, but it would not be wholly wrong to say that the disabilities of caste were considerably less severe in their provinces than in some other parts of the country.

Anyone who has travelled in the different parts of rural India will have noticed that the ritual restrictions on contact are far less severe in the north and the east than in the south. These regional differences are today less clear than they were fifty years ago because of the many changes since Independence, among which perhaps the most important in the present context is the replacement of traditional forms of untouchability by modern forms of atrocity. But they can still be observed if we take the trouble to look beneath the surface, and the entire ethnographic record upto the time of Independence confirms the same pattern of regional variation.

J.H. Hutton, who was in charge of the census of 1931 which began the exercises out of which the current lists of the scheduled castes have emerged, was a noted anthropologist who published in 1946 a book on caste in India. In that book he paid careful attention to what he called caste restrictions in the light of regional variations, and noted that those restrictions were much more stringent in the south than in the north or the east. Hutton was by no means the first ethnographer to present this kind of picture. While many of his predecessors had noted pollution practices in both the north and the east, the choicest examples of the practice of untouchability almost always came from the south, particularly Kerala.

If we now examine the regional distribution of the scheduled caste population as given by the 1981 census, we find a pattern that is, at least in appearance, very puzzling. The proportion of the scheduled caste population to the total population is 15.75 per cent for India as a whole, but the state which has the highest proportion, namely 26.87 per cent, is, to the surprise of the old-fashioned ethnographer, Punjab. West Bengal, though not in fact second, follows close behind with a figure of 21.99 per cent, which is far higher than the all-India figure. To confound the ethnographer still further, Kerala, long considered the citadel of the worst excesses of untouchability, shows a figure of 10.02 per cent, which is well below the all-India figure, and Maharashtra, where the Poona pact was made, shows an even lower figure, namely 7.14 per cent. There are some differences between the 1971 and the 1981 figures but these differences are minor, and the broad pattern is the same.

How are we to account for this anomaly? How has it come about that Punjab, where the rigours of untouchability were believed to be so mild, has now such a high proportion of scheduled caste persons in its total population, whereas Kerala, where its rigours were believed to be so severe, has such a low proportion? It cannot be that the entire body of accumulated knowledge about regional variations in the rigours of untouchability rests on an illusion. Can it then be that how we assess the rigours of untouchability is one thing, and how we count the scheduled caste population is a very different thing?

An argument which seeks to delink the practice of untouchability, particularly the past practice of it, from the enumeration of the scheduled castes, would be difficult to maintain. Firstly, it would fly in the face of the very historical conditions which compelled the creation of the category we now designate as the scheduled castes. Secondly, it would be inconsistent with the provisions of the Protection of Civil Rights Act which makes membership of a scheduled caste the touchstone of offences deemed to be committed on the ground of 'untouchability'.

The existing lists of the scheduled castes are arranged state by state. It is not necessary to labour the point further that these lists are not fully consistent either with each other or with the social reality they are presumed to reflect. It is true that there is no foolproof criterion by which we can specify either the practice of untouchability or the groups that have been its victims. The Protection of Civil Rights Act and its earlier incarnation, the Untouchability (Offences) Act, wisely refrained from trying to provide a definition of untouchability. Even with the best of intentions it will be difficult if not impossible to construct a fully consistent list of the scheduled castes for the country as a whole, one which will incorporate only the real victims of untouchability. But can we really say that only the best intentions have entered into the construction of these lists?

To point to the artificial or even the arbitrary nature of the existing categorization into the scheduled castes is not to argue against either measures for the eradication of untouchability or measures for the welfare of its past and present victims. However hard it may be to define untouchability to the complete satisfaction of judges and scholars, no one can be blind to its existence or its consequences. No cost can be counted too high for protecting and promoting the interests of its real victims who number in the millions. But having said this, we must be careful to distinguish between considerations of social welfare which should be enlarged and calculations of political gain which have to be restrained.

It should not be a matter of surprise that political calculations have been mixed together with considerations of social welfare in matters relating to the scheduled castes. They have been mixed together from the very start. It is undeniable that many of those who served the colonial government, of whom J.H. Hutton was one, had the welfare of the 'exterior castes' at heart. But they had at heart other interests as well. They would not be human if they were to miss the chance of using 'minority politics' to undercut 'nationalist politics'. One hardly needs to stress the point that in a democracy, where numbers count for so much, the census is always a handy instrument of politics. The British had the foresight to realize this even before India became a democracy.

What began during British rule did not end with British rule. Political calculations have continued to play a part in and sometimes even to dominate policies and programmes designed for the welfare of the backward classes. This is seen most clearly in the case of the Other Backward Classes, but evidence of it is not difficult to find for the scheduled castes and scheduled tribes as well. The existing lists of the scheduled castes and scheduled tribes are in the process of being revised. There is reason to believe that there will be pressures from the state governments to revise them upwards by the inclusion of new castes and communities: many want to be counted in; few, if any, want to be counted out. It is to be hoped that if an attempt is made to bring about uniformity, this will not be done by revising the lists of all the states so as to make them match the proportion of the scheduled caste population to the total population in Punjab.

21 March 1985

Caste in the Indian Census

A move is afoot to include caste in the forthcoming census of India. The enumeration, classification and ranking of castes became a major part of the census of population periodically undertaken by the colonial government since the end of the last century. The practice was discontinued, as a matter of principle, when the country became independent. Bringing caste back into the official census of population will in my judgement be a retrograde step in the light of our constitutional commitment.

It is said that liberal intellectuals act against their own principles in opposing the collection of a wider body of information: they ought to support and not oppose the move by the government to make more information on caste available to the public. This is a shallow argument. The question is not simply whether to have more information, but how and by whom such information should be collected and presented. Information on caste collected by the census will no doubt be very large in quantity, but, going by past experience, its quality will be open to very serious doubt.

It goes without saying that caste is an important part of our present reality. Nothing would be more perverse than to put a ban on investigations into caste. Sociologists have actively studied caste for the last fifty years, and their studies have provided many valuable insights into Indian society. I support the continuing study of caste by private individuals, universities and independent research centres. I am at the same time opposed to the state giving recognition to caste for official purposes without special and valid reasons. In a liberal democracy, the state should not be directly involved in every type of investigation; some types of investigation are best left to independent agencies.

Many members of the public take a somewhat simple view of what the census does. A census does not merely enumerate, it also classifies; and a classification presented by the census has the authority of an official classification. Every individual carries in his head some kind of a map of his own society which provides him with a sense of its main contours and cleavages. These maps are usually partial and fragmentary, and they change over time. The colonial administration sought for its own reasons to create a definitive map of Indian society whose principal demarcations were to be the cleavages of caste and community. Fifty years after Independence, do we need to start that same exercise all over again?

Even while they greatly value tradition, Indians appear to pay scant regard to history. It will be a pity if we forget the history of caste in the decades preceding Independence and the part played by the census in that history. Some of the earlier commissioners of census, such as H.H. Risley and J.H. Hutton, were men of great intellectual ability, and they used such resources as they could muster to bring into full view what they considered to be the real significance of caste in Indian society. They did not stop with making lists of the castes they enumerated, but sought in various ingenious ways to classify and rank them. They also came to be used as courts of appeal in matters relating to the social standing of castes.

A hundred years ago, those responsible for using the census operations for the study and management of caste could not anticipate the full range of claims and counter-claims to which the official involvement with caste would give rise. Even if they could foresee the future, they would not all have been equally alarmed, for some clearly found the policy of divide and rule to their advantage. We are not now in the position in which the country was a hundred years ago. We cannot say that the official involvement with caste will be a harmless exercise in fact-finding; and why should an elected government seek to foster divisions among its own people?

Attempts by the census authorities at the classification and ranking of castes led to the most extravagant claims from the most unexpected quarters. If the census becomes involved once again in the enumeration and classification of castes, it will be difficult for the authorities to turn a deaf ear to contending claims from interested parties. No doubt there will be a difference. Whereas in the past, castes with the most humble antecedents sought to register themselves as Kshatriyas, now politically dominant castes will vie with each other to be classified as Backward, More Backward and Most Backward.

The increasing attention paid by the colonial government to caste led to changes in its nature and practice. What took place has been described by some sociologists as the 'substantialization of caste'. To be sure, the census alone cannot be held responsible for heightening the competition between castes for status and power. But it certainly contributed something to it. If we wish to reduce instead of increase that competition, we should give serious thought to the reasons that led the first government of independent India to turn its back on the policy of recording caste in the census.

I would like in the end to dispose of one argument that is persistently made to justify the inclusion of caste. That argument is that since we include language and religion, which can also be socially divisive, it would be inconsistent to exclude caste. This again is a misleading argument. Caste cannot have in any modern society the place that belongs rightfully to language and religion, whether or not they are socially divisive. The makers of the Constitution of India sought to create a casteless society; they did not by any means seek to eliminate or even diminish the significance of religion or language.

Language and religion are and have been important constituents of culture everywhere and at all times. Not only that: liberal Indians take pride in the fact that their country is the home of many languages and many religions. The plurality of languages and religions is what gives to Indian society its special place in the comity of nations. We not only record but also celebrate the presence of many languages and many religions in our land. Who celebrates the division of Indian society into the thousands of castes, subcastes and sub-subcastes that have long outlived such social utility as they might have had in the past?

11 June 1998

Myth of Indigenous People

The idea of 'indigenous people' has become a rallying point for social and political movements in many parts of the world. When an idea becomes a political force, it often becomes detached from its historical context. It then becomes necessary to go back to the context to see how far the idea can be regarded as valid.

When about a hundred years ago, western anthropologists began the systematic study of what were then called 'primitive cultures', they were naturally struck by the great difference between those cultures and their own. Early anthropological studies established certain conventions, and in using those conventions—as with words such as 'tribe', 'aborigine', 'indigenous people'— we must keep in mind their original context. Anthropologists of the past studied race, language and culture together, since it appeared natural for them to assume that the differences between themselves and the people they studied were not merely of language, religion and culture but also of race. The assumption of a close relationship between language, religion and culture on the one hand and race on the other, often led to a serious misrepresentation of the relations between social groups. It has left behind a substratum of belief that tribal and non-tribal populations belong to distinct racial stock; though plausible in some contexts, this belief is generally misleading in others, including India.

In many parts of the world, European settlements were superimposed upon pre-existing communities through a unique historical process. That process witnessed the encounter of two distinct populations—of settlers or immigrants on the one hand and native or indigenous people on the other—that differed radically in race, language and culture. Not only was the difference very marked at the initial encounter, it was often perpetuated though careful segregation. As a result, in Australia, for example, and to a lesser extent in North America, there was little fear of confusing between settler and indigenous populations. When anthropologists went out to study tribal communities in these countries, the identification of such communities presented no serious problems.

The relationship between tribal and non-tribal populations has been of a very different kind in the ancient civilizations of India, China and the Islamic world. This is true to such an extent that in India, for example, it is generally difficult to draw a sharp line of distinction between tribal and non-tribal communities on the basis of race, religion or language. In Australia, the term aborigine has a very definite meaning; it is difficult, if not impossible, to give such a term a definite meaning in India.

Anthropological practice in India gradually led to the designation of some communities as 'tribes' or 'aboriginal tribes' as against others. This practice was initiated by colonial administrators, some of whom had considerable familiarity with anthropological usage in the rest of the world. When we now look back on the earlier accounts of Indian communities, we are struck by a pervasive ambiguity in the use of the terms 'tribe' and 'caste'. Communities such as the Jats or Ahirs were freely referred to as 'tribes' although today we would describe them as castes.

The great paradox of Indian society is that, despite its rigid rules for the maintenance of social distance between communities, there has been pervasive interpenetration between tribal and non-tribal populations for well over 2,000 years. This can be seen if we compare tribal and non-tribal ways of life in most regions. If we take only the extreme, for instance the food-gathering Birhors and the landowning Brahmins in Bihar, the contrasts are no doubt sharp. But the extremes are almost everywhere mediated by a large number of communities between which the contrasts are often muted. The coexistence of tribal and non-tribal communities, population movements of both tribals and non-tribals, and the displacement of one type of community by another were no doubt accompanied by a great deal of exploitation and expropriation, but they were slow and gradual rather than sudden and cataclysmic as in the New World.

Throughout inner India, in Bihar, Madhya Pradesh, Rajasthan, Gujarat and elsewhere, there have been movements of both tribal and non-tribal populations from time immemorial. Some tribal populations have displaced other tribal populations and have in turn been displaced by non-tribal populations. Many tribal groups in Rajasthan, Gujarat, Tamil Nadu and elsewhere have spoken some variant of the regional language as far as living memory goes. Sometimes tribal chieftains or headmen have been implicated in regional political structures by tradition, and elements of a common ritual idiom may be found among tribals and non-tribals in more than one area. Where the same traits of material or non-material culture are common to both tribal and non-tribal groups, it is by no means easy to determine who borrowed which trait from whom. The inter-penetration of tribal and non-tribal modes of life is of course not equally manifest everywhere, being most conspicuous among the larger tribes of inner India such as the Bhils, the Gonds and the Santhals.

It needs to be stressed that what is at issue is the status as indigenous or immigrant not of a particular individual or household but of a whole community. The current talk about 'indigenous people' is a talk about rights, of which the core is a right by birth. Further, one is 'indigenous' by virtue of being born into a particular community and not a particular place. Someone else born in that same place cannot be regarded as indigenous even if his parents or his grandparents or his great-grandparents lived and died there, for his forefathers might have come from elsewhere; the forefathers of the first person might also have come from elsewhere but that will not matter if the community to which he belongs is designated as 'indigenous'. Where historical records are scarce and historical memory is short, the idea of 'indigenous people' provides abundant scope for the proliferations of myths relating to blood and soil.

The political argument about the rights of indigenous people is not necessarily wrong, but it can be easily misplaced. It obviously has a certain cogency in countries such as Australia, Canada and the United States, but it now threatens to become a universal slogan. It has extended its appeal to Indian intellectuals with a strong sense of social justice. However, the many implications of the distinction between indigenous and immigrant peoples are not always kept in mind.

In the south, the idea of the Brahmins as aliens of Aryan descent who came from the north and imposed their hegemony over the indigenous Dravidian people has been current for some time. To the extent that it presupposes a difference of race between Aryans and Dravidians, it is a myth and not a scientific truth. But it can easily acquire fresh sustenance from the present worldwide concern for the rights of indigenous people. As the south Indian example shows, the idea of an indigenous people rooted in the soil and with prior claims on it presupposes the other who is defined as the immigrant, the alien or the usurper. We have only to consider the view, freely expressed in certain quarters, that Muslims in India are immigrants and usurpers, to recognize the dark face of the myth of the indigenous people.

5 January 1993

Colonial Construction of Tribe

The Anthropological Survey of India has given a new lease of life to the old belief that, basically, the people of India are made up of castes ad tribes. It is hard to ignore the presence of castes in the social landscape of contemporary India. Their continuing importance is regularly confirmed by our newspapers, in their reporting of electoral matters and in their matrimonial columns. At the same time, the castes of today are not what they were in their original or pristine form, or even in the form in which they existed till a hundred years ago. Many of them have discarded their old names and adopted new ones. They have also changed their identities to a greater or lesser extent in response to changes in economic and political life.

Some scholars now argue that castes acquired a new—and in some sense more rigid—identity as a result of the persistent efforts of the colonial state to enumerate, classify and rank all the different castes throughout the country. The effect on caste identity and caste consciousness of the censuses and surveys undertaken by the colonial state came to be recognized only gradually in the period since Independence. Some American anthropologists have gone so far as to write about the 'colonial construction of caste', although this has to be taken with many qualifications. For while the colonial state, with its marked predilection for clear definitions and neat classifications, might have done something to reinforce the identities of caste, it also introduced changes in education and employment that undermined the traditional distinctions of caste.

No matter what importance we assign to the part played by the colonial state in reinforcing the identities of caste, we cannot say in any literal sense that the category of caste was an artefact of colonial rule. We can say that much more confidently in regard to the category of tribe. It is surprising that those who have written about the colonial construction of caste have had so little to say about the colonial construction of tribe.

When the British began to take a new look at caste, its manifold divisions and their functions and ranks, they did not begin on a clean slate. A complex and sophisticated literature dealing with all these questions in one way or another had been in existence for two thousand years. Nor was familiarity with the category of caste confined only to the intelligentsia; it was also a part of the thinking of the common man long before the British came on the scene. Every Hindu knew not only that he belonged to a particular caste but also that others belonged to other castes of whose respective places in a broader scheme of things he had some idea, whether vague or stereotyped. Hardly anything corresponding to this existed in the case of those we know today as tribes. The consciousness of the distinct and separate identity of all the tribes in India taken as a whole is a modern consciousness, brought into being by the colonial state and confirmed by its successor after Independence.

To be sure, each tribe taken by itself had a sense of its own identity long before the work of the surveys and censuses began. The Santhals had a sense of their own identity as Santhals; the Garos of theirs as Garos; and the

Todas of theirs as Todas. But Santhals, Garos, Todas and the hundreds of other tribes now existing in the different parts of the country had neither a sense of commonality nor the sense of interdependence by which castes have been characterized, at least within the region, for a very long time. There was no tribal literati to reflect and write about the nature of tribe, corresponding to the Brahminical literati who reflected and wrote about the nature of caste. Discussion of the nature and significance of tribe as a distinct social category had to await the coming of colonial rule.

The colonial state was only partly successful in giving a clear and definite identity to the tribal population of India. This population is too large and too differentiated to be easily defined in terms of any single criterion or set of criteria, and there are too many cases where it is hard to decide whether to count a particular community as a tribe or a caste. Nevertheless, the category of tribe has today become a part of the established order, but more as a political than as a social fact. Having become established, that identity is now in the process of being reformulated, with a distinct tendency to describe the tribal population as a whole and irrespective of its location as the indigenous people of India.

The term 'indigenous people' has acquired wide currency throughout the world during the last decade, mainly on the initiative of international agencies. It can, of course, be legitimately used in certain contexts where a clear distinction has remained between a population inhabiting the land since time immemorial and a population of more or less recent settlers, as in the case of Australia or Canada. The use of the term in other contexts is misleading and can be mischievous.

Every population or part of it is indigenous to some

area, just as every person is a native of some place. So when we categorize a particular section of the population of a land, to the exclusion of other sections of it, as indigenous, we must know how those other sections stand in relation to the one designated as indigenous. Taking India as a whole, it would be absurd to designate as indigenous only the tribal population, leaving out all the others. As a matter of historical fact, several of the contemporary tribes of India moved into the country across its northeastern frontier long after the areas into which they moved had been settled by peasants who are not now designated as tribals. The Mizos certainly are not more indigenous to the areas they inhabit than the Gujaratis are to Gujarat.

We know too little about the history of population movement in India to be able to decide with any confidence who has lived for how long in any given territory. The claim of occupation since time immemorial is based more often on mythology than on history. Population movements have taken place among both non-tribals and tribals, and it will be a mistake to maintain that those movements have always been more extensive among the former than among the latter. There is no reason to believe that the Santhals have lived longer in the Santhal parganas than the Bengali peasants of Hooghly district have lived in that district; or that the Oraons have lived longer in Ranchi district than the Tamil peasants of Tanjore have lived where they now live. It is true that population movements have led repeatedly to the displacement of tribals by non-tribals; but they have also led to the displacement of some tribes by other tribes.

The political demands of the present cannot alter what took place in the past. The idea that the tribes are the indigenous people of India has grown in response to a political demand. That demand can alter perceptions to some extent, but it cannot wish the facts of demography out of existence.

19 June 1995

Religion in a Secular Society

Not long ago, as I was struggling to formulate a somewhat involuted argument about religion and society, my interlocutor, a sagacious person with a wide experience of men and affairs, cut me short and said, simply, 'Secularism is India's destiny.' That is indeed so, and arguments that secularism is difficult to define, that the concept is inherently ambiguous or that it means different things to different persons take nothing away from the force of the statement.

The conviction that secularism will make room for itself increasingly and inevitably in Indian society does not require the belief that religion will disappear from the lives of the Indian people. It would be strange for a sociologist, however strong his desire for secularism, to hold such a belief. Sociologists have studied the relationship between religion and society for a hundred years now, and even those among them who have written about a long-term trend towards secularism have rarely considered religion to be a dispensible feature of collective life. The sociology of religion as a serious academic discipline must be distinguished from the construction of utopias from which social classes, the state and religion are made to disappear.

Granted, then, that religion will continue to have an important place in the lives of people, or of most people, the question that arises is whether and to what extent a society can accommodate institutions such as universities, hospitals, banks, and civil and military bureaucracies that must necessarily arrange their affairs without regulation by religious doctrine or religious authority. It is in this sense—the building of secular institutions and their insulation from the demands of religion—that one speaks of secularization as a worldwide tendency.

The growth of secular institutions is a slow, laborious and painful process whose sources of nourishment still remain largely obscure. Judicious action by the government may smoothen its course, but thoughtless interference may also obstruct it. People often feel about their religion as they do about their family, that it is something sacred, and they resent interference in it by politicians and officials, particularly when they regard them, as they increasingly do in India, as venal and corrupt. At the same time, it does not help when free-wheeling intellectuals declare that secularism is a western idea, alien to the Indian spirit, and that we do not need secular institutions but should create our own alternatives to them. It is not all that easy to create an alternative to the modern world.

It would be easy to argue that interference by the government in religious affairs should be limited and restrained, except for the fact that sometimes the very existence of a government may be threatened by the play of religious passions. The hope of secularism is not that it will eliminate religious passion from human affairs, but that it may to some extent neutralize and soften its expression in public life. However ardently one may desire the separation of religion and politics, it is impossible in a democracy to prevent political leaders from exploiting religious sentiments or religious leaders from seeking political alliances. Democratic politics thrives on social divisions, whether of class or religion or race, but it need not—indeed should not—make the manipulation of only one kind of social division its sole obsession.

It is said all too frequently that we are different culturally from western countries such as Britain and France. It will not do to forget that we are also different demographically. India's religious minorities may comprise only a small proportion of the total population, but in absolute numbers they are very large, taken together, and, in some cases, even separately. There is no question here of the differences of religious identity becoming obliterated through either peaceful assimilation or forceful conversion in either the short or the long run. Thus we need secularism in order to ensure that no religious doctrine or community exercises unwarranted dominion over any other, and not only in order to nourish institutions that are by their nature indifferent to religious demands.

Secularism in the sense of equal respect for all religions and in the sense of indifference to religion in selected spheres of social life are not exactly the same, but the practical implications of the two are often, though by no means always, similar. Secularism in both senses is a philosophy of moderation, and that makes it particularly compatible with democratic as against revolutionary politics. The attack on religion made in the name of secularism by the votaries of revolutionary politics is contrary to the spirit of secularism. It is in fact another form of sectarianism which is an enemy of both traditional religiosity and democratic politics from whose apparent incompatibility it hopes to benefit.

Secularism is undermined when political parties heighten or exploit religious differences for the mobilization of political support. It is also undermined, though in a less obvious way, when the government is confused as to how it should discharge its responsibilities towards the equal treatment of all religions. Equal treatment may be interpreted negatively as disengagement from the affairs of all religions equally, or positively as equal support and encouragement for all religions, their institutions and their leaders. In India, even when the intentions of the government have been honest, it has wavered between disengagement and encouragement. The active encouragement of religious practices by the government, no matter how even-handed, cannot promote secularism in any meaningful sense and is bound to be self-defeating in the long run.

It is a truism that reform has been a continuous feature of all great and living religions. But the reform of religion on the initiative of the government of the day is always of doubtful value. Religious reform can be successful and long-lasting only when it comes from within. There is little reason to doubt the presence of sufficient religious energy among the people of India for a meaningful reform of religion which is a very different thing from the use of religion for the assertion of political power.

From very early times, religious worship in Hindu temples has been conducted by members of certain castes or subcastes and not others, just as in Muslim mosques Friday prayers have been conducted by only men and not women. Some Hindus have now begun to believe that the office of temple priest should be made open to members of all castes, although it is difficult to tell how well that belief reflects the sentiments of those Hindus who regularly visit temples for their devotions. Clearly, there is some room for reform in this regard, but equally clearly this is a matter that ought to be settled between Hindus, particularly those Hindus who are of an actively religious disposition. Of course, a well-intentioned government may feel inclined to give the tendency for reform a friendly push in the cause of secularism. But such a move might be ill-conceived, especially when no government, whether at the centre or in any state, will have the audacity to legislate that mosques should engage women as well as men to lead the Friday prayers. The moral of the story is plain. If secularism means the equal treatment of all religions, then it may be best for the government to adopt a minimalist policy in regard to religious affairs internal to a community. For when it provides aid or encouragement to one community, it soon discovers that it is difficult, if not impossible, to provide aid and encouragement of the same kind or to the same extent to every other community.

18 December 1993

Retreat from Secularism

Is secularism good for India? Educated Indians seem more inclined to equivocate over an answer to this question today than they did some years ago. If this indicates a serious and sober reflection on the nature and significance of secularism, its social presuppositions and its political implications, it is perhaps a good thing. But if the equivocation over secularism is merely the effect of a loss of nerve in the face of the social and political turmoil of the last few years, then it becomes a source of misgiving. The social and political turmoil in the country does not make the case for secularism weaker, it makes it stronger. Indian intellectuals will do little good to themselves or their country if they espouse secularism in fair weather and disown it in foul weather.

There can be little doubt that intellectuals in the broad sense played a leading part in creating the vision of India as a secular society. It is true that they believed, perhaps a little too eagerly, that the ingredients of such a society were widely available in the tolerant and pluralistic traditions of Indian civilization. In trying to bring a secular India into being, Nehru and his generation of leaders believed that they were working along and not against the grain of the Indian tradition, and they certainly did not wish to turn their backs on religion in either its philosophical or its popular form. Perhaps they thought too well of their people and seriously misjudged the strength of the dark forces lodged in the depths of their society.

The idea of a secular India is a modern idea, and it took shape in the course of the nationalist movement. Those who were fighting for the independence and unity of India could hardly have taken a different stand, for at that time the repudiation of secularism would have meant the rejection of the very idea of India's unity. The colonial administration derided the idea of either a united or a secular India. Among the nationalists, on the other hand, the attachment to secularism became not only a matter of practical politics but also one of national honour. That attachment found its most complete expression in the Constitution of India which refused to subordinate the rule of law to religious doctrine.

It takes more than a Constitution to create a civil society based on the rule of law. In India, the idea behind secularism was not to banish religion from the life of the individual or the family, but to insulate it from public affairs. Already, before Independence, Indians had experienced some of the consequences that followed from the mixture of religion and politics. Religion at its deepest level is a matter of personal faith, and it is an unsteady faith that requires the support of politics—or of the state—for its sustenance. Perhaps what troubles the intellectual opponents of secularism today is that their own religious faith has become unsteady; but they are deluded if they believe that it can be revived by politics.

Religious faith certainly binds people together, but it also creates a sense of difference among those who adhere to different faiths. The sense of difference among the religious communities did not disappear after Independence. On the contrary, the political process was used in such a way as to encourage its all-round growth.

The politics of post-Independence India made it easy to combine the advocacy of secularism with the practice of communalism, so much so that some began to view secularism and communalism as two sides of the same coin. It is this that has led some well-meaning intellectuals to lose heart in the prospect of a secular society in India. They wondered first whether secularism was possible in India, and then whether it was necessary or even desirable. Secularism, some suggested, was all very well for the West, but India had a different historical tradition and perhaps a different destiny.

Others who have sought to remain steadfast to secularism have been inclined to prevaricate in the face of evidence of a pervasive sense of difference among India's religious communities. Their selective use of historical evidence to prove that religious communities have always lived in harmony and amity has failed to convince the sceptics who can easily find evidence of the opposite kind. Secularism is a modern and not a medieval value, and it must address itself to India's contemporary predicament. The problems that India faces today can hardly be solved by deciding whether Akbar or Aurangzeb was the more representative medieval monarch. And nothing can be more futile than to try to secure the future by whitewashing the past.

Advocates of secularism often say that all that it requires is a certain fairness in the treatment of all religions which is essential in a country where so many religions co-exist. Had there been nothing more to secularism than the requirement of fairness, it would be difficult to account for the growing sense of resentment towards it among those who are religiously inclined. Although secularism does not seek to interfere with the private practice of religion, it does require the emergence of certain spaces in society that will be free from the claims of religion. In a secular society it is impassible for every domain of life to be permeated by religion. The exclusion of religion from certain areas of life is not simply a matter of religious neutrality, it is a basic requirement of institutional arrangements of a particular kind. The question therefore is not whether religion should be banished from society, but whether those who speak in the name of religion will tolerate the presence in society of any space over which it will have no authority.

No discussion of the place of religion in contemporary Indian society can be fruitful if it ignores the differentiation of institutional domains within it. It will be idle to pretend that religion can have uniformly the same place in every institutional domain in so large and complex a society as the Indian. Religion has always had a central place in the Indian family, whether among Hindus, Muslims or Christians, and the family continues to be a very robust institution in both rural and urban India. It is difficult to see why the insulation of politics from religion should lead to its displacement from the home. But it is equally difficult to see how other institutions, essential to the survival of any modern society, can function if they are to yield to the demands of religious ritual and doctrine.

We have only to think of a modern university or hospital or bank to recognize how difficult it would be to ensure the satisfactory working of such an institution on a religious basis or on any basis other than a purely secular one. Indian intellectuals who have been sustained by such institutions but are now a little tired of secularism must ask themselves what their lives would be like if these institutions did not exist or were constituted on a religious rather than a secular basis. One has the right to ask whether those who call for a retreat from secularism have any definite idea of what will replace it in their working lives, or whether the call comes merely out of a sense of defeat.

Perhaps it is the sense of defeat that leads some intellectuals to look back on peasant religiosity as a secure basis for a complete life. They see the city as a site of total disorder and the middle classes as completely corrupt, and attribute it all to secularism. They have left the life of the rural community too far behind to carry a living sense of its dreariness, its pettiness and its intolerance. Peasant religiosity is rooted in a kind of life that is far removed from the world of the scientist in his laboratory, the doctor in his hospital or the accountant in his bank. It will be disingenuous to pretend either that we do not really need such institutions or that we will find some way of fitting them all into a world that will be governed by a simple religious faith.

The life of the intellectual would be worth little if it remained an unexamined life. Surely, the intellectual has a right to repudiate secularism, but he must examine his own life—as physicist, historian, sociologist, or whatever—and ask what that life would have been like without the support of institutional arrangements that are irrevocably secular in their orientation and ethic. The repudiation of secularism cannot be undertaken lightly. A great many things that are essential to the life of the mind must go if secularism is to go. Intellectuals must consider deeply and dispassionately what they are abandoning and asking others to abandon when they call for a retreat from secularism.

7 August 1993

V
Reservations

Reservations constitute an important policy issue on which sociologists and other social scientists have commented widely, particularly since 1990. Some of the articles in this section go back to the tumultuous days of the Mandal agitation when the lines were sharply drawn between the supporters and the opponents of reservations. But my interest in the subject goes back to a much earlier period, and, indeed, the very first newspaper article I published, in the *Indian Express* in August 1961, was a critique of the recommendations of the ill-fated Nagan Gowda commission for extensive caste quotas in what was then Mysore state.

The issues in reservations in education and employment are difficult, not to say intractable. Positive discrimination, of which caste quotas are a particular form, may be viewed as an attempt to create special opportunities for some over and above the equal opportunities for all guaranteed by the Constitution. It is essentially a balancing act. The makers of the Constitution were not unaware of the precarious nature of the balance being created. Dr Ambedkar wanted special provisions for groups that had suffered from severe disabilities in the past; but he also wanted to ensure that those provisions did not 'eat up' the general provision of equality of opportunity for all.

Reservations are supported most characteristically in the name of social justice. Supporters of the policy say that it is only through reservations in education and employment that disparities between groups will be reduced, and unless that reduction takes place, there can be no real equality of opportunity between individuals. Opponents of reservations say that they negate the very principle of equality of opportunity and at the same time enhance, rather than reduce, caste consciousness. I have always maintained that reservations have to be assessed in a differentiated way, so that distinctions are maintained, firstly, between the different forms of reservations, such as political reservations and job reservations, and, secondly, between the different claimants for reservations, namely, the scheduled tribes, the scheduled castes and the other backward classes.

The articles on reservations presented here are exercises in what I would call policy analysis rather than policy prescription. I am somewhat sceptical of the conception of sociology as a policy science for I do not believe that it has much to contribute directly to policy prescription. At the same time, policies of the kind discussed here are social facts and, as such, have social causes and social consequences which ought to be analysed by the sociologist.

The Gains of Reservation

One of the main objectives the country set before itself at the time of Independence was to reduce if not remove inequality through a process of planned social change. Inequality was conceived in a broad sense to include not only the disparities of income and wealth but also the traditional feudal or hierarchical relations between people and the attitudes sustaining those relations. Progress in realizing the objective of greater equality has been halting and uneven, partly because of a lack of will and partly because of obstacles whose nature and significance had not been foreseen in advance.

Among the many efforts to bring about a measure of equality in a society saturated with hierarchical distinctions, the programme of positive or compensatory discrimination for the backward classes occupies an important place. In its scope and reach it stands comparison with the programme of agrarian reform. Positive discrimination, like agrarian reform has received considerable attention from the legislatures, the courts and the executive, and both have given rise to a voluminous literature. In what follows I shall discuss the problem of assessing the part played by positive discrimination in reducing social disparities.

Positive discrimination may be described as a way of reducing social disparities by creating special opportunities for some in addition to the equal opportunities created for all. Obviously there is a tension between the two principles—equal opportunities for all and special opportunities for some—and success in realizing the larger objective of reducing disparities will depend on the care with which a balance is struck between the two. It is thus that one may support the creation of special opportunities in certain spheres for the scheduled castes and scheduled tribes while at the same time opposing the creation of such opportunities in the same spheres for the other backward classes.

Positive discrimination in favour of the scheduled castes and scheduled tribes has generated less public controversy in independent India than positive discrimination in favour of the other backward classes, and I shall concern myself solely with the latter. These other backward classes are not all defined in exactly the same way in the different parts of the country, but by and large they are an assemblage of castes or caste-like groups. The special measures adopted or recommended for their advancement are many and diverse, but by far the most important among them are reservations in educational institutions, especially in professional and technical colleges and in government service.

Opinions differ quite widely regarding the social benefits as well as the social costs of reservations for the other backward classes. In the years immediately following Independence opinion in the country, at least outside peninsular India, was on the whole unfavourable to the extension of the benefits of reservation to others besides the scheduled castes and scheduled tribes. The first Backward Classes commission recommended extensive reservation in 1955, but there were several notes of dissent and the chairman of the commission himself strongly attacked the reservation of posts in the government on the basis of caste. Throughout the fifties and into the sixties the Union home ministry opposed the use of caste in making concessions to the other backward classes.

The tide began to turn sometime in the seventies. In several north Indian states leaders of intermediate castes began to claim special concessions for their members on the ground that they were being excluded from the benefits of development. The crucial position occupied by Charan Singh in the Janata government helped to give these claims a focus. A new Backward Classes commission was set up by the Union government in January 1979 under the chairmanship of B.P. Mandal, which submitted its report in December 1980. The second Backward Classes commission has shown none of the hesitations and equivocations of the first. Mr Mandal has recommended extensive and comprehensive reservations in favour of a large number of castes and communities throughout the country as a necessary if not inescapable step towards the realization of social equality.

Earlier recommendations regarding the other backward classes, whether for or against reservations, were frequently criticized for lacking an adequate empirical basis. The Mandal commission has sought to make good this lack by collecting and compiling a large body of data on a variety of topics. It has tried to use these data to forestall all possible objections to the use of caste quotas in education and employment. More recently, an American student of the subject, Marc Galanter, has brought together a formidable body of material in a book which might give some support to Mr Mandal's case. Professor Galanter seems to follow Mandal in his view that objections to reservation as a method of attaining equality arise largely from lack of information and from bias among the intelligentsia who belong largely to the upper castes.

For all the work put in by his commission, Mr Mandal has ignored certain obvious questions which might in effect undermine his advocacy of caste quotas as a necessary step towards equality. If the use of caste quotas is the only way of reducing social disparities between groups, what has been the record of those states which have refused to use such quotas except for the scheduled castes and scheduled tribes? There are such states in India, and it cannot simply be assumed that they are all indifferent to the objective of reducing social disparities.

West Bengal offers a test case to those who maintain that there is no way of reducing social disparities except through positive discrimination, and it is remarkable that both Mr Mandal and Professor Galanter have so little to say about it. Successive governments in that state have refused to introduce reservations for the other backward classes, and it does not appear that the people as a whole in West Bengal have been greatly aggrieved by this. A committee was set up on 1 August 1980 to look into the problems of the other backward classes and it submitted its report within a month, recommending against the use of caste quotas in government service in favour of the other backward classes.

The Mandal commission had a comparative study made by the Tata Institute of Social Sciences of the four states of Karnataka, Tamil Nadu, Bihar and Uttar Pradesh. Since these states have all adopted caste quotas in one form or another, the study failed to consider whether there are viable alternatives to reservation for reducing disparities in society as a whole. A comparison between, say, Karnataka and West Bengal would have revealed not only what reservations have actually achieved but also what may be achieved without reservations.

There are no doubt enormous difficulties in comparing regional patterns of inequality in a systematic and objective way. But on the face of it there is little reason to believe either that West Bengal has been less concerned about reducing social disparities or that Karnataka has actually achieved greater success in that respect. Here we have to take into account not only disparities in the distribution of wealth and income, but all those inequalities in social life which were characteristic of the traditional hierarchical order. There is enough evidence of significant changes in social relations and social attitudes in West Bengal as in other states like Punjab which have shown little enthusiasm for job reservation.

It we look at regional variations in patterns of positive discrimination it will be obvious that the decision to adopt reservations on a large scale is governed by various considerations, although an attempt is invariably made to justify the decision by an appeal to the principle of equality. Political parties have not adhered to a uniform position on this. In West Bengal neither the Congress nor the Communist party has shown much enthusiasm for reservations, whereas in Kerala both the CPI and the

CPM have supported caste quotas, as has the Congress in Karnataka.

Variations in patterns of reservation tell us less about regional structures of inequality than about regional political alignments. Reservations were introduced into peninsular India during British rule less as an instrument for attaining equality than as a device for maintaining a balance of power between the various communities. It is now forgotten that what the Supreme Court struck down in the Champakam Dorairajan case in 1951 was not so much a rule of positive discrimination as a system of communal quotas. Under the old dispensation in Madras all positions in specified areas were filled by rotation between the different communities. This is no longer possible under the new Constitution. But where, as in Karnataka, more than two-thirds of the positions are reserved under the umbrella of positive discrimination, one is only a short step away from a system of communal quotas.

6 September 1984

Caste and Politics for All

In assessing any scheme of reservations today, we have to keep in mind the distinction between those schemes that are directed towards advancing social and economic equality, and those that are directed towards maintaining a balance of power. Reservations for the scheduled castes and scheduled tribes are, for all their limitations, directed basically towards the goal of greater equality overall. Reservations for the other backward classes and for religious minorities, whatever advantages they may have, are directed basically towards a balance of power. The former are in tune with the spirit of the Constitution; the latter must lead sooner or later to what Justice Gajendragadkar had called a 'fraud on the Constitution'.

Supporters of the Mandal commission's recommendations would like to group the other backward classes together with the scheduled castes and scheduled tribes. This is an error of judgement, not always made in innocence. The other backward classes have a very different position in Indian society from that of the scheduled castes and scheduled tribes. It is true that their traditional ritual status was low and that they were latecomers to the competition for university degrees and government jobs. But only the Harijans and Adivasis have been for centuries the victims of active social discrimination, through segregation in the first case and isolation in the second. They alone have suffered the kind of psychological and moral injury that justifies their being treated now with special consideration. The castes and communities grouped together as the other backward classes have not suffered collectively that kind of injury in either the recent or the distant past. They include locally dominant castes, some of whose leaders are among the worst tormentors of Harijans in the rural areas today.

The other backward classes should be grouped, not with the scheduled castes and scheduled tribes, but with the religious minorities. The students' union of Aligarh Muslim University drew attention to this obvious fact when it welcomed the recommendations of the Mandal commission and added that the benefits proposed by it should be extended also to the Muslims. If the idea behind reservations is that power should be so distributed as to maintain a balance between all castes and communities, then the plea of the Muslim students is not unreasonable. But that was not the basis on which reservations were adopted by the Constitution; the basis there was to provide special opportunities for the most disadvantaged sections of society.

It is essential to remember that reservations were first introduced by the British. The colonial policy of reservations, which was administered extensively in peninsular India, was governed mainly by considerations of the balance of power. That being the case, there was nothing incongruous about the fact that the old Madras Presidency had 100 per cent reservations for a time, or quotas for both 'forwards' and 'backwards'. There was indeed a certain unity and coherence in the policy of the colonial administration: job quotas for all on one side, and separate electorates for religious groups on the other.

The colonial administration was not in any way hampered by the principle of equality of opportunity. Article 16 of the Constitution (together with Article 15) altered dramatically the scope for reservations in independent India. What was possible under the British was no longer possible in the new order. Reservations could now be justified only by the argument for greater equality and not by any argument for the balance of power. The provisions in the Constitution relating to job reservations do not come anywhere near to even mentioning numerical quotas. Those on reservations in the legislatures specify such quotas as clearly as possible, but are, on the other hand, strictly time-bound. The Constitution maintains a consistent distinction between the two kinds of reservations, dealing with them in two separate places. But the executive, with some help from the judiciary, has succeeded in obscuring that distinction in the public mind.

The Indian Constitution is committed to two different principles that both relate to equality: the principle of equal opportunities and the principle of redress. It is difficult, even under the best of circumstances, to evolve a coherent policy that will maintain a satisfactory balance between the two. The present policy of massive numerical quotas in public employment is a perverse application of the principle of redress that threatens to eat up the principle of equality of opportunity.

The principle of redress is a broad one that can be translated into many kinds of affirmative policy action. For instance, there can be substantial investment, on a preferential basis, to raise the levels of health, housing and elementary education among the weaker sections of society. Job quotas in public employment are by no means the best way of reducing social and economic disparities between castes and communities, and they have serious institutional costs that far outweigh the benefits they bring to some individual members of backward castes.

Preferential policies may be considered as a way of creating special opportunities for some over and above the equal opportunities available in principle to all. The tension between 'special opportunities for some' and 'equal opportunities for all' is too obvious to be ignored. If that tension is to be kept under control and not allowed to subvert the institutional system, preferential policies must be used judiciously and with restraint.

Paradoxically, caste has increased its hold over public life, despite such modernization as there has been in India since Independence. At the time of Independence, many Indians believed that caste was on its way out, and they had some evidence to support their belief. The many ritual rules by which distances between castes had been maintained in the past were declining or dying out. The restrictions on commensality were rapidly breaking down; marriages were taking place between subcastes of the same caste, and it was hoped that this would show the way to inter-caste marriages on a wider scale. However, there was one sphere of life, that of politics, in which caste not only held its ground but began to strengthen its hold. If caste has acquired a new lease of life in independent India, this is almost entirely because of the increasing use made of it in politics.

In the last forty years, and particularly since 1977, a tacit consensus seems to have emerged that all political bodies—zilla parishads, state cabinets, party committees —should be so constituted as to represent the major castes and communities. Representation in India has come increasingly to mean the representation of castes and communities. Two questions arise from this. The first relates to the purely political domain: does a political body become representative only when its composition matches the distribution of castes and communities in the larger society? Secondly, should all public institutions, irrespective of their functions, be constituted in the manner of political bodies? What is disquieting is the growing belief among leaders of all political parties that if caste balances are good for the domain in which they operate, they ought to be good for all institutional domains.

Much of the current debate on reservations is focussed on the question of employment: how much employment can and should be provided to our educated men and women, whether new jobs can be created to maintain the existing level of employment among the forward castes despite job reservations, and so on. But there are other issues, besides the distribution of jobs among castes, that we must consider if we are to assess the long-term implications of reservations. The most serious implication of extending caste quotas is that all public institutions will by that process come to be cast in the mould of political councils and committees. Universities, hospitals, scientific research laboratories, defence establishments and courts of justice will all come to look more and more like representative political bodies. If, like our present political bodies, they are constituted so as to maintain a balanced representation of castes, it will not be long before they begin to function like them. Every public institution will then be riddled not only with caste but also with politics, for caste has no place in these institutions except as an instrument of politics.

11 September 1990

Social Backwardness

While re-examining the three sets of criteria used by Mr Mandal's commission to determine which castes and groups of castes should be designated as 'backward', my attention naturally rested on those criteria that are described as 'social'. Among these, I was struck by one in particular, the criterion relating to age at marriage. A caste or community is regarded as socially backward where a substantial proportion of both its male and female members are married while below seventeen years of age. To what extent are we justified in using a low age at marriage as a criterion of social backwardness where that is identified to a large extent with low social status?

Let me say at once that the commission's use of low age at marriage as a criterion of social backwardness corresponds reasonably well with the common sense of urban, educated, middle-class Indians. In the social circles in which I move, most people would regard as very backward families in which boys, or even girls, are married off before they are seventeen. Indeed, it is typical of my wife to condemn as 'backward' people of her acquaintance who get their daughters married before they leave their teens; and my mother did just the same. Yet my mother's own mother, as well as my wife's mother's mother, both married well before they reached the age of seventeen. Their fathers, who had arranged those marriages around the turn of the century, both happened to be Bengali Brahmins of the Rarhiya sreni, and they would have been confounded by our common sense which tells us that a low age at marriage for girls is an indicator of low social status.

How can we say that nothing has changed in India when even what may be regarded as common sense has been so vastly transformed within a couple of generations? I would like to argue that the idea that it goes against common sense to get your daughter married before she is thirteen is both very new and very widely established among Indians in public life today. One can hazard that in this regard Atal Behari Vajpayee's common sense is the same as V.P. Singh's and the late B.P. Mandal's, although the two former belong to 'forward' castes while the latter belonged to a 'backward' caste. How has it come about that something that was taken for granted by our grandmothers (or even our mothers) has become virtually incomprehensible to our daughters?

As is well known, traditional Hindu society set a very high value on the purity of women which was in some sense made the foundation of its institutions of family and marriage. It is true that the purity of women has been a preoccupation in all pre-industrial civilizations, but the Hindus carried that preoccupation further than all the others. The *Dharmashastra* and the Grihyasutras explain in detail why marriage at a very low age is essential to safeguard the purity of women and of the family, and they also specify the sanctions to be imposed on fathers who allow their daughters to remain unmarried beyond the onset of puberty.

Now, the point is that these shastric injunctions, which prevailed among Hindus until a couple of generations ago, were designed with particular reference to Brahmins and other twice-born groups. For two thousand years, in both principle and practice, they were a mark of upper-caste, and not lower-caste status. It is well known that the lower castes enjoyed greater freedom—or were prone to greater laxity, depending on the point of view—in regard to all the observances by which the so-called purity of women was protected. Divorce and widow-remarriage were common among them, and girls married at a relatively higher age. The greatest departure from the norms of orthodox Hinduism was among the tribals, followed by the untouchables and other Hindu castes deemed to be low in status.

It is now a commonplace of the sociology of India that the lower castes sought to emulate the customs and observances of the higher castes. The process through which they did this has been made familiar to us under the name of Sanskritization by M.N. Srinivas. A central part of Sanskritization had to do with marriage, particularly as it affected women. It involved the prohibition of divorce and widow-remarriage, and, very commonly, a lowering of the age at marriage for women. It has to be repeated that a caste or community undertook to lower the age at marriage for women with a view to raising and not lowering its social status.

Although Sanskritization in the manner described above took place throughout Indian history, its scope was greatly extended by the forces set in motion during British rule. Earlier, changes in styles of life were slow and imperceptible, and subject to community sanctions that bore particularly heavily on castes with a very low status. British rule opened up new possibilities for these castes and quickened the tempo of change. The record clearly indicates that Sanskritization in this sense was in full cry in the first two or three decades of the present century. At any rate, in 1931, when the last census that enumerated caste was taken, a low age at marriage for girls was still widely, though no longer invariably, associated with high caste status or the aspiration towards such status.

The point I wish to make is a simple one. There was a clear tendency in Hindu society that persisted into the early decades of the present century to regard a low age at marriage for girls as a mark of superior social status; but some time between then and now, that tendency reversed itself, so that today the same observance is viewed as a mark not of high social status but of social backwardness. When did this reversal, so crucial to our understanding of contemporary India, take place? It is impossible to assign exact dates here because these tendencies can never be recorded or described with the precision of natural science. Suffice it to say that so far as caste observances go, it is extremely hazardous, from the viewpoint of method, to treat data from 1931 and from today as if they both related to the same unchanging universe.

A second criterion of social backwardness used by the Mandal commission relates to the participation of women in work. A caste or community whose women are engaged in outside employment to a significantly larger extent than the average is taken to be socially backward. Here again we are on slippery ground, for although work by women outside the home may indicate low social status in some cases, it may indicate the opposite in others. Much depends on the nature and context of the work. Where women work as agricultural labourers on low wages and under humiliating conditions, they and the families to which they belong are usually assigned low social status. But it may be very different where they work as doctors, school teachers or even gram sevikas.

The whole question of determining the criteria of social backwardness is a vexed one, as a comparison of the two criteria to which I have just referred will show. First of all, it always remains a little unclear by whose standards—the actor's or the observer's—a particular practice is judged as socially backward. I am not convinced that those who get their girls married before they reach the age of seventeen necessarily regard themselves as socially backward on that account. The judgement must be that of Mr Mandal and his commission. As it happens, I concur in the judgement that getting girls married at a very young age is a bad practice that is out of tune with the modern world, although I would hesitate to use the term 'backward' to describe it.

I certainly do not concur in the judgement that it is socially backward for women to engage in gainful employment outside the home. No doubt the commission's effort to use the criterion as a way of identifying social backwardness was well-intentioned. But the consequences of our actions are often different from the intentions behind them. When we link the idea of social backwardness with the employment of women outside the home, we give tacit support to a social outlook that is itself pernicious and ought to be demolished and not reinforced. If we believe that women often have to work under oppressive and degrading conditions, we ought to do something to alter those conditions instead of giving public support to antiquated social myths. No useful purpose can be served by labelling as socially backward those families that must, under pressure of economic necessity, send their wives and daughters to work under oppressive and degrading conditions.

It would be unfair to put all the blame on Mr Mandal's commission for the intellectual and moral confusions to which I have drawn attention. Those confusions are inherent in the very concept of 'social backwardness'. The commission went about its work of identifying the criteria of social backwardness in an ad hoc manner without the benefit of an adequate social theory to which those criteria could be logically related. It did not have the benefit of such a theory for the simple reason that it does not exist. It is the responsibility of the social theorist to point this out to the public, and to recommend the use of criteria such as poverty and illiteracy whose use involves the least amount of moral and intellectual confusion.

6 November 1990

Millstone of Reservations

Forty years ago the Indian intelligentsia started with a certain faith in the capacity of the state to play the leading part in the transformation of society and culture. A great many things needed to change, and it was natural to believe that a national government would do all the things that its colonial predecessor had either failed or refused to do. It will be difficult to appreciate the faith reposed by the Indian intelligentsia in the government if we fail to keep in mind the auspices under which it assumed office at the time of Independence. In the years preceding Independence, the landlords and the capitalists had acted badly by the people of India; those who took charge of the new government had, as leaders of the nationalist movement, acted well by them.

This faith in the capacity of the government to change all things for the better found its characteristic expression in the idea of centralized planning. That idea reached well beyond the limits of a technical economic exercise; it came to signify a whole philosophy. Without much experience of the practical limitations of economic planning, it was not too difficult to believe that it could be used not only to raise the national product or lower unemployment, but also to establish equality and social justice. In the fifties and sixties, the Indian intelligentsia placed much faith in economic rationality, but their faith was in the rationality of the plan as against that of the market.

By the eighties, the limits of a centrally-regulated economy had begun to manifest themselves. Knowledgeable persons, including some civil servants, were saying that the government had landed the economy in a mess. But established habits of mind do not change very easily or all at once. The responsibility for the failure on the economic front was assigned first to individual politicians and bureaucrats and then to the whole political class. It was not immediately apparent that the fault lay deeper in the fact that the government had, in the name of socialism, vastly overextended its activities. Thus, even those who became progressively disenchanted with each successive plan often felt that things could be set right with bigger plans and more effective regulation.

But the climate of thinking in the world as a whole has now become more favourable towards liberal economic systems. In one country after another, including China and the Soviet Union, the negative economic consequences of always promoting the bureaucracy at the expense of the market have been dramatically brought to light. In eastern Europe, the accumulated resentment against the bureaucracy for its mismanagement of the economy has created the danger that a blind faith in the state may be replaced by an equally blind faith in the market.

Fortunately, in India, the excesses of the state in the name of socialism have been mild in comparison with the Soviet Union and other East European countries. The question here is not of doing away with the role of the government in the economy, but rather of limiting it to those areas in which it can be most effective. Even the strongest advocates of liberalization or a market-friendly approach have not called for an end of either planning or the public sector. What they want is more freedom for economic activities to establish themselves in their own domain and to operate according to their own logic.

It is in this context that we have to appreciate the relief with which the new package of economic policies introduced by the government since July has been received both within and outside India. Its success will depend on a number of factors apart from the economic ones in the narrow sense of the term. Above all, it will depend on a new set of attitudes and orientations and a new framework of roles and relationships. What has been lacking in our economy so far is dynamism, and it cannot be too strongly emphasized that economic dynamism is more a matter of attitudes, values and institutions than of material resources. Forty years of political and bureaucratic patronage have stifled and suffocated all those qualities that stand for economic dynamism in human terms. The real obstacles that the new economic policy will encounter will be from ingrained attitudes and relationships that are inimical to enterprise, initiative and flexibility.

The social and psychological preconditions for a turnaround in the economy are probably well understood in the ministry of finance. All the talk there has been about initiative and enterprise, about allowing the best talent to make room for itself in every field through open competition. At the same time, the government's policy on caste quotas in public employment is bound to choke the very processes on which the new turn in the economy is vitally dependent. It hardly needs to be emphasized that recruitment through caste quotas is the very antithesis of selection on the basis of success in open competition. From where will the much-needed dynamism in the economy come if employment remains entangled in caste quotas?

The economic ministries have at last begun to view quotas with misgiving and suspicion, whereas thirty or forty years ago, one only spoke against them in a weak voice. Liberal economic doctrine views quotas as obstacles to the smooth functioning of the market and requires that they be reduced to the minimum. If quotas are bad in general, quotas based on caste and community are particularly retrograde. They not only stifle initiative but make factional strife endemic. As caste quotas come to be extended indefinitely, they turn every organization from a work site into a bargaining centre. It is characteristic of the politics of reservation that, whereas V.P. Singh's government wanted quotas to the extent of 49.5 per cent, the present government has offered to increase them by another 10 per cent; the introduction of some economic restrictions does not substantially alter the fact that not merit but some other criteria will be the principal basis of recruitment for reserved positions. An economy cannot be made competitive by persons who owe their positions in an organization to birth rather than achievement.

It can, of course, be said that economic efficiency will be looked after by the private sector while the public sector attends to social justice. Indeed, so intense has been the reaction against corruption and inefficiency among politicians and civil servants that there are now some who are prepared to write off the public sector and get on with their business. Educated Indians have begun to prepare themselves mentally for caste quotas in the civil service, not because they believe that caste quotas are good, but because they think that the civil service is so bad that it is almost beyond recovery. Those who see the bureaucracy as a source of rental income are likely to agree that the rents should be shared more widely among the different castes and communities.

But such a view of the relationship between the private and the public sectors—or between enterprise and governance—would be short-sighted. No matter how much we welcome the opening up of the economy, we cannot do without a public sector in India. The public sector will continue to occupy a significant space in the Indian economy, and it is important to ensure that it does not become choked by an employment policy that is inherently defective. A public sector in which employment is governed by caste quotas will sooner or later infect the whole economy with its own inefficiency and corruption.

Nor is it a question of the public sector in only the narrow economic sense of the term, but of public institutions in the widest sense. Caste quotas threaten the health of a whole array of administrative, educational, scientific, legal, financial and other institutions in India. These institutions have a vital role to play in the modernization of Indian society without which no programme of economic liberalization can prosper.

12 October 1991

Caste and the Intellectuals

Indian intellectuals have a peculiarly ambivalent attitude towards caste. It makes them uneasy to have to explain or even describe the system, particularly in the presence of foreigners. I can hardly think of any who will attempt to justify it. At the same time, most of them feel that it is in some obscure sense an important part of life in India. As a professional sociologist who is not a Hindu and has no caste, I have often been struck by the inability of educated Indians to provide a coherent account of the system. Most of them, including many with university degrees in sociology, present fanciful accounts that correspond little with caste as it is today or as it was in the past. Why should this be so if it is still a significant reality?

There have been some curious reversals of the intellectual position on caste in the last year or so. Marxists had in the past tended to dismiss caste as a factor of any great importance in Indian society; but the commitment of the left parties to caste quotas in education and employment has led Marxist intellectuals to find all kinds of new evidence of the continuing significance of caste. Bourgeois sociologists and social anthropologists had, on the other hand, been consistently devoted to the analysis of caste in the last forty years, drawing attention to its great adaptive capacity; but, being on the whole opposed to caste quotas, they have now begun to argue that many factors other than caste are responsible for the continuance of inequalities in contemporary India.

Part of the reason behind the confusion is that caste itself is changing, in some ways very markedly. Caste continues to be an important social fact, but it is ceasing to be a social institution. Or, to vary the language, the morphological structure of caste—the division of society into castes and subcastes—is still visible and prominent, whereas its normative structure, or the ideas, beliefs and values by which those divisions were sustained in the past, is clearly in decline. Intellectuals may have experience of caste, but they are unable to describe that experience coherently; even if they are able to describe it, they do not know any longer how to justify it. Their forebears knew not only how to describe the caste system but also how to justify it.

Under colonial rule, the census operations had played a large part in drawing public attention to the multiplicity of castes and subcastes in every part of the country. This had been a thorn in the flesh of the nationalist intelligentsia. When India became independent, it was decided to exclude caste from the national census of population. But we do not need the census to tell us about the continued presence of caste on the social landscape. That presence has been recorded in hundreds of case studies and social surveys made by social anthropologists and sociologists in the last forty years.

There is, thus, no dearth of evidence of the continued presence of the morphological side of caste. But in the traditional order, and upto the nineteenth century, caste had not only a morphological side but also an ideological one. In other words, society was not only divided and subdivided into groups that were ranked, but these divisions and their ranks were acknowledged, upheld and reinforced by law, religion and morality. We cannot say that there was always in the past perfect correspondence between the social morphology of caste and the prevalent social ideology. Neither remained completely unchanged over time, but, despite the changes that occurred, a broad correspondence between the two remained until the middle of the nineteenth century when it began to break down with the emergence of a new set of ideas, beliefs and values. It is in this specific sense that caste was a social institution in the past and is no longer one today.

In the traditional order, caste distinctions were enforced by both shastric and customary law. The *Dharmashastra* dealt mainly with 'varnadharma' or conduct appropriate to the different varnas, although it also acknowledged 'sadharanadharma' or conduct appropriate to human beings as such. Every Hindu was required to have a caste, and expulsion from it amounted to civil death. Only ascetics and criminals were without caste, and they too regularly became organized into groups that had many of the features of caste. Today, the prescriptions of caste no longer enjoy any legal sanctions, and expulsion from caste means little, at least among the middle classes where the upper castes predominate.

Comparative sociologists from Max Weber to Louis Dumont have argued that the real basis of caste lay in Hinduism, or that caste was merely the social expression of the Hindu religion. If caste and religion were in fact inseparable, we would expect the contemporary proponents of Hinduism to strongly defend the caste system. That in fact has not been the case. Reformers of Hinduism from Dayanand to Vivekananda have attacked the caste system and not defended it. Even Mahatma Gandhi, who believed strongly in the organic unity of

Hindu society, was ultimately obliged to abandon his defence of varna. It would be safe to say that the public defence of caste has virtually disappeared from religious discourse in contemporary India.

It is easy to show that the legal and religious foundations of caste have been undermined, but difficult to show that this has happened also to its moral foundations. For one thing, Indian intellectuals, whether liberal or radical, are often unable to perceive that caste ever had any moral foundations. For another, it is difficult to find unequivocal evidence of a change in moral values in a society as large and differentiated as the Indian. Nevertheless, it will be conceded that the sense of obligation to one's caste, so widespread in the traditional social order, has definitely declined, more conspicuously at the top than at the bottom of the social hierarchy.

How has this steady decline in the ideological side of caste—its legal, religious and moral foundations—come about? If there are any old-fashioned Marxists left, they will say that it has been the inevitable result of changes in the material forces of production. Undoubtedly, economic changes, particularly changes in property rights and in the occupational structure, have played their part in undermining caste. But new ideas, beliefs and values have played an equally important part.

As has happened many times in history, in India too, people have abandoned the social theory before abandoning the corresponding practice. However strong the evidence of the continuance of the practice of caste may be, its theory stands completely discredited in the eyes of reflective Indians. Indeed, those who are most active in producing evidence of the continuing practice of caste are the very ones who have clearly rejected its theory.

India has had a long intellectual tradition in which theoretical reflection and dialectical skill have been very highly valued. The social theory of caste was constructed within that tradition of which it became an important part. Caste was a Brahminical system only in this restricted sense that its theoretical elaboration and justification were largely the work of Brahmins. Visitors to India have through the ages marvelled at the theoretical ingenuity of the Brahmins in explaining and justifying the caste system even when they did not find the explanation or the justification to their taste.

Sometime in the course of the nineteenth century, a great change came about in the intellectual orientation to caste. A new intelligentsia, in many ways the heir to the old one, turned a critical gaze on the system and, instead of defending it, began to attack it. It is not as if this had never happened in the past, but the scale of the attack and its momentum were unprecedented. Undoubtedly European teachers, missionaries, civil servants and others played an important catalytic role in bringing about this change of intellectual orientation to caste, but it was mainly a catalytic role. The important social fact is that by the end of the nineteenth century, the caste system appeared indefensible in the eyes of Indian intellectuals themselves, and slowly but unerringly, they began to dismantle its theoretical basis.

Today caste remains a peculiarly prominent part of our social landscape, something that everybody is prepared to attack and nobody is prepared to defend, at least in public. It would be a travesty of the truth to maintain that the destruction of the theoretical basis of caste was the work of popular political movements. That destruction began a hundred years ago, and the initiative for it came from the intelligentsia, most of whom were members of the upper castes. Their names are too many to list and are in any case too well known. It is strange that liberal intellectuals in India should still carry such a burden of guilt about the caste system whose ideological foundations they have helped to undermine more than anyone else.

30 November 1991

Caste and the Politicians

In the years immediately following Independence, educated Indians, barring a few anthropologists, were inclined to believe that caste was on its way out. They rebuked or ridiculed the anthropologists for ferreting out all kinds of evidence of the continuing importance of caste, which they believed belonged to India's past rather than her future. For them, the future would be shaped by technological change and economic development and these, together with the new Constitution and the new laws, would leave little room for the archaic social practices of caste.

Today, Indian intellectuals take a less rosy view of the future and are rather more resigned than they were a generation or two ago to the continuing, if not increasing, importance of caste in public life. Why did they so seriously misread the future forty years ago? We must remember that in the years immediately preceding Independence, caste had been a subject of great interest among British civil servants, several of whom were outstanding ethnographers. They had amassed an enormous body of material on caste practices that enabled them to argue that caste was present everywhere and virtually indestructible. That argument, whether right or wrong, always made nationalist Indians uncomfortable.

Part of the reason why Indian intellectuals misread the

future of caste around the time of Independence was wishful thinking. Their colonial masters never tired of reminding them of the continuing presence of caste, and it hurt their pride and dignity to be reminded of something that they themselves had come to regard as 'feudal' and 'backward'. But there were other reasons as well for their failure to read the signs of the future. Caste had been for a long time represented as a religious phenomenon, sustained by a unique set of ritual beliefs, attitudes and practices relating to purity and pollution. The British themselves represented caste in that way in the accounts they wrote of it, dwelling at inordinate length on the innumerable ritual prescriptions and proscriptions that they believed were the essence of the system. Now, had that been all that there was to caste, the Indian intellectuals would have been right in their reading of the future, for who can deny that there has been a steady and irreversible decline in the ritual aspects of caste and in the preoccupation with purity and pollution?

But, of course, that was not all that there was to caste. Even while the innumerable rules relating to purity and pollution were breaking down, caste was acquiring a new lease of life from politics. Whatever might have been the source from which caste drew its sustenance in the past, it was to draw its strength in the future from politics—the mobilization of support, the manipulation of interests and the struggle for power.

By and large, the Indian intelligentsia failed to see clearly at the time of Independence the tremendous part that politics would play in the future in keeping alive the identities of caste. If they did have any premonitions about this, they did not wish to make too much of them, and here both radical and liberal intellectuals appear in retrospect to have been equally myopic.

But it was not the Indian intellectuals alone who misread the signs, their colonial masters appear to have done the same. I have already indicated that in the many accounts of caste written by the ICS ethnographers, the ritual side was strongly emphasized and the political side hardly noted. It is tempting to believe that they failed to write about the political side of caste because, wittingly or unwittingly, they were playing a significant part in bringing that side to life. Caste did not enter Indian politics after Independence; it was introduced into it before Independence by the colonial administration, but it found a vastly extended field with each successive general election.

Nationalist historians have been very severe with colonial administrators for playing politics with caste and community. I think that it is unjust to maintain that they always or even mostly acted in bad faith. There clearly was some genuine anxiety about securing justice and fair play among the many castes and communities into which Indian society was divided. It is unlikely that the colonial government could always foresee the long-term political consequences of measures introduced to secure social justice even to the extent that we are able to do today. But even if all did not act in bad faith, many were suspected of doing so, and some clearly did, taking delight in confounding the nationalists by pitting community against community and caste against caste.

The British in India did not have to justify every policy that took caste and community into account with the argument that it would ensure greater social equality for all. They were not even convinced that Indians really wanted greater social equality. It was enough for them to maintain that caste and community had to be taken into account to ensure a satisfactory balance of power. They were not in India to bring about a social revolution, or to transform India society from a hierarchical to an egalitarian one. Their task was to hold the country together and they were not entirely averse to exploiting the divisions of caste and community for that purpose, even if that weakened the country in the long run, for they were not going to be there for ever.

Things changed after Independence. Those who had fought against the use of caste and community in public life now found themselves in office. They made a new Constitution which prohibited discrimination on grounds of caste and guaranteed equality of opportunity irrespective of it. It is not that caste could never be used in public life any longer, but its use was covered by restrictions and had to be justified within the framework of the Constitution. It imposed limits on the new government to the use of caste in public policy of a kind that did not exist under the colonial regime. Under it, caste could be taken into account by the government in education or employment only if it promoted equality and justice and not merely to ensure a balance of power.

For some time after Independence, there was some hesitation to use caste openly in the political process in many if not most parts of the country. This does not mean that it was not used at the time of elections, for even the undivided Communist party of India was using caste for the mobilization of political support in Kerala and Andhra Pradesh in the fifties. But party leaders were reluctant to admit in public that they were doing this, just as they are even now reluctant to admit that they use religion extensively to mobilize political support.

One by one, the political parties have dropped their inhibitions about the use of caste in the electoral process.

Each party can argue, with some justification, that it has to do what the others are doing if only in the interest of political survival. But more than that, they have all discovered that there is only a thin line that separates the use of caste in the interest of a balance of power from its use in the interest of social justice. Thus, all parties have become deeply involved in the politics of backwardness. They are all committed to using caste in defining social backwardness because they have all realized that that is the quickest way of securing electoral support; and they have also come to feel that opposing such a definition is the surest way of courting electoral disaster.

To say that all parties are now engaged in the politics of backwardness is not to say that they are all equally enthusiastic about it. All are engaged in it on grounds of Realpolitik, but some are engaged in it also on ideological grounds. The stand taken by the Communist parties, which have long been the favourites of the intellectuals, has been a source of some surprise. In the past, they have had some hesitation, on theoretical grounds, about representing caste quotas as a form of social justice. Now the Communist leadership even in West Bengal has lost that hesitation. Perhaps this merely means that Leninism is giving place to Lohiaism in radical politics in India.

29 December 1991

Reviewing the Constitution

The ongoing crisis in coalition politics has led many persons to call for a comprehensive review of our present Constitution. It is rightly believed that such a review is an essential condition for devising a more coherent, a more effective and a more stable system of governance. At the same time, there is a danger that the discussion may become too narrowly focussed. It will be a pity if all other issues are crowded out by the compulsion to dwell only on the comparative advantages of the presidential and the parliamentary forms of government.

It will not do to forget that ours is an ambitious Constitution. It is not a bare blueprint for just a particular form of governance, but a bold and challenging design for a new type of society based on the equal rights of individuals in place of the old one based on the hierarchy of castes. The transformation of a whole society is a more far-reaching project than the creation of an effective form of governance. Naturally, many unsuspected obstacles have appeared in the path of this transformation, and the Constitution has had to be amended some fourscore times in less than fifty years. Have all these amendments carried us forward, or are some of them going to set us backward?

The Constitution of 1950 sought to establish not only a new conception of the state but also a new conception of citizenship. In the present preoccupation with alternative forms of governance, we should not lose sight of the possibility that we may be drifting away from the conception of citizenship that was the point of departure of the Constitution. In our modern political order, as against its traditional counterpart, the powers of the state have to be matched by the rights of the citizen. But to appreciate what is owed to the citizen as an individual is not easy in a society that has been dominated by caste, clan and community for two thousand years. The claims of the individual are overlooked and disregarded, and this undermines the value placed on citizenship which is the bedrock of our legal and constitutional order.

In the old order, the relationship between the individual and the king was mediated by kin group, caste and community; the idea of an unmediated relationship between the individual as citizen and the state did not exist. At least among Hindus, expulsion from caste literally meant civil death; the rights of the person expelled were automatically extinguished. The passage from such an order to one in which the individual is treated on merit, without consideration of race, caste or creed, is of the most momentous social and political significance. But one might well ask if the move itself is not being aborted by the increasing demands of caste, community and now gender, as against the claims of individuals as citizens.

The demand for restrictions on what is due to the individual as a citizen is typically made in the name of equality. This makes the demand almost irresistible, for who would like to be counted as an opponent of equality in public? The demand for equality appears compelling because the marks of the invidious social distinctions inherited from the traditional order are visible everywhere. There are all kinds of social disparities that require serious attention. It is important to devise policies that will lead to the reduction if not the elimination of those disparities over time. But those policies cannot be grounded on the assumption that disadvantaged castes and communities have rights that can override the ones conferred by the Constitution on individuals as citizens. The enthusiasm for quota justice has in fact given wide currency to such an assumption. Quotas based on caste, community and gender directly threaten the conception of citizenship on which our Constitution rests.

In the first ten to fifteen years after Independence, the extension of caste quotas in the name of equality was viewed with suspicion and mistrust. Kaka Kalelkar, the chairman of the first backward classes commission had written in 1955 that nothing should be allowed to organize itself between the individual at one end and the nation at the other 'to the detriment of the freedom of the individual and the solidarity of the nation'. Justice Gajendragadkar had in 1962 condemned the reckless extension of caste quotas as a 'fraud on the Constitution'. Both were concerned about the rights of individuals as citizens. But their warnings were not heeded.

The Mandal commission has extended quotas based on caste and community to just below 50 per cent. Where there is a demand to go beyond that limit, as in Tamil Nadu, recourse may be had to the Ninth Schedule. How can one, in these circumstances, speak of the relationship between the citizen and the state as an unmediated relationship?

We ought to have learnt by now that there are no short cuts to equality, and that quota justice is for the benefit of the politicians and not the people. And yet, the juggernaut of reservations moves forward. The Women's

Reservation Bill will be another milestone in its progress. The reservation of seats in Parliament is bound to be followed by demands for the reservation of jobs in the government. The climate has changed since 1974 when the committee on the status of women had recommended against reservations for women in Parliament and in the state assemblies. It had argued that women must stand on their own merits and intensify their political and social life. It sought to make the rights of women as individual citizens more secure, and thought that there were better ways of doing this than through quotas.

There is today some controversy over quotas for women. The leaders of the women's movement are often well-educated, upper-caste and upper-middle-class persons. They themselves believe no doubt that they speak for all Indian women, but their opponents, perhaps with equal sincerity, think otherwise. Some of the leading champions of the backward classes say that if there are to be quotas for women, the beneficiaries of those quotas should be women from the backward classes, and not from the upper castes. In other words, they would like to exclude the 'creamy layers' of women, or at least to ensure that such women do not corner all the reserved positions. The issue of 'creamy layers' bristles with difficulties. Its legal, political and social implications will have to be examined far more seriously than has been done so far. In the meantime, the battle for quotas will continue. It is hard to tell who the winners will be in this battle: the loser will be the Constitution of India.

5 August 1998

VI
Politics and Power

Politics and power are discussed in several of the articles in the preceding sections since they permeate so much of public life in contemporary India. How can one discuss the Indian university or the policy of reservations without taking politics into account?

The articles in the present section focus attention on specific aspects of politics, such as agrarian politics and youth politics. The first two articles deal with aspects of the agrarian social structure, a subject on which I was engaged in research between 1968 and 1970 as a Jawaharlal Nehru Fellow. Unfortunately, my research interests turned to other subjects in subsequent decades, and I was never able to return to the study of agrarian questions. But the agrarian class structure remains an important feature of the Indian social structure and deserves as much attention as the structure of castes and communities.

Although I never undertook any research on the politics of youth, like many others, I became fascinated with the subject during the JP movement in the mid-seventies. The rhetoric of youth power had an ominous ring in my ears, and I may not have been the only one to have had misgivings about what might happen in states such as Bihar where the JP movement had at that time a particularly strong appeal. I have had a move enduring interest in white-collar trade unionism and its larger social and political implications which I discuss in the article entitled 'White-collar Trade Unionism'. It appeared to me that university and college teachers were not unique in taking recourse to the kinds of industrial action they engaged in; doctors, engineers and others who demanded professional autonomy as a vital condition of their work, also undertook very similar kinds of industrial action.

Industrial action is of course an exercise, or an attempted exercise, of power. When workers in a private firm go on strike, they are challenging the power of the capitalists. When professors in a university or doctors in a public hospital go on strike, it is not always clear whose power they are challenging. By continuously challenging the power of the establishment, professors, doctors and others weaken the authority structures of the institutions of which they themselves are in some sense the custodians. Two of the articles in this section discuss the relationship between power and authority, and the implications of the thesis of empowerment for the authority structure of institutions.

Agrarian Unrest in Tanjore

The district of Tanjore has recently attracted attention for two reasons. The success of the package programme has led some to speak of a green revolution in the area, although the rise in the yield per acre of paddy, the principal crop, has not been as spectacular as might appear at first sight. The district has also been marked by a rather unusual degree of bitterness and violence in the relations among the agricultural classes. Two episodes in this conflict were the burning alive last year of forty-two persons in a hamlet inhabited by Harijan labourers and the more recent agitation by agricultural workers against the use of tractors.

Since both the increase in production and the conflict between landowners and labourers are readily observable, it might appear natural to view the two together as cause and effect. Certainly, the increased pace of economic activity has led to changes in the relations between the owners and the tillers of the land or at least has made these relations appear in a new light to the parties involved. But beyond this there are specific political and social conditions, in some respects unique to the area, which require to be analysed in order to place these conflicts in their proper perspective.

In large parts of Tanjore district the landowners as well as the landless are politically organized to a degree which is unusual in rural India. It should be remembered that the year 1967 witnessed not only a change in the pace of agricultural production but also the return of the communists to a position of increased strength in the eastern taluks of the district. The CPI(M) won the crucial Assembly constituencies of Nagapattinam, Thiruvarur and Kuttalam in the fourth general elections and succeeded remarkably well in organizing the kisans or agricultural workers for militant political action.

Along with the success of the agricultural programme there has been an increase in agricultural wages in the district during the last two years. However, it would be a mistake to think that this increase has followed directly or automatically from the rise in agricultural production. On the contrary, it has been brought about to a considerable extent by means of organized political action on the part of the kisans and their leaders. In this regard Tanjore provides a significant contrast to other package districts such as Ludhiana, for instance, where organized political action has played a small part in raising the agricultural wage rate or in changing the relations between the landowners and the landless in a general way.

In Tanjore political action by agricultural workers has involved both organized collective bargaining at the district level and widespread agitation at the village and farm levels. The two methods can in fact be viewed as complementary. In January this year the District Collector met representatives of landlords and labourers and fixed a new set of harvest wages which was marginally higher than what was prevalent earlier. Such 'tripartite agreements' have become a well-known feature of agrarian relations in Tanjore district.

In agriculture as opposed to industry wage agreements are difficult to reach because of the diversity of local conditions which vary not only from one village to another but even from farm to farm. Wages of course differ from one operation to another even when the work involved is similar, and for the same operation they differ from one part of the district to another. Wage disputes are particularly acute at the time of harvest when the demand for labour is high and the work has to be accomplished quickly. Even for a single operation such as harvesting the wages specified in the tripartite agreement of January 1969 vary from four and a half local measures of paddy to six.

If wage agreements are difficult to reach they are even more difficult to enforce. The tripartite committee could not agree to a uniform or fixed rate of wages but provided instead for certain increments over wages prevalent at the time. This has left the door wide open for disagreements at the farm and village levels between landlords and labourers. Landlords, where they are strong, are able to pay as little as four and a half measures by claiming that they were paying less before. Where labourers are strong in number and well organized they can demand six measurers and more by the argument that they were getting almost as much in the past. Under such circumstances the conciliation committees find it difficult to decide in each individual case what the correct wage should be.

Both landlords and labourers are particularly well organized in the eastern taluks of the district. Labourers are at places able to prevent or at least delay by means of united action the work of harvest on farms belonging to intractable landowners; in extreme cases standing crops have been destroyed on such farms. Landowners in their turn have on occasion succeeded at short notice in organizing farm work without labourers or by bringing labourers from outside, sometimes at considerable expense.

Both landowners and labourers have formal organizations for articulating their respective interests. The landowners are organized in the Paddy Producers' Association and the labourers have their Agricultural Workers' Union. These associations have played an important part in reinforcing a sense of unity within each class and one of opposition between the classes. Interestingly, it is in the eastern taluks that both these associations have their greatest strength. In the New Delta, by contrast, where the workers are not organized to any significant extent, the Paddy Producers' Association also plays an insignificant role.

The agrarian unrest in Tanjore district is to be explained in large measure by the extent to which both landlords and labourers are politically organized. But this itself cannot be satisfactorily explained by the recent economic changes which have been introduced in the district. For one thing, such changes have also been introduced in other parts of the country where their consequences have been different. For another, conflicts of a similar nature have existed in Tanjore district for more than twenty years. One must at this point bear in mind that these conflicts have been largely confined to the eastern taluks and have played very little part in the New Delta where the same programme of economic development is being implemented.

The different lines of political development in the two parts of the district are to be explained by certain basic differences in their social structure. The New Delta is an area of small and medium farms owned largely by members of the cultivating castes and operated mainly by family labour. In the eastern taluks on the other hand there are many large farms owned often by members of the non-cultivating castes and operated characteristically by means of hired labourers. The proportion of agricultural labourers in the total agricultural population is not very much higher in the New Delta than it is in the state as a whole. In east Tanjore it is substantially higher, being more than half the agricultural population in practically all the taluks.

In the eastern taluks the economic, social and cultural differences between landowners and labourers are sharp and clear cut; here, if anywhere, they form a pair of mutually exclusive classes. In the New Delta like elsewhere in general these distinctions are spread over a continuum instead of being sharply polarized. Political polarization was easily achieved in the eastern taluks because economically, socially and culturally the classes were already polarized to a considerable extent.

In east Tanjore manual work is generally avoided by landowners, particularly when they belong to the higher castes or have large holdings. This provides an important basis for social and cultural distinction between them and the landless. The overwhelming majority of them are 'pure' agricultural labourers who have no farms to operate either as owner cultivators or as tenant cultivators. They are an economically homogeneous class of people whose common material interests are not difficult to identify or organize. Elsewhere it is not uncommon for the same individual to combine a number of roles—as owner cultivator, tenant cultivator and agricultural labourer. In such cases the interests of different social categories are difficult to identify and organize for the same individual is governed at different times by different interests.

The economic homogeneity of the agricultural

labourers and their common material interests are underpinned by a measure of cultural unity which again is more pronounced in this area than elsewhere. This large population of landless wage labourers consists predominantly, and in some places exclusively, of Harijans. Elsewhere landless labourers are not only a mixed category economically but are also socially and culturally heterogeneous, being divided generally between caste Hindus and Harijans and occasionally between Harijans and Adivasis.

The Harijans are culturally differentiated from the rest of the population throughout the country but generally to a much greater extent in south India than in the north. In Tanjore district this cultural differentiation is intensified by a high degree of residential segregation. The Harijans live in separate hamlets known as cheris which are often at considerable distance from the main village. These cheris provide unique opportunities to political agencies concerned with the organization of classes. For here landless agricultural labourers live in what may be described as 'natural communities' bound together not only by common material interests and a common culture but also by a multiplicity of kinship and other social ties.

20 June 1969

Implementing Land Reforms

There is a new wave of concern in the country today over inequalities in the agrarian system. In many parts of India much of the land is owned and controlled by a small section of people who enjoy considerable economic and political power. Such areas also contain a fairly large class of sharecroppers and agricultural labourers who have hardly any rights in the land and lead a precarious material existence. In the years since Independence the disparities between the two have not been substantially reduced; some have indeed argued that they have to some extent been increased.

It would be wrong to suggest that the concern over these disparities is entirely new. Shortly after Independence the different states prepared and enacted a voluminous body of land reform laws which on paper at least appeared very impressive. There were first the laws aimed at the acquisition or abolition of estates, followed by, and in some cases combined with, laws designed to bring about a redistribution of land by imposing ceilings on individual holdings; finally, there were laws seeking to improve the conditions of cultivating tenants or sharecroppers by giving them security of tenure and reducing their rents.

Neither the laws relating to ceiling and redistribution nor those relating to the rights of sharecroppers have achieved very substantial results. An amazing variety of devices have been contrived for evading the ceiling laws. The ones which are more widely known include partition and backdated transfers within the family, 'benami' transfers, creation of religious and charitable endowments, and recording of agricultural lands as fisheries, orchards and the like. Similarly, tenancy laws have been evaded by getting tenants to sign deeds of relinquishment by the use of bribes or threats, which are later used to evict them.

The default of the administrative machinery in implementing the land reforms has been widely condemned. There can be no doubt that both corruption and inefficiency have prevailed on a large scale. Those responsible for implementing the land reforms, particularly at the lowest levels, are ill-paid and ill-equipped, and it is hardly surprising that their work has suffered due to bribery and dilatoriness. Yet it seems futile to explain away the failures of such an elaborate programme by passing the entire blame on to the bureaucrats. The constraints which it has to cope with are built into the economic system on which this society is based and the laws by which it is governed.

Whatever the merits of the case, there has been widespread disenchantment with the possibility of bringing about a more equitable pattern of agrarian relations solely through administrative means. This disenchantment has been particularly marked in states like West Bengal where the evasion of land reform laws and its adverse effects on the landless have been well known and widely discussed. In such areas the feeling has grown that these reforms will never be fully effective unless the economically weaker sections are able to acquire the political strength to be able to fight for their own rights.

In West Bengal the two peasant associations affiliated to the CPI and the CPM have taken some such position for some time. They have maintained that the implementation of land reforms is not simply a matter of legislation but also one of political organizàtion. The coming into power of the two United Front governments in West Bengal provided opportunities for trying out the possibilities of this alternative means for making the land reforms effective.

During the last three years political agitation in the countryside has revolved around two principal issues concerning, first, the redistribution of land, and, second, the rights of the sharecropper. The parties involved in the two cases have often been the same. The large landowners generally called jotdars have become the principal targets of attack both for evading the law on ceiling and for violating the conditions of the barga tenants and being given some share of the land recovered from the bigger jotdars.

It is true that in some sense the land reform laws and the political movements against large landowners have common objectives. Both aim to bring about a more equitable distribution of economic opportunities. Both seek to reduce the powers of the large landowners and to improve the conditions of the landless. In fact, peasant associations in West Bengal often emphasize that their first objective is to implement the land reforms, but to do it more speedily and effectively than would be done by the ordinary administrative means. However, an examination of the facts on the ground will show that there are basic contradictions between the two approaches and that, beyond a certain point, the one can be used only by foregoing the other.

The organizational structures associated with the two

approaches are markedly different. If the first is over-rigid and weighed down by rules of procedure, the second is amorphous and not easily subjected to disciplined control. There are basic differences in the personnel used by the two types of organization and it is difficult to arrange for party activists and petty officials to work in concert at the ground level, whatever be the ultimate objectives of the organizations for which they work.

It has often been said that the sharecropper and the poor peasant can hardly look to petty officials to have their rights established. But can they depend to any greater extent on the peasant associations? It should be realized that this is not a question merely of the good intentions of those who direct these associations but also of their organization and strength. There is little doubt that in placing their trust on party activists, the landless people often forgo such claims as they have on the petty officials as well as on the landowners who provide them with work, credit and the other means of livelihood. So it is important to know to what extent the cadres of the peasant associations are capable of giving protection to the landless when such protection is needed.

During the 1969-70 agricultural season the general climate in the countryside was definitely against the large landowners. The eviction of sharecroppers was no longer very easy and it became increasingly difficult to hold on to such land as was held in excess of the ceiling. This kind of land was in many areas forcibly taken and cultivated by the landless and it was not uncommon for standing crops to be cut down and taken away. Far from being able to demand more than was allowed by the law, some landowners got less than their due and, in a few cases, nothing at all. In many areas in West Bengal the organized support of the local units of the Kisan Sabhas gave the sharecroppers a bargaining advantage for the first time.

Will they be able to maintain this advantage? What little evidence is now available seems to show that this is far from certain. No doubt it is difficult to generalize for the whole of West Bengal. The pattern varies from one district to another and even within the same district there are sharp differences. Very much depends on the organization and strength of the local Kisan Sabhas.

I do not think that it would be wrong to interpret the available evidence as showing that on the whole the advantage has shifted away from the landless and is now once again with the jotdars. There are various ways in which the latter are once again beginning to deal, on their own terms, with the former. A common practice is to keep sharecroppers out of the land by invoking Section 144 against them; very rarely are the bargadars so well organized as to be able to go on working on the land in defiance of an order under Section 144. Another common way in which a jotdar takes advantage of a bargadar in distress is to get him to sign an istafanama or a deed of relinquishment in return for a small consideration; this practice, though by no means new, seems to have become more widespread.

It is not difficult to determine the principal factors behind the default of the peasant associations. In the first place, they have not as yet really established themselves as an integral part of the rural social structure except in a few areas. Many of their activists are still middle-class people from the towns and cities. Their relations with the people among whom they work are on the whole intermittent. The activists and cadres come when a movement or an agitation is launched but they are not always there when their help is most urgently needed. The success of their mission would seem to require the continuous presence in the rural areas of workers of the peasant associations in sufficient numbers.

There are some areas where they are present in sufficient numbers but here they are sharply divided among themselves. In the 24-Parganas district, which is well known for its agrarian movements, the bargadars have not one but four peasant associations to look after their interests. Apart from the two Kisan Sabhas affiliated to the CPI and the CPM, there are the Krishak and Khetmajur Federation affiliated to the Socialist Unity Centre and the Agragami Kisan Sabha affiliated to the Forward Bloc. The cadres of each of these have to contend not only with the jotdars but also with cadres of the rival associations. Each Kisan Sabha accuses the other of working for the jotdars. This is probably not true in a literal sense, but, ignoring intentions, if we look at the consequences of this kind of inter-party rivalry, we will have to conclude that it helps the jotdars much more than the bargadars.

9 September 1970

Democracy and Development

Democracy rests on a tension between two different principles. There is, on the one hand, the principle of equality before the law, or, more generally, of equality, and, on the other, what may be described as the leadership principle. The first gives priority to rules and the second to persons. No matter how skilfully we contrive our schemes, there is a point beyond which the one principle cannot be promoted without some sacrifice of the other.

Alexis de Tocqueville, the great nineteenth century writer on democracy, maintained that the age of democracy, whose birth he was witnessing, would also be the age of mediocrity: in saying this he was thinking primarily of a regime of equality governed by impersonal rules. Despite his strong attachment to democracy, he took great pains to point out what he believed to be its negative side: a dead level plane of achievement in practically every sphere of life. The age of democracy would, in his view, be an unheroic age; there would not be room in it for either heroes or hero-worshippers.

But modern democracies have not been able to do without heroes: this too was foreseen, with much misgiving, by Tocqueville. Tocqueville viewed this with misgiving because he believed, rightly or wrongly, that unlike in aristocratic societies, there was no proper place in a democracy for heroes and, hence, when they arose they would sooner or later turn into despots. Whether they require heroes or not, democracies certainly require leaders, and, in the contemporary age, breed them in great profusion; the problem is to know what to do with them.

In a world preoccupied with scientific rationality the advantages of a system based on an impersonal rule of law should be a recommendation with everybody. There is something orderly and predictable about such a system. When life is lived mainly in small, self-contained communities, men are able to take finer personal distinctions into account in dealing with their fellow men. They are unable to do this in a large and amorphous society, and organized living would be impossible here without a system of impersonal rules. Above all, such a system guarantees a kind of equality to the extent that everybody, no matter in what station of life, is bound by the same explicit, often written, rules, and nobody is above them.

But a system governed solely by impersonal rules can at best ensure order and stability; it cannot create any shining vision of a future in which mere formal equality will be replaced by real equality and fellowship. A world governed by impersonal rules cannot easily change itself, or when it does, the change is so gradual as to make the basic and fundamental features of society appear unchanged. For any kind of basic or fundamental change, a push is needed from within, a kind of individual initiative which will create new rules, new terms and conditions of life.

The issue of leadership thus acquires crucial significance in the context of change. If the modern age is preoccupied with scientific rationality, it is no less preoccupied with change. To accept what exists on its own terms is traditional, not modern, and it may be all very well to appreciate tradition in music, dance and drama, but for society as a whole the choice has already been made in favour of modernization and development. Moreover, in countries like India the gap between ideal and reality has become so great that the argument for development and change is now irresistible.

In countries like India no argument for development has greater appeal or urgency than the one which shows development to be the condition for the mitigation, if not the elimination, of inequality. For there is something contradictory about the very presence of large inequalities in a society which professes to be democratic. It does not take people too long to realize that democracy by itself can guarantee only formal equality; beyond this, it can only whet people's appetite for real or substantive equality. From this arises their continued preoccupation with plans and schemes that will help to bridge the gap between the ideal of equality and the reality which is so contrary to it.

Where pre-existing rules give no clear directions of change, leadership comes into its own. Every democracy invests its leadership with a measure of charisma, and expects from it a corresponding measure of energy and vitality. Now, the greater the urge for change in a society, the stronger the appeal of a dynamic leadership in it. A dynamic leadership seeks to free itself from the constraints of existing rules; in a sense that is the test of its dynamism. In this process it may take a turn at which it ceases to regard itself as being bound by these rules, placing itself above them. There is always a tension between 'charisma' and 'discipline' in the case of a democratic leadership, and when this leadership puts forward revolutionary claims, the tension tends to be resolved at the expense of discipline.

Characteristically, the legitimacy of such a leadership rests on its claim to be able to abolish or at least substantially reduce the existing inequalities in society. To make its claim plausible, it is then led to oppose substantive equality to formal equality. From the argument that formal equality or equality before the law is but a limited good, it is often one short step to the argument that it is a hindrance or an obstacle to the establishment of real or substantive equality. The conflict between a 'progressive' executive and a 'conservative' judiciary is but one aspect of this larger problem. This conflict naturally acquires added piquancy when the executive is elected and the judiciary appointed.

Two kinds of uncertainty are built into such a situation. Firstly, the elected leadership, for all its claims to represent the will of the people, may from the start be corrupt and act in bad faith, seeking above all to increase its own power and the privileges that go with it. But the leadership may act in good faith, at least to begin with, and this may in the end turn out to be the more difficult case. For such a leadership is more likely to carry conviction with the people, including the intelligentsia, that it has at its command some special formula by means of which it will be able to establish a reasonable measure of substantive equality, if only it is given a free hand to push aside some minor obstacles on its path.

But in general no such formula exists, although it is a common error to believe that such a formula must exist simply because people might be made so much more happy by its existence. In the modern world no leadership can afford to do without a theory or model of social and economic change, so sooner or later it mobilizes the services of intellectuals who apply themselves to the job of squaring the circle. There is no dearth of intellectuals in this country or elsewhere who are able to delude others about what a model or a theory can do, and the fact that they delude themselves in the process can hardly be a comfort to anyone. To be sure, there is a large body of social science literature on modernization, development etc., but that part of it which claims to deal with scientifically established laws of social and economic change is mainly bluff and verbiage.

The art of squaring the circle ceases to be an innocent intellectual pastime when its practitioners become instruments in the struggle for power. The layman would be surprised, were he to be told, how little the experts really know about the laws by which societies change; if such laws exist, the experts are nowhere near to having discovered them. The process by which real or substantive equality gains ground is a slow, painful and—let us admit—largely unpredictable one. The Emergency will have served as a lesson and a warning if people learn from it, at least for a time, what it costs to kick aside formal equality in the hope that if only they make this small concession to their leaders, they will establish real equality here and now.

6 June 1977

Youth Power

About ten years ago large parts of West Europe and North America were swept across by great waves of youth power and student power. The consequences of this were, by any reckoning, not all very happy. In India today some of the most prominent public figures—including elder statesmen—are paying homage to youth power, seeing it as a main basis for creating a new society by quickening the energies of the people.

One may not need to ask why students and other sections of the youth should wish to pursue the path of power, but one must certainly ask why their elders should wish to put them on this path. Is the expression of this desire genuine? How much of it is born out of hope, and how much of it reflects fear? In talking or even thinking about youth power today one would be ill-advised, even in a peace-loving society such as ours, to ignore the linkage between power and violence. Indeed, for the sociologist the concept of 'non-violent power' is almost a contradiction in terms. Once again, then, why do even the known adherents of non-violence speak about youth power, especially now?

The relations between age and youth, and, more generally, between the generations bear in each society the marks of its particular historical development. In what are called traditional societies age dominates over youth, and this kind of dominance often has a deadening effect on both. In the so-called modern societies the boot is often on the other foot: I remember the great sense of surprise with which I first read in a well-known American textbook of sociology that in American society 'one is generally considered better, superior or more worthy if he is . . . young rather than old'. While the tyranny of age over youth has to be deplored, nothing can be more abject than when the old submit to the tyranny of the young.

In Indian society, caught as it is between tradition and modernity, the relations between age and youth are charged with tension. One is at a loss for a satisfactory model to follow. Clearly, there is no going back to a tradition which made the old complacent because the young were docile. At the same time, there will be little to look forward to if an irrational reverence for age is replaced by an even more irrational cult of youth.

To come to the crux of the matter, what is power? Leaving aside the metaphorical uses of the term (as in the power of words, or the power of ideas), we are dealing with power when some men are able to impose their will on others, despite the latter's resistance. In the social context, a relation of power is a relation of command and obedience. Commands may of course be implicit and obedience rendered with a show of affection, but it would not make sense to talk of command and obedience unless they were backed by the use of force, or, what is more commonly the case, the threat of its use.

The most easily recognizable form of power is state power, or the power of established authority. Recently in this country many people have learnt, to their cost, about the linkage between this kind of power and violence. But this is not the only kind of power or the only source of violence. Populist movements, when they mobilize the energies of large masses of people, can also be coercive in effect, if not in intent, generating their own forms of violence. True, such movements need not necessarily become violent, but when their leaders and followers both learn to acquire a taste for power, individuals may find such power no less irresistible than the power of established authority.

Nobody can deny that in countries like India the youth constitute a vast reservoir of energy. It is no easy task to direct this energy to the ends of social reconstruction in a purposeful manner. On the other hand, it is both easy and tempting to try to use it as an almost inexhaustible resource in the struggle for power. Any human resource which is used in this way inevitably lays claim to its own share of the spoils in return for its contribution to the struggle. Those who pay homage to youth power can hardly claim not to know what is, after all, a commonplace, that the youth can be as ruthless in the pursuit of power as any other section of society.

It would be a serious mistake to think of the youth, particularly in a country like India, as a homogeneous category. There is urban youth and rural youth; student youth and non-student youth. These distinctions are important because there are enormous differences in the extent to which the various sections of the youth can be organized, and there can be no effective exercise of power without organization. To put a complex matter in simple terms, in the context of youth power it is the urban youth, and, in particular, the students, whose role is and always has been decisive. To all intents and purposes, youth power virtually signifies student power. Now, in almost every country, and certainly in countries like ours, the students comprise only one section, and not necessarily the largest section of the youth.

Although they comprise only one section of the youth, the absolute number of college and university students in India is very large and is rapidly growing. It must also be remembered that as an organized category with a bargaining power of their own in the political market they are a relatively recent phenomenon in Indian society. They are a recent phenomenon not only as a political resource but also as an economic problem. Graduate unemployment is today a reality for lakhs of young men and women, and a prospect for millions of them. It is in this context that it might appear tempting to try to use the political resource and to solve the economic problem at one and the same time by sending out millions of student youth into the countryside to revitalize our decaying and moribund rural society.

Nobody could disagree with the view that it is necessary to think of more creative ways to utilize the capacities of our educated youth than have been tried out so far. Our educational system is lopsided; our manpower planning is deficient; and our economic growth can barely keep pace with the growth of our population. But by any reasonable reckoning these problems will only be aggravated and not mitigated by creating a wave of youth power and letting it sweep through the countryside after taking over the control of our colleges and universities. An experiment which has cost even the rich countries of the West so dearly is not one which a poor country like ours can afford to plunge into on an impulse.

There is no doubt the example of China where not many years ago the schools and colleges were closed down in order to enable the youth to usher in a great cultural revolution. Indeed, the Chinese case was cited in an important national broadcast only a short while ago. Those who know more about these matters will have to tell us how much of what happened in China a decade ago was even intended to bring about a new type of culture, and how much of it was just part of a sordid struggle for power among those who stood around Chairman Mao. Indeed the various gangs which were conveniently revealed after the Chairman's death were surely not innocent spectators of the drama which was being enacted by the Chinese youth a decade ago.

But then the Chinese case is different because the leader of the Chinese revolution was different. No one in recent history, not even Lenin, has had a more clear-sighted view than Chairman Mao of the substance and logic of power. Power, in his saying, flows out of the barrel of a gun; and what applies to power in general must surely apply also to youth power. We may or may not admire Chairman Mao, but surely it is impossible to combine Maoism with Gandhism; we must view with deep suspicion any attempt to dispense non-violence with one hand and youth power with the other.

23 May 1977

The Theory of Empowerment

After the destruction in Ayodhya and the violence that followed in Bombay and other parts of India, many persons have begun to be seriously alarmed over the destructive threat of populism. Populism is a release of the energies of large masses of people in the service of an overpowering idea that sweeps away the established institutions of society and its constituted authorities. It sees bureaucracies, legislatures, courts of justice and other such institutions as dispensable obstacles in the way of what it declares to be of supreme importance: religious dignity, national honour or civilizational destiny. It speaks in the name of the people against rules, regulations and the laborious attention to routine. It wants justice for the people, and not procedures that differentiate, separate and judge each case on merit.

Intellectuals, whether in India or elsewhere, do not like to be called populists; that is a term they reserve for others who are the objects of their contempt or reproach. Of course, many of them also like to speak in the name of the people, but when they do so, they see themselves as radicals, egalitarians and champions of social justice. Populists and radical intellectuals share in common a hatred of elites of every kind, whether aristocratic or meritocratic; and this hatred, when persistently expressed, can alter people's perceptions of what is intolerable in society, and hence dispensable.

An idea that has spread increasingly and lodged itself in many minds is that of the empowerment of the people. It appears to me that some of those who were most enthusiastic about the idea of empowerment are now terrified in the face of its close cousin, populism. Perhaps they had reckoned that they would have a creative role to play in the process of empowerment, but now find that the people whose energies they had hoped to mobilize may not need them for the time being.

When the country started on a new course after Independence, there was at first general enthusiasm over parliamentary democracy, economic planning and social engineering. The experience of independence proved to be different from the expectation, and many of the old problems remained while now ones made their appearance. Poverty did not disappear but appeared to increase; vast masses of people remained illiterate; and the marks of social and economic inequality could be seen everywhere. People blamed in succession the capitalist class, the political class, the bureaucracy and the intelligentsia, or, in short, the elite which included anyone who was doing well or appeared to be doing well.

It is true that even at the time of Independence there were those who put little trust in parliamentary democracy and thought, instead, of class war; but theirs was a small voice. On the whole, the intelligentsia, including the left intelligentsia, thought in terms of a socialistic pattern of society in whose creation the state was to play a leading role. Indeed, a strong state that would control the commanding heights of the economy was considered to be both necessary and desirable for keeping the capitalist class at bay, and also for protecting and promoting secularism.

The year 1977 may be regarded as a turning point, not

only in our political but also in our intellectual life. The old left ceased to be the sole or even the principal exponent of radicalism whether in politics or in ideas. Oppression, exploitation and injustice were no longer defined solely in terms of class, but increasingly also in terms of such identities as those of tribe, caste, community and gender. The weakness and vulnerability of the state and its institutions—the corruption of the legislature, the obstructiveness of the bureaucracy and the confusion of the judiciary—came to be increasingly exposed and attacked from both within and outside. Finally, prominent intellectuals, some of them enjoying as well as dispensing official patronage, began to speak of 'people's power' as against 'state power'.

In the last fifteen years, the idea of the empowerment of the people has come to be linked very closely with the idea of social justice. It is not easy to give a clear definition to the concept of social justice, but in the Indian context it has tended to shift the focus of attention from individual to collective identities, so that those who speak most often of it dwell on the rights of the indigenous people, of the dalits, and of various castes and communities. A persistent point of attack against the existing system is that it hās failed to give these communities their fair share of power. From this point of view, how power is distributed within and between institutions is less important than how it is shared by various groups in society. This displacement of attention from the distribution of power in institutions to its distribution between castes and communities represents a shift from the liberal to the populist conception of democracy.

One would of course expect politicians, particularly while in opposition, to dwell on the empowerment of the people. But the talk about empowerment is today no longer confined to politicians in opposition, but has become current coin in the gathering demand for social justice. V.P. Singh has said, as prime minister of India, that what he wanted to give to the backward communities was a share in the power structure. More recently, the Supreme Court has added its authority to the argument for empowerment. In the Mandal case decided last November, the majority judgment written by four judges, including the Chief Justice, stated that 'the objective behind clause (4) of Article 16 was the sharing of State power'; or, in other words, 'the empowerment of the backward communities'. Characteristically, the Court spoke not of authority, which one associates with office, but of power, which in this view ought to be shared between communities. In an article published in the *Times of India*, a former Attorney General has hailed the judgement as the triumph of social justice, and supported its stand on empowerment.

The words of judges and attorneys are carefully chosen and uttered with restraint. That is not always the case with others who prefer to think and speak of empowerment in a more vivid way. For them the idea conjures up many images. There are sinister as well as benign images of power. The sinister images are of vast quantities of it, controlled by a small number of persons: capitalists, ministers, bureaucrats and others, collectively known as 'elites' and presumed to belong to one or more privileged communities. The structures of institutional authority in offices, factories, banks, hospitals, universities, and so on are of small importance in this view, for institutions are seen as instruments which elites manipulate for their own ends. Power will acquire its benign form when it is gathered up from its privileged possessors and distributed to the people who will then share it among themselves according to agreed principles of social justice.

To be sure, when judges speak of empowerment, they have in mind backward, disadvantaged and disprivileged communities; but, so indeed do politicians. No one would ask for empowerment in the name of advanced, advantaged or privileged communities. The real blunder is to believe that anyone can have the last word in deciding which communities will consider themselves disadvantaged and disprivileged. Who can deny that millions of Hindus have in the last four years been persuaded to believe that they are the disprivileged and the disadvantaged who have been deprived of their fair share of power through the machinations of misguided elites? It is true that this kind of populism is not to the taste of the original proponents of the idea of empowerment. But it is doubtful that we can go on promoting that idea without undermining institutions and clearing the ground for populism to come into its own.

12 March 1993

Power and Authority

There has been some anxiety over the increasing burden being placed on the courts by requiring them to decide on matters that might be regarded as political rather than legal in the strict sense of the term. The Supreme Court has found itself more than once in an awkward situation, and its typical response has been to adopt an ambivalent stance. This ambivalence is nicely brought out in the leading judgment in the Mandal case decided in November 1992. The judges appeared to find it irksome to have to decide on issues that they said 'could have been settled more satisfactorily through political processes'. At the same time, they seemed pleased by the thought that the public reposed so much confidence in their fairness and their wisdom. The public seems to have lost its confidence in the political process, but if the courts take to intervening in that process, the lack of confidence might extend from the political to the judicial organs.

It is, even in the best of circumstances, difficult to draw a clear line between law and politics, and particularly difficult to maintain the distinction between the two in the context of a changing society. In the real world they interact and shape each other continuously. Nevertheless, it is important to remember that they are distinct and separate. The failure to distinguish in principle between law and politics may in the long run cost us as dearly as the failure to separate politics from religion.

Politics has been described as the science of power, its pre-eminent concern being with the distribution of power and the processes through which that distribution is maintained or altered. The concept of power is a very broad one, and there are many forms of it such as coercion, domination and manipulation. As against power, which is the broader and more inclusive concept, we might speak of authority which has a more restricted meaning. Authority is a form of power, but not the only form of it. It may be described as that form of power which enjoys legitimacy and is associated with established chains of command and obedience in institutions such as civil and military bureaucracies, universities, hospitals, banks, and so on. While the distinction between power and authority is an important one, it is not clear that the courts always keep it in view.

Social and political theory is concerned with the distribution of power in the broadest sense, whereas the central concern of the law is with the scope, the limits, the use and the abuse of authority. Obviously, the exercise of authority in institutions will be governed to some extent by the distribution of power between groups, classes and categories in the wider society, but the success of liberal democracy requires us to pay attention to distinctions and boundaries. It is a mistake to believe that the structure of authority in an institution ever reflects exactly the distribution of power in the wider society; and the effort to bring about an exact correspondence between the two is bound to be both futile and costly.

The actual distribution of power between the groups, classes and categories in a society nowhere remains fixed for ever, and it rarely corresponds to one's ideal conception of it. But the proper way to change the distribution of power in a democracy is through the political and not the judicial process. Parties of the left have sought to bring about the empowerment of workers and peasants, and other political parties have advocated the empowerment of religious groups or ethnic communities that are or regard themselves as socially disadvantaged. There are rules for regulating the political processes through which changes in the distribution of power are brought about, and the courts should intervene when those rules are violated. But when they move beyond that, and seek to regulate the distribution of power directly, they enter unfamiliar waters where they will sooner or later find themselves out of their depth.

In the leading judgment referred to above, the Supreme Court took the unusual step of endorsing the theory of empowerment as a justification for caste quotas in employment. For all the length at which the learned judges expressed themselves, their interpretation of Article 16(a) as recommending 'the empowerment of backward communities' is more surprising than convincing. That article has received the Court's attention on more than one occasion, but its interpretation in terms of the theory of empowerment is a new departure in our legal discourse. If the courts have views regarding the correct distribution of power in society, it is surely their responsibility to present those views clearly and candidly.

Large-scale job quotas are likely to have two related though distinct implications that have to be considered separately. Firstly, there is the distribution of authority in and among institutions subjected to job quotas. There is, of course, some inequality in the distribution of authority in all institutions. What we have to consider in the first instance is the effect that caste quotas are likely to have on their structure and functioning. It may certainly be argued that a better mix of castes and communities in public institutions is likely to soften the internal hierarchy without any significant cost to efficiency. A public institution with a more mixed composition may, in addition, be able to deal more effectively with a very large and heterogeneous public.

However important such changes in the membership of public institutions might be to their structure and functioning, it is not clear what they will contribute to changes in the distribution of power in the wider society, or to the empowerment of backward communities in general. One might of course view public institutions as resources at the disposal of their members for altering the distribution of power in directions that they consider desirable. It is to this possibility and its implications that the courts must devote their most serious attention.

It is widely alleged that certain castes and communities have persistently taken advantage of their strategic presence in public institutions to use them as resources for consolidating and maintaining an unjust distribution of power in the wider society. It is said, for instance, that the civil service whose members are predominantly upper caste men will, consciously or unconsciously, seek not only to maintain a general balance of power in favour of men and of the upper castes but also to obstruct legislative or executive measures designed to alter the balance in favour of groups to which they do not belong. Clearly, those responsible for protecting the public interest must identify such obstructiveness and deal with it firmly and unequivocally.

The courts have not shown any great ingenuity or enterprise in dealing with invidious discrimination and other abuses of authority by members of public institutions belonging to advantaged groups. It will be a mistake to believe that the only way in which these deficiencies can now be remedied is by changing the distribution of power in society as a whole. And the mistake will be compounded if the judiciary takes it upon itself to initiate that change. No doubt societies require changes in the distribution of power, but in a democratic order, the initiative for such change does not lie with the judiciary. Moreover, the need for a radical redistribution of power in the wider society should not become an alibi for not doing anything to set right the pervasive abuse of authority within institutions to the benefit or the detriment of individuals belonging to particular castes or communities.

It would be folly to maintain that the misuse of authority in public institutions by members of some castes and communities can be corrected by extending the opportunities for such misuse equally to members of all castes and communities. Yet, the case for 'the empowerment of backward communities' seems to hover around that very idea. Having opened up the case, the courts must now take the responsibility for examining closely and candidly its implications for the governance of public institutions.

20 April 1993

White-collar Trade Unionism

Anotable feature of trade union activity in contemporary India is the growing strength and prominence of what may be called white-collar trade unionism as against the trade unionism of manual workers. Office workers, teachers in schools, colleges and universities, doctors and many others have become increasingly unionized, and their agitations for better pay and conditions of work have altered, expanded and redefined the meaning of 'industrial action'. Frequent and protracted strikes by professionals, such as doctors and professors, who are well paid, well educated and enjoy high social esteem, have raised questions of political morality that are quite different from those raised by trade union activity in its classical form.

Trade union activity has had a very close historical association with the working class movement. Much depends of course on how we think of workers, and here we encounter variation and change in social convention. The French sociologist Raymond Aron had pointed out, not without irony, that in the United States, most people, including many manual workers, viewed themselves as belonging to the middle classes, whereas in France, many persons in non-manual occupations, including intellectuals, identified themselves as workers. In India, the situation is both complex and ambiguous. College and university teachers declare themselves as workers during rallies and strikes, but the same persons take great care to maintain very respectable middle-class lifestyles at home.

The *locus classicus* of trade union activity is the capitalist enterprise. There are specific economic, political and moral conditions under which capitalists and workers negotiate the terms of their relationship in such an enterprise. In the early stages of industrial development, these conditions gave every advantage to the capitalist while placing the individual worker in a position of acute and severe disadvantage. The capitalist defined the interest of the enterprise as *his* interest, refusing to be bound by any obligation to take separate account of the interest of the worker. By acting on behalf of combinations of workers, trade unions were able to moderate, at least to some extent, the asymmetries between the principal parties. There can be no doubt that trade union activity has over the decades contributed much to the betterment of the economic and social situation of the working class in large parts of the world. One could even argue that without trade unions, it would be difficult for workers to secure their status as full citizens in the advanced industrial democracies.

Starting with manual workers in the capitalist enterprise, the trade union movement extended its scope in several ways. As is well known, there has been in the last hundred years a steady increase of non-manual workers in proportion to manual ones in all industrial societies. Office workers and other non-manual workers have become progressively unionized in the twentieth century, and in this process they have taken over some of the techniques of collective bargaining from the class of manual workers and added some new ones. The activities of trade unions have led to some convergence between higher manual and lower non-manual workers, but many differences still remain, and these become most evident when we compare the lower ranks of manual workers with persons in professional occupations.

A change takes place in the character of trade unions when they incorporate employees in various non-manual occupations. A larger change takes place when they organize themselves, not against private capital but against the government or some branch of it. In India, the growth of a very large and very active public sector, employing millions of persons in a variety of occupations, has given a distinctive orientation to trade union activity as a whole. It should not be difficult to see that a trade union of teachers employed under the government in West Bengal today operates in a very different environment from a union of miners employed by private capitalists in nineteenth century Britain.

It is often said that the trade union movement is weak in India due to paternalistic interference by the state. Where the state is such a large employer, directly and indirectly, there is bound to be some accommodation between it and the trade unions. This accommodation has not always been to the advantage of the working class as a whole, but it has certainly benefited those employees such as doctors and university teachers who have been able to use their strategic locations in society to catch the government on the wrong foot. The late Ashok Rudra pointed out how differently the government had acted in dealing with the railwaymen's strike in 1974 and the strike by college and university teachers in 1987.

Engineers, doctors, professors and others have a kind of social and cultural capital that they are able to use far more effectively than uneducated workers in stretching the government to the full, and calling its bluff. A strike is often a game of nerves, and with a little experience, well-educated persons are able to play that game quite skillfully, no matter on which side they happen to play. Strikes by professionals may or may not bring substantial benefits to them, but, unlike those by manual workers in private employment, they are largely cost free. Though without much apparent cost to those who engage in them, strikes, whether actual or threatened, by doctors, professors and others, have done much to undermine the credibility of our public institutions.

A strike, if it is serious, is designed to hurt. One can see that striking workers in a capitalist enterprise wish to hurt the owners of the enterprise, and, depending on the circumstances, one can even sympathize with the workers. But when doctors in a public hospital or professors in a university go on strike, whom do they aim to hurt? It is of course possible to represent the government as the ally of capitalists or even as their agent, but the plain fact is that when doctors go on strike, the ones who are most directly and immediately hurt are their patients, just as the ones who suffer most from a strike by teachers are their students.

Nothing brings out the contradictions of white-collar trade unionism more clearly than a strike by university teachers. In a university, the distinction between employers and employees, or between management and workers, is an artificial if not a notional one, at least as far as the professoriat is concerned. Professors sit on the executive council which makes appointments, they act as members of selection committees which recommend those appointments, and, as heads of departments or deans of faculties, they participate in university governance; yet, they also go on strike when their union gives a call. Being sagacious people, they are able to use their weight in the governing bodies of the university to protect themselves and their colleagues from punitive action after the strike.

Autonomy and self-governance are an essential part of the ideology of professionals. A university (or a hospital) is not a factory, and it cannot be treated as one. Doctors, scientists, professors and others must enjoy a certain freedom in defining the work that they do, how they do it and when they do it for it to be fruitfully accomplished; their work cannot be circumscribed in the way in which work in a factory or even an office is circumscribed. Professionals in India are at one and the same time jealous of their individual and institutional autonomy, and tempted by the easy attractions of industrial action. Whatever may be the short-term gains from this urge to eat one's cake and have it too, it can, in the long run, lead only to a loss of their social credibility.

2 May 1995

Burdens of the Pay Commission

The economic changes of the last three or four years have created a mood of euphoria in some sectors and, as is bound to happen in such a large and heterogeneous society as ours, a mood of depression in others. There are rumours of six- and even seven-figure salaries for corporate managers, newspaper editors and frontrunners in the media. Civil servants and others in public employment have begun to wonder how and where the government will find the resources to match these salaries and so enable them to maintain their status and dignity in society.

The malaise among government employees has not arisen only from the imminent increase in salary differentials between those in private and public employment. It has grown over a period of time and from a variety of causes. The two significant trends in public employment since Independence have been: (1) a continuous and unregulated expansion of posts at every level, and (2) a steady decline in salary differentials among government employees. These two trends now need to be seriously reviewed and reconsidered. It will be readily conceded that the expansion of staff and the levelling of incomes cannot continue indefinitely, but that does not mean that the government is now ready to bear the political cost of putting its own house in order. The fifth pay commission has to take a clear view of these matters, and to make its recommendation with courage and a sense of responsibility.

India has many able civil servants, and the best of these can compare with the best anywhere in the world. Indian officials who do very well in assignments abroad find it hard on return to cope with the disorder and anomie of their offices at home. Very often the problem with getting work done in government offices in India is not that there are too few people to do it but that there are too many. Such offices swarm with underemployed, discontented and fractious section officers, upper- and lower-division clerks, peons, daftaries and many others who come and go as they please and attend to their work only fitfully and intermittently.

The drive for the expansion of staff in government offices has now acquired a life of its own. It is sustained by a variety of forces: the lure of patronage, trade union pressure, and ill-conceived ideas of social justice. Everybody who is entrusted with an important public office asks, almost as a matter of routine, for a large establishment with a substantial staff. I will give only one example. After it assumed power in 1977, the Janata party set up a new commission for scheduled castes and scheduled tribes. The first thing that the chairman of the commission did on assuming office was to put forward proposals for staff: 141 gazetted officers, 567 non-gazetted officers and 900 group D employees. One has only to compare these numbers with the corresponding numbers in the older constitutional office of the commissioner for scheduled castes and scheduled tribes to get a sense of the scale on which expansion was being proposed. It is easy to multiply such examples, and every public servant has his own favourite story of the runaway expansion of staff in one or another department or ministry.

Quantitative expansion has been accompanied by a decline in quality. The two things are not unrelated. Where fifteen people congregate to do work that can be done by five, it is not easy in the long run to maintain either discipline or morale. But other factors have also contributed to the decline in quality. Over the years, providing secure employment to increasing numbers of 'deserving' persons has come to be viewed as a part of the government's commitment to welfare and social justice. The hard part is to find a job in the government. Once that has been found, pay, promotion and other benefits are guaranteed more or less independently of effort and ability. The last nail in the coffin has been the recent increase of caste quotas in public employment. It was hard enough to run offices when under a quarter of the posts were filled through quotas. It will be next to impossible to run them when more than half of the posts are filled in that way. The most damaging effect of caste quotas has been the wilful denigration of effort and ability in the name of social entitlement. The consolidated fund of India has been treated as an unlimited resource for drawing salaries for socially deserving government employees. After proposing a dramatic increase in the proportion of reserved posts in 1990, V.P. Singh coolly announced that there should be no cause for alarm since he was going to create additional posts to take care of deserving candidates from the forward castes.

Responsible and conscientious civil servants regret all this, but many of them have come to regard it as inevitable. There are indications that the best products of our colleges and universities are turning away from careers in administration to those in management. In this climate, some have begun to believe that efficiency should be left to the private sector which should be given more scope for expansion, and that the concern of the government should be less with efficiency than with social justice.

Nothing could be more shortsighted than the belief that India can afford to neglect its public institutions so long as it continues to make room for the market. Strong public institutions are essential for the health and well being of any modern society, and they require attention on their own right. These institutions have fallen in the public esteem, and it is no longer uncommon to hear civil servants attack their own service for its corruption and inefficiency. They must be helped to regain their rightful place in society. For that to happen, public services have to be made efficient and not just socially responsive; indeed, they cannot be socially responsive if they wilfully neglect efficiency.

It is the responsibility of the pay commission to assert once again the central significance for Indian society of public institutions in general and the civil service in particular. But that assertion will not carry much conviction unless it turns against the drift of the last several years. A robust civil service can carry only a certain amount of fat, and ours has accumulated too much of it for its own good health. The pay commission must give a clear signal that the runaway expansion of staff in government offices must be halted and reversed. It must also make it clear that government employment cannot be treated as a source of rental income, and that salaries are not a form of social entitlement but must be earned through work. No doubt managers and officials have different kinds of work to do, but that does not mean that effort and ability should count for less among the latter than among the former. It should be possible in public administration, and not just in private management, to sort the sheep out from the goats. There must be large increases in salary for positions that call for great initiative and responsibility, but such increases cannot be conceded all across the board simply as a price for political peace. The pay commission must not fight shy of recommending increases in salary differentials where these differentials are justified by the requirement of responsible and efficient administration.

2 December 1994

VII
Institutions

In the last ten years I have written increasingly on institutions. An institution is a social arrangement which has a distinctive identity and a certain continuity over time. It outlives or is expected to outlive its existing members who may be viewed as links between its past and future members. While it is true that an institution is shaped to some extent by its members, it is also true that those members are in turn shaped by the institutions in and through which they live and work. For my part, I cannot say how much I have contributed to making the Delhi School of Economics what it is; but it has certainly contributed a very great deal to making me what I am.

Institutions are of many different kinds, and as a society changes, old institutions are gradually replaced by new ones, although some of the institutions of kinship and religion have shown a remarkable capacity for endurance. The focus in these articles is not on all institutions but on those of a particular kind, which may be called open and secular institutions, such as universities, colleges, hospitals, municipal corporations, political parties, banks, chambers of commerce, and so on. These institutions are of great significance in the transformation of a closed and hierarchical society to a more open and egalitarian one.

The modern institutions of which I speak are open in the sense that entry and exit as well as promotion in them are governed by impersonal rules that do not take kinship, caste and community into consideration. They are secular in the sense that they are governed by rational, man-made rules and not by religious doctrine or authority. In modern constitutional democracies, they play a crucial part in linking the citizen to the state. In such a democracy, citizenship does not depend on race, caste or gender, and the state too is indifferent to those distinctions. Open and secular institutions which mediate between the citizen and the state constitute the backbone of what I understand by civil society.

Modern institutions are of relatively recent origin in India. Their principles of operation often run contrary to the principles by which much of the wider social environment is governed. Their success since Independence has been uneven, and their very legitimacy in Indian society is sometimes questioned. At the same time, it is difficult to see how a modern economic and political system can operate without them.

Rules and Persons

Societies differ in the extent to which they are governed by rules and by persons. In small-scale, traditional societies based on agricultural production, the personal factor plays an important part in every sphere of life. By contrast, life in the modern industrial society is ordered to a much greater extent by impersonal norms and standards.

The difference between the two modes of life can perhaps be best illustrated with an example. In the traditional Indian village each individual had a place within his family, his kin group and his caste or community. When in need he could seek help from his kinsmen, his caste fellows or his patrons. These links could be used for practically every purpose and they invested the individual with a certain sense of security. Now there are whole areas of life in the modern industrial society where such links are in principle irrelevant.

In Indian as in other traditional societies people are accustomed to getting things done through persons rather than rules. To say this is not necessarily to pass a moral judgement. In a society where kinship, caste and community have a high value the use of personal ties for achieving individual objectives would appear to be both proper and expedient. Where however, the norms are defined differently, the dependence on such ties creates a variety of problems.

I would like to emphasize that for the individual the moral issues involved are neither clear nor simple. As a university teacher I have been approached many times by people to use my personal influence to get a relative or a friend admitted to a particular course. Those who are related to me by blood or marriage or went to school or college with me or come from the town where I was born feel that they have a moral right to make such claims on me. In a society where kinship, caste and community have an intrinsic value, these claims are not easy to deny. In some societies to make such claims would appear improper; in others, to deny them might seem unreasonable.

Moral problems (as also problems of efficiency) arise when values which are appropriate to one kind of society are carried over into organizations which are meant to work according to norms of a different kind. What we see in India in this respect is not unique. It is everywhere a feature of the transition from a social order based on family, kin and community to one in which impersonal rules play a more important part. In such periods of transition the individual has often to cope with the worst features of both types of system. He cannot be sure that his personal links will be wholly effective; nor can he depend fully on the appropriate system of rules. This is one important reason why our contemporary life is beset with so much uncertainty.

Those of us who live in large cities have to depend upon a variety of public utilities. These are so organized as to serve citizens uniformly, irrespective of personal considerations. There are rules of procedure according to which every citizen is entitled to make claims on certain services. In practice, however, when someone wants to get something done, he rarely depends on the rules alone.

He tries in addition to approach someone in the right quarters through a relative or a friend, or a friend of a relative, just in case the rules do not work or do not work quickly enough for his needs. Those who have no relatives or friends (or 'connections', as they are called) find themselves left out in the cold. But it is really amazing how almost everyone in India is able to activate some personal links with at least some persons of consequence.

Thus, most Indians get used to operating a dual system and try, so to speak, to have one foot in each world. Very few seem to believe seriously that things can be done without any kind of personal influence; and few of them doubt the ultimate efficacy of personal influence whether or not they can make it work to their own advantage. As a consequence, even among the most 'modern' sections of our population, the commitment to impersonal norms is weak. And this operates as a kind of vicious circle. If I feel (perhaps with some reason) that I cannot attain a particular end without manipulating personal ties then I make it to that extent difficult for others to avoid doing the same thing for themselves.

I would like to dwell a little on this ambivalence which is so pronounced among the western-educated middle classes in our cities. In the traditional village community when a man used the ties of kin and community to get something done he did not feel he was doing anything wrong; he was not beset by a sense of guilt. Nor would he in general find it improper or immoral if others did the same thing to achieve their ends. The modern, educated Indian finds himself in a somewhat more intractable moral universe. He is a victim of both guilt and self-righteousness. Even when he makes use of the ties of family, kinship and community he does not do so with an entirely easy conscience. And when he finds others manipulating these ties against his own interest he becomes easily self-righteous.

In countries like India which are trying to achieve rapid economic change, much depends on the efficacy of administration, using that term in its widest sense. We are often told that our failures in the economic front are failures not of planning but of its implementation. Obviously these are basic problems to which no easy solutions will be found. But if in the kind of society we are trying to create we cannot build up a sufficient commitment to impersonal norms, our administration will continue to be corrupt (in the specific sense described above) and inefficient.

Much of the 'corruption' and inefficiency one sees in India today follows from a half-hearted commitment to the norms which ought to govern the working of a modern administrative system. It is not enough to build up organizations; unless the appropriate values and norms are also there, these organizations can never be effective. If you wish to open an account in the State Bank or in a post office, or if you wish to have a passport made, the first thing that the clerk concerned will tell you is how difficult and complicated the whole business is going to be. If he happens to be a friendly person (and if you can convince him that the work is very important), he may tell you that there is a fellow-Bengali or a fellow-Tamilian who will get the job done immediately if he can be approached through a personal acquaintance. Very often the person who is meant to operate the rules does not himself have faith in their effectiveness.

Those who have dealings with government departments in India complain of the formidable body of rules they are required to cope with. There are innumerable forms to be filled and each form asks for detailed particulars which very few people can supply both honestly and accurately. Visitors from western countries complain of the complexity of our administrative procedures and wonder how they can work in a society where such a large proportion of the population is illiterate.

One could say with some reason that in India people are inclined to bypass the rules because they are so cumbrous and difficult to operate. But I think that the opposite argument would also have a measure of plausibility. Rules are made cumbrous and outmoded ones are allowed to remain unchanged because those who make them or are responsible for their enforcement do not give them the kind of serious consideration they deserve. One reason for this is perhaps the assurance that if people find the rules too obstructive they will in any case have recourse to other means.

This attitude of drift leads to a number of evils among which corruption and inefficiency are the most conspicuous. I am not suggesting that it is the only or even the most important cause of these two evils. But corruption is bound to flourish where so much depends on personal favours which cannot, as in the traditional system, be claimed as a matter of right. This, I repeat, is not to deny that in any economy of scarcity there are other, independent causes of corruption. Efficiency also suffers for a variety of reasons. One obvious factor is the low rate of literacy and education in the country. People cannot be expected to operate a system of rules smoothly when so many of them do not understand what the rules are about. But when they do achieve this minimum

understanding of what they mean, will they also acquire a
moral commitment towards them?

4 November 1968

Modern Institutions

The common man's life in India is beset with many uncertainties. Some of these follow from our close dependence on the forces of nature over which we have little or no control. The rains do not come on time, or they do not come at all; the rivers rise in flood, and wash away crops, cattle and habitations; or epidemics ravage the countryside. The Indian peasant has lived with these uncertainties from time immemorial, and has dealt with them in his own way, either by trying to control them through magical techniques or by facing them with resignation in the hope of a better life hereafter.

But there are other uncertainties, arising from the vagaries not of natural forces but of social arrangements, and it is to these that I wish to draw attention. It is a truism that the individual human being cannot pursue his aims entirely on his own and that he has to act through a variety of social arrangements which we call institutions and organizations. These arrangements, which are a universal feature of collective life everywhere, may be viewed as either constraints or facilities. They are facilities to the extent that in the absence of such institutions or organizations, the individual would often not know what to do or how to do it. But they are also constraints to the extent that each institution or organization has its own rules of operation by which those who participate in it are to some extent bound.

Although institutions and organizations are, in the ultimate analysis, created by individual human beings, the rhythms of their life are not the same as the rhythms of individual life. While they too have their states of health and of sickness, these are far more difficult to detect than the corresponding states in the individual. Individuals can speak for themselves, institutions cannot, and those who speak on behalf of institutions often give contradictory messages. Just as it is a sign of sickness in an individual when he thinks all the time that he is sick, so also it is a sign of sickness in an institution when its members regard it as only a constraint and not a facility.

The uncertainties of contemporary life are to a large extent a reflection of the weakening of the social arrangements through which individuals conduct their everyday pursuits. Every society has a variety of such arrangements which acquire a kind of dependability through continued, if not long usage. An institution is nothing but a framework of activities whose rules of operation are tacitly accepted by those who participate in them. There are times when a society finds itself in a situation where its individual members no longer feel committed to its old institutions but are at the same time unable to provide firm foundations for new ones. We are in that situation today. Our old institutions do not inspire much confidence in the modern world; yet, the new ones we have created or tried to create do not seem to hold together.

It would take up too much space to make even an inventory of the new institutions that we have tried to establish during the last hundred years or so. Legislatures, political parties and universities may be taken as good examples, and one could add many more. Everyone seems to agree that these do not work at all well, or as they ought to, and a hundred instances could be given of the malfunctioning of each. If we compare these with our traditional social institutions, such as those associated with family, marriage and kinship, or with the village community, especially as they existed in the past, we will see at once the difference between insecure and dependable social arrangements.

It is not simply that these new social arrangements do not function as they ought to, but that our confidence in their capacity to function adequately is growing thinner everyday. I think it would be fair to say that thirty-three years after Independence we have less rather than more confidence in the Indian university as a dependable framework for the pursuit of higher education. The same fate seems to be overtaking our legislative and related institutions, and it is no doubt this erosion of confidence that has taken shape in the wild thought that the country's social, economic and political problems will come to an end by a switch from the parliamentary to the presidential form of government.

Our great success in the past in creating and maintaining the institutions of family and community seems to be matched by our conspicuous inability to manage the new type of institution which survival in the modern world demands. One sort of explanation for this is that these new institutions, such as Parliament, political party and university, are foreign plants on the Indian soil, and as such they are destined to sicken and wither away. But it is a shallow argument that ideas or institutions cannot work except on the very soil on which they take birth: Christianity did not originate in France, nor capitalism in Japan. At the same time, it is true that two of the basic preconditions for the success of modern institutions, viz. attention to the individual and regard for impersonal rules, are very weakly developed in our society. The success of those institutions that stood the test of time with us—family, caste and community—depended on exactly the opposite conditions, i.e. the subordination of the individual to the collectivity and of impersonal to personal considerations in social interchange.

Our inability to manage or even to understand the requirements for managing the new institutions we have set up means that they are inefficient or unproductive. But it also means that the quality of personal life in them acquires a very different character from what one expects it to have in such institutions.

Whether we take a students' union, a social welfare agency, or a scientific research laboratory—and in whichever part of the country—we will find it to be divided into factions; and we will find these factions to be of exactly the same kind as the factions that have existed in our villages from time immemorial. No matter what they say or how loudly they say it, the plain fact is that Indians love factions. I do not mean simply that they make use of factions as means for furthering their material ends, but, rather, that from the social point of view they regard the life of the faction as an end in itself. One may say, with but a little bit of exaggeration, that the faction is the only form of social life that engages at one and the same time both the intellect and the passions of the Indian in his workplace today.

But, for all the pleasures that it might give, factionalism, with its intense preoccupation with persons, obstructs a clear appreciation of the rules by which modern institutions are governed. The criteria of fairness are quite different in a factional system from those in an institution that puts a premium on impersonal rules.

Individuals, whose aims and pursuits are blocked by the operation of such rules, automatically believe and persuade others to believe that there is a conspiracy against them. Lack of faith in the rules of the system and the misuse of those rules reinforce one another. The rules may be misused wilfully or negligently, but in either case the misuse tends to confirm suspicions of sinister forces at work. The readiness to ascribe everything to conspiracies is the other side of the failure to conduct institutional life according to the principles proper to its constitution.

It would appear that more and more people are coming to believe in the existence of a hidden hand as a source of all misfortune. If the hospitals do not work because the doctors are on strike, there is a hidden hand behind it; if the law courts cannot dispose of all their accumulated cases, there is a hidden had in it; and if students sit in the cafe instead of attending class, there is a hidden hand there as well. Belief in the hidden hand is in some sense a secular counterpart of the belief in witchcraft. Witchcraft accusations become endemic in certain types of societies under certain conditions, and they have been studied in detail by anthropologists, sociologists and historians in both contemporary Africa and early modern Europe. These studies show that witchcraft accusations are a symptom of the uncertainties of everyday life caused by the weakening of the institutional order. Above all, they show that witchcraft is one of the deadliest inventions of man, for it deranges both accuser and accused.

4 December 1980

Factions and Their Legitimacy

There is much disagreement among students of Indian society as to whether its true basis is constituted by caste or by class. While both caste and class are undoubtedly important in the larger social and historical context, the immediate environment of a great deal of everyday life in contemporary India is neither the one nor the other, but the faction. Class and caste have been studied in detail, but factions have not received much scholarly attention and very little can be said to account for either their pervasiveness or their persistence. The faction represents the private and largely unacknowledged side of our collective life; we recognize it easily enough among others but refuse to acknowledge it among ourselves.

There are two misconceptions that need to be removed if we are to understand factions for what they are. The first is that factions are primarily a rural phenomenon, that they are an expression of peasant social life or the peasant mentality, and that their presence among educated people in professional, managerial or executive occupations is nothing but a survival of an ancient or traditional mode of social existence. The second misconception is that the faction appeals only to the baser side of human nature, that it has no concern whatever for any code of morality.

I would like to argue that factions are an inseparable

part of our modern social life, being, if anything, even more characteristic of the present than of the past social order. One of the early prose writers in Bengali, Bhabanicharan Bandyopadhyay, a contemporary of Rammohun Roy, wrote an account of Calcutta in the form of a set of dialogues in which he gave a prominent place to the dal or faction in the new social life then taking shape in the city. The account is detailed and matter-of-fact, and it points to the distinction between single-caste and multi-caste factions.

The literary representation of factions in early nineteenth-century Calcutta highlights one important basis of their existence, namely, the distribution of patronage. These factions were built around important personalities, each of whom attracted his own coterie and sought to outdo his rivals in lavish and ostentatious expenditure. In the nineteenth century the city of Calcutta provided much scope for ostentation and display, and having a large circle of dependents was in some ways the most satisfying part of it all. The wealth that was used in the support and entertainment of dependents then was mainly private wealth. In our time the scope for using public resources for creating and maintaining the ties of patronage has become greatly enlarged.

The use of public resources for the creation of personal support is seen best in the political party. This is to some extent true everywhere, but nowhere more so than in India where the party divides itself into factions with the regularity of a law of nature. This simply means that a framework of impersonal rules counts for little in the life of the party in comparison to personal ties of loyalty and dependence. Moreover, the patronage structure of the party is replicated in almost every kind of organization that has anything to do with the control and distribution of public resources. Anyone who is in a position to make or to influence the making of appointments is recognized as a patron and acts as one. It is remarkable how responsible people in public institutions believe that if they have appointed someone to a position of responsibility, a binding obligation is created on the one appointed to remain personally loyal to the one who has appointed him.

It is a mistake to believe that what people value most in public office is the opportunity it provides for material gain, legitimate or otherwise. They value far more the scope it offers for helping others by securing appointments or promotions for them in their own organization or in other organizations in which they have influence. One cannot but be impressed by the lengths to which Indians in positions of responsibility are prepared to go in seeking out avenues of employment for their deserving dependents. A man who holds an important position in a public institution but is unable to find jobs in it for any of his dependents is a man of no account.

A factional tie may be initiated by an act of patronage, but that alone cannot account for either the durability or the pervasiveness of factions in their new social environment. The source of their strength lies in the nature of this environment itself which is at one and the same time both pliable and uncertain. This is an environment in which the traditional obligations of kinship and community have become loose without the obligations appropriate to the modern workplace becoming firm. In such an environment people fall back upon the faction because they have little else to fall back upon; it offers scope for patronage, but, more than that, it provides social security.

Our urge for modernization has led us to construct a large number of institutions with whose management we have very little experience. Whether we take our civic institutions, or our nationalized banks, or our colleges and universities, we will find each of them to be faced with critical problems of governance. The rules that were devised for their governance have all suffered serious loss of credibility by being frequently ignored or bypassed, and what had once looked like becoming viable institutions now appear increasingly as scissors-and-paste jobs. At the same time, more and more people have to make their livelihood in and through these institutions. When they find that the rules adopted for their operation cannot be relied upon, they turn for protection to personal loyalties and attachments.

The only ties on which people really depend in this society are still the ties of family and kinship: professional and other associational ties count for little beside these. This has a great deal to do with the way in which children are reared and socialized within the household, including the way in which they are taught to acknowledge their obligations to relatives outside the household. This is not to say that relatives in fact do always help each other or ever did, but only to maintain that the social obligations of kinship have in our society a kind of precedence over all other obligations.

In the traditional order many types of social activities, including economic activities, were organized on the basis of kinship. The domestic group was not only the unit of consumption, it was also frequently the unit of production; and people turned first to their relatives for companionship in both work and leisure. Even where the real ties of kinship have a limited range, the idiom of kinship might extend quite far. To extend the idiom of kinship means simply to define the reciprocity between persons in a particular way. It is common in the Indian village even today to extend the idiom of kinship across caste, even though everyone knows that real kinship can hardly exist between members of different castes.

The modern workplace cannot easily accommodate the ties of real kinship, and it is not clear what place even the idiom of kinship can legitimately occupy in it. It is not simply that there is a difference in the scale of activities, but the very principles of recruitment, placement and promotion are different in the modern workplace as compared with the traditional. But the old idiom of relationship does not disappear simply because the context has altered. Rather, the uncertainties inherent in the altered context give a new lease of life to the old idiom even when its claims can no longer be publicly acknowledged.

Thus, what appears as a faction from the outside appears from the inside as a dependable and even a humane arrangement for mutual support and protection. The real strength of the faction is that it is an association with a human face, and not merely an instrument for the calculated pursuit of personal gain. It serves to mediate between the domain of family and kinship—where alone Indians feel truly secure—and the domain of office and factory where they must earn their livelihood. But factional ties in the new institutional context can only simulate the ties of kinship, and, for all the benefits it may bring, pseudo-kinship can never have the moral authority of real kinship.

Pseudo-kinship offers more scope for the manipulation of human relations than real kinship. These manipulations are a source of both pleasure and profit, and that is why factions thrive. But in the end, they are parasitical on the institutions and organizations within which they grow, and parasites cannot fatten except by feeding upon their hosts.

5 January 1981

Alternatives to Bureaucracy

One hears it frequently said of our public institutions that they are too bureaucratic, that nothing gets done in them because of bureaucracy: in India when people are not complaining about intellectuals, they are bound to be complaining about bureaucracy. And just as it is the intellectual himself who speaks most fluently about the futility of every kind of intellectual activity, there is now a rising generation of civil servants who are ready to hold forth on the inherently unproductive nature of bureaucratic activity itself.

The problem with our public institutions is not that there is too much bureaucracy in them but that there is too little. Their troubles are not due to bureaucracy, they are due to the decay of bureaucracy in a tropical environment. If one may speak of a life cycle for such institutions, then the phase in which the rules of their operation become too many, too cumbersome and too rigid is followed by a phase in which these rules are circumvented, violated and then simply ignored. From the viewpoint of individual morality it is bad when those in responsible positions in an institution violate its rules in the interest of personal gain. From the viewpoint of the institution itself, it is worse when these rules are simply ignored.

Bureaucracy simply means administration in

accordance with impersonal rules. It presupposes competence in dealing with paperwork and a degree of reliance on the written word. It is not the only possible form of administration, but the only one suited to a large-scale society with pretensions to economic progress and political democracy. Now, most Indians try to run public institutions not through the written word but by word of mouth, not by means of impersonal rules but by means of personal approach and access. This is not bureaucracy but its opposite.

It is common knowledge in these institutions that administrative action of even the most routine kind cannot be ensured only through correspondence. If the building has to be repaired or if furniture needs to be bought or if a temporary appointment has to be made permanent, one cannot rely upon correspondence alone to accomplish the task even when it falls within the scope of provisions already made or agreed upon. One has to telephone the official concerned, or send an assistant to speak to his assistant, or go there personally to get the job done. In India the movement of files from office to office achieves no result unless accompanied by a corresponding movement of persons.

It must be understood that this perpetual movement of persons from office to office does nothing to diminish the volume of correspondence or of paperwork. Not only is the volume of correspondence handled by every office very large, but an extraordinarily large part of it is marked 'urgent', 'most immediate', 'out today', etc. etc. But as every office assistant in India knows, these markings by themselves do not mean much and need not be taken too seriously. If the matter is really urgent then someone will be bound to come and see him or his superior, and then will be the time to bestir oneself.

Clearly, no system of administration can function solely through the movement of files; there has to be also some movement of persons. But in the West the historical role of the bureaucratic system has been to give precedence to impersonal rules in administration and to confine personal intervention to a limited sphere. If we, on the other hand, are unable to manage any of our affairs without recourse to personal access and personal contact, it is hardly reasonable to put the responsibility for this on to bureaucracy.

An administrative system which is supposed to work according to impersonal rules but in fact works through personal contact provides much scope for manipulation. Everyone knows that there is some advantage in this for those who occupy key positions in the administration, for at least in the short run they gain rather than lose by manipulating the system. Everyone also knows that in a labour surplus economy one has to employ armies of peons, clerks and assistants who have to be kept busy by being sent from one office to another. But over and above all this is our inherent mistrust of the written as against the spoken word: we only half believe what we see written, we believe it fully only when someone says it to us. Now, bureaucracy can never work properly in a culture in which the written word is taken so lightly.

Thus, along with the quantity and volume of paperwork, we have to consider its meaning and function. It is impossible to explain fully the peculiarly light-hearted attitude to paperwork in the Indian office, but we have to note the fact that, for all its richness and variety, the Hindu intellectual tradition has always given precedence to oral over written communication. Some of the paperwork done in the office today is used for facilitating administrative action, some for obstructing it, and a great deal of it is of no use at all. In terms of human interest it is this last that is the most intriguing, for, however strongly we might deplore calculated obstructiveness, it is not difficult to understand it, and at times even to sympathize with it.

The consequence of excessive paperwork is that administrative procedures become complicated beyond the point of convenience. People simplify procedures and make them convenient only when they want to use them. When they feel that they can get by without having always to use them or to use them consistently, they do not mind if the procedures are inconvenient. To those who have acquired the habit of evading the rules, it is in fact an advantage when these rules are complicated, inconsistent and unintelligible.

It is not as if the rules and procedures—the files and the paperwork—can always be ignored even when one has the best of personal relations with those with whom one has to work. One has to acquire a certain agility to be able to move successfully through the administrative jungle, for there are snares and pitfalls at every turn. In course of time people who work through the system come to acquire a distinctive orientation towards its rules and regulations, treating them for practical purposes as weapons of offence and defence.

While most people who work in an office have to acquire some of the skills required in evading, circumventing and bypassing the rules, there are a few who become true virtuosos in the art. Such virtuosos are to be found at every level, from the head of the institution to the junior assistant, and they are viewed by everyone with a mixture of admiration and envy. They know the rules backwards and the loopholes in each one of them, and whenever they are faced with a problem, they go straight for the loopholes in the rules. Of course, they use their virtuosity for advantage to themselves and their friends, but beyond considerations of material advantage, there is the sheer aesthetic pleasure of beating the system.

It is a truism that no institution can work entirely according to its formal rules of procedure. These formal rules have to be capacious enough to accommodate informal arrangements to deal with contingencies of various kinds. But the informal arrangements cannot be allowed to supplant the formal rules of procedure. At any rate, when the impersonal rules by which public institutions are meant to be governed are supplanted by private arrangements of an informal kind, what we have is not a bureaucracy but its opposite.

To deny its due place to bureaucracy is to seek to evade the responsibility of living in the modern world. We have to accept the responsibility of conducting our public affairs according to objective and impersonal rules even though this means some sacrifice of the comfort and security that have in the past been guaranteed by the attachment to family, caste and community. It is true that this is not an easy sacrifice to make, and perhaps the sneer at bureaucracy merely conceals our inability to make it. At the same time, we must recognize that there are no short cuts for the entry into the modern world of a society as large, as heterogeneous and as disorderly as ours.

In this light the argument for a committed bureaucracy appears somewhat disingenuous. The Chinese made a bold attempt to commit their bureaucracy to a cause, and how far they got in that we are bound to discover before long. We are not likely to get even that far, for in India commitment to a cause is only a thin disguise for attachment to faction, community and caste. It is hard to see how we can rid ourselves of these millstones if we continue to hold bureaucracy in contempt. In India the alternative to an impersonal bureaucracy will be not a committed bureaucracy but an administration in the service of caste, community and faction.

16 February 1981

Government and NGOs

When the country became independent, many Indians looked to the government to play a leading and beneficial role in transforming the collective life of the nation. The leaders of the nationalist movement had spoken and written tirelessly about what needed to the done to enable India to take its rightful place in the comity of nations. There had been one insuperable obstacle in the way, and that was the presence of an uncaring and oppressive colonial power. A national government would do everything that the colonial government had been unable or unwilling to do.

The conviction that a national government would play a major part in the regeneration of Indian society was very widespread among the Indian intelligentsia. Many of the brightest and the best students in the metropolitan universities aspired to careers in the civil service, not simply in the interest of personal gain, but also because they believed that such a career would enable them to lead fruitful and constructive lives.

The attitude to the government and to public service through the organs of government began to change, slowly at first and then with increasing rapidity after 1977. The trauma of the Emergency was followed by the disorder of the first non-Congress government in New Delhi. The post-Emergency period brought in a culture of public exposure whereby the misdeeds of the government and its functionaries began to be widely exposed, sometimes in an exaggerated form. This led to a general loss of esteem for the institutions of governance. It also reinforced the turpitude and venality that were already there among civil servants, for it is a truism that men behave badly when they lose their self-esteem, and public servants easily lose their self-esteem when they are deprived of public esteem.

I was for many years a regular visitor to the Lal Bahadur Shastri National Academy of Administration at Mussoorie where I often discussed the state of the nation with the probationers and the course directors who were mostly members of the various services. From the late seventies onward, I detected a growing disenchantment with the services among the latter. I was told repeatedly that professional laxity and corruption had become endemic in the services. I sometimes found myself in the peculiar position of a university professor having to defend the Indian Administrative Service from trenchant attacks against it by its own members.

It was in Mussoorie that I first learnt about the good work being done by the NGOs, and the tremendous opportunities being opened up by them for public service in various fields. In the discussions there, a sharp contrast was often made between the dull and confined routine of the bureaucrat working for the government and the freedom and initiative of the social activist serving the NGO. Some civil servants resigned from the government to work for one or another NGO, and others set up their own NGOs on retirement. In this and other ways, the NGO has come to occupy an established place in public life in India.

Looking back on those discussions of twenty years ago, I am reminded of the dialectic of church and sect that has been a part of many religious traditions. In this dialectic which has been extensively studied by sociologists of religion, the church has been viewed invariably as conservative and hierarchical, and the sect as radical and egalitarian. The distinction just noted has been especially emphasized by the founders of new sects.

Sects have had highly varied historical fortunes. Many have died or disappeared without leaving much trace. Some have grown and prospered. Their development from origin to maturity has shown certain common patterns across the different religions. Growth and prosperity have led, with unfailing regularity, to changes in both doctrine and organization. With success, the sect becomes less doctrinaire and more pragmatic, and less fluid and more organized. This dual process may be described as routinization. Through it, the successful sect comes in course of time to look more and more like the church, the disenchantment with which was the original cause of its foundation.

What kind of relationship—of complementarity or competition, of mutual help or mutual hindrance, of convergence or divergence—are the NGOs likely to develop with the governmental organizations that work in broadly the same fields into which they are entering? The successful NGO tends to extend its operations, and, in doing so, it has to come to terms with the very problems of funding, management and accounting that bedevil the work of the government.

The acquisition and management of large funds requires both time and effort. The move from social activist to fund raiser and fund manager has been made with ease by many, but it has also brought about some change in their orientations. In my limited experience, the prime movers of successful NGOs do not like to talk about the sources of their funding, preferring to dwell instead on the work their organization is doing and the work that remains to be done.

Then there is the question of organization, division of labour and remuneration. Not everyone can afford to work without pay. The successful NGO needs to have administrators, accountants, project officers and field staff. Their terms and conditions of work have to be specified in a more or less formal way. Even the most dedicated promoters of social causes have to make some concessions to the demands of bureaucratic routine.

Modern organizations have certain common characteristics, whether in the public or the private domain, in the governmental or the non-governmental sector. Here, as important as the sector in which the organization operates is the scale of its operation. It is at this point that the NGO comes to replicate, not just the way of functioning but also the forms of organization of agencies of the government. This cannot be an argument against the existence or even the expansion of voluntary activity in the social field outside the government's ambit. Such activity plays a vital part not only in the regeneration of society but also in the health and well-being of democracy. The public will no doubt appreciate the good work that is being done by the NGOs. But they in their turn must be ready to submit themselves to the same exacting scrutiny and assessment that they expect the public to exercise over the work of the government.

10 March 1999

Between State and Market

When the country became independent, people looked forward to a social transformation in India, and they expected the state to play a leading part in this transformation. Those who were placed at the helm of affairs were persons of great ability and integrity, and it was assumed that it was within their capacity to transform India from a backward hierarchical society into a modern democratic one. The Constitution and the laws on the one hand, and centralized planning on the other were seen as the major instruments through which the state would usher in the new society.

As we now know, things did not happen as they were expected to. The state increased its power and at the same time reduced its capacity to meet the expectations of the people. The idea of socialism has lost much of its shine, and the talk today is about liberalization and the possibilities that may be opened up by freeing the market of the many constraints imposed upon it by the state. A change of orientation has certainly come about, but what it signifies for the future of Indian society is not easy to determine.

Can the market be expected to bring about the kind of social transformation that the state failed to bring into being? With the advantage of hindsight it is easy to see the mistake made in assigning to the state a kind of miraculous power as an agent of social transformation. It would be an even graver mistake to assign such a magical power to the market, and to treat the state as dispensable.

Market and state are both very important, but they do not between them make up the whole of society. Today all the talk is about liberalization and control, or the relative advantages of state and market, and in this talk the enormous significance for society of its various institutions tends to be lost to sight. A society such as ours has a great variety of these, ranging from domestic and religious institutions to educational, scientific, medical and civic institutions. Some of these go back to our ancient past, while others are of more recent origin. It is the modern institutions of a more or less public character that call for serious attention from us. To be sure, the state itself is an institution and the market may also be viewed as one, but here I wish to dwell upon institutions other than state and market.

In an essay published before Independence in a Bengali magazine, N.K. Bose had put forward the provocative argument that modern Bengal had produced many great individuals but hardly any institutions of lasting value. He had illustrated his argument with three examples: Calcutta Corporation, Vishva-Bharati and the University of Calcutta. He had said that Calcutta Corporation had been overshadowed by the towering personality of C.R. Das, Vishva-Bharati by that of Rabindranath Tagore, and the University of Calcutta by the personality of Sir Ashutosh Mukherji. With the demise of these personalities, the institutions associated with them went into decline. When I look at the public institutions with which I am familiar, I realize how prescient Bose's observation, made more than fifty years ago, had been.

Educated Indians today care a great deal about family and perhaps also about religion, but they do not seem to care very much about the institutions in and through which they secure their livelihood. I have in mind such institutions as colleges and universities, hospitals and laboratories and municipalities and corporations. The creation of these institutions in the nineteenth century was a part of the modernization of India, and a large number of new ones were added after Independence. It does not require a professional sociologist to discover that most of them are in a state of decay and disintegration. The decay within is signalled by the poor state of physical maintenance and the derelict external appearance of so many of our public institutions.

The modern university is among institutions occupying spaces in society that are not or ought not to be regulated wholly by either the state or the market. There are many such institutions, but I will concentrate on the university for reasons of convenience. It does make a difference to these institutions whether or not the state and the market function effectively as parts of the external environment. But their own health and well being can be guaranteed only if they are able to develop and sustain ways of functioning that are to some extent independent of the state and the market.

As an institution, the Indian university is in a poorer condition than it was fifty years ago. This truth is most evident in the case of the university for the simple reason that it operates in a conspicuously open space: virtually anybody can walk into a university and see the disorder and apathy prevalent there. Vice-chancellors and the proverbial 'deans and dons' will say that the poor condition of the Indian university is due to their being starved of funds by the government. Others, apparently more adventurous in their ideas, say that the universities should shake off their dependence on the government, raise their own funds, and become more responsive to the laws of the market. Both views are essentially shallow, for the principal ailment is an institutional one, arising from the displacement of academic values and commitments by other interests, whether in social justice or in profitability not only outside the universities but also within them. I consider the main problem with the university to be not of finance but of morale: increasing numbers of both students and teachers have come to regard as trivial or even meaningless the everyday work of the classroom, the library and the laboratory.

It is one thing to set up lecture rooms, libraries and laboratories, although now even that is not without its difficulties. It is quite another to create the feeling that the work that is done there may be not just profitable but also meaningful, and that it has to be governed by its own norms and values which are different from those of both administration and management. Teachers and students often lament the breakdown of the regularity and routine of academic life in the universities, but that lament does not by itself create a caring attitude towards the institutions of which they are members. Such a caring attitude takes a long time to grow, and perhaps it never struck such deep roots in our universities—and other modern public institutions—as to make them self-sustaining.

Indian academics write a great deal on an endless variety of subjects, and that indeed is what is expected of them. Yet it is remarkable how little they have written about the universities in which they live and work. It has struck me that every college in Cambridge and Oxford has its own biography, and some have more than one, whereas one hardly finds a biography of an Indian college or university. The fact that so few scientists, doctors, architects, lawyers or journalists have written about the institutions in which they have spent the better parts of their lives must surely tell us something about how much—or how little—their lives have been touched by those institutions. In the end, institutions are damaged much more severely by lack of care from within than by lack of support from outside.

18 January 1995

Waning of Charisma

In the last five years we have had a government in New Delhi whose leadership has not been marked by any vivid or memorable qualities of personality. Both the prime minister and the finance minister, whose economic policies have received much praise at home and abroad, are men of modest demeanour and speech. They do not make a great impression before either the camera or the microphone. Compared to V.P. Singh in 1989 or Rajiv Gandhi in 1984, P.V. Narasimha Rao in the last five years has done little to enthuse any section of the Indian public by his personal style.

The waning of charisma, by which people generally mean the kind of personal quality that secures instant and unquestioned devotion to a leader among his followers, is now a general feature of our national political life. It has affected the leadership of all the major national parties. What is more, charisma appears to be in decline among democracies the world over. Not only is there no Nehru today; there is no Churchill and no de Gaulle. The implications of this for the prospects of democracy merit careful consideration.

There is widespread and growing dismay over the utterly lacklustre quality of the political leaders of the day. People transfer their adulation to movie stars, sadhus, sants, and the heroes of the sporting field whose magnetic presence is now easily conveyed by the media: NTR missed being prime minister of India, Imran Khan aspires to be prime minister of Pakistan. Charisma never disappears altogether from society, at least not from our kind of society; it moves over from one arena to another.

Charisma betokens not only the presence of certain qualities among leaders, but also a thirst for those qualities among their followers. Perhaps Indians have lost the thirst for political leaders of exceptional quality that was carried over from the nationalist movement into the decades immediately after Independence. Intellectuals are understandably disappointed that our political leaders have all revealed their feet of clay and that we no longer have any national heroes left in our legislatures and political parties. But is the absence of the heroic mode from democratic politics necessarily to its detriment?

It is in some sense paradoxical that many of those who lament the lack of a strong political leadership today were the very ones who were first dismayed and then embittered by Mrs Gandhi's use of the iron hand in the days when she held the country in thrall. Mrs Gandhi believed that so long as she had the people of India behind her—as she largely did have at the height of her power—she could throw to the winds the intelligentsia and their cumbersome institutions. Today we have to ask ourselves whether this was an aberration of charismatic leadership or its essence. The charismatic leader has very little use for the niceties of parliamentary procedures or institutions. He shows the path to the people, and they in turn render their unquestioning allegiance to him. History shows that charismatic leaders are not so much the sustainers as the destroyers of institutions.

Those who yearn for the return to the national scene of strong leaders who will once again galvanize the people by the force of their personality no doubt hope that such leaders will also act with the highest respect for the proprieties of democratic life. Such a hope is likely to be without much substance. Charismatic leaders do not act by the rule book; were they to do so, they would almost certainly lose their charisma. The regularity and routine of everyday politics has little attraction for forceful personalities who scale the pinnacles of political power. It is not that such people are devoid of all moral sense. Their morality is nourished not by the external rules of society but by an inner voice that urges them to clear away all the deadwood from a society that they see as moribund. Their role is crucial in some phases in the development of society, but not in all its phases.

Perhaps it is a good thing to be freed, at least for some time, from the distractions of spell-binding political personalities who promise much but deliver little, and uproot both the dying and the newborn arrangements of society. While in the popular mind the idea of charisma is inseparable from exceptional individuals, the scholar who contributed most to its use in political analysis in fact distinguished between individual and institutional charisma. If charisma is the sort of quality that automatically imposes its majesty and inspires deference, respect, awe and loyalty, that quality might inhere in institutions as well as individuals. In a democracy with established traditions, a certain amount of charisma inheres in Parliament and not just in the exceptional prime minister. Individual charisma is intense and concentrated, whereas institutional charisma tends to be subdued and dispersed.

In the early years of independence, the pre-eminent site of charisma was in the political domain. No film star or athletic hero had the magnetism of the leaders of the nationalist movement recently come to power, and in particular Jawaharlal Nehru. Nor was it only a matter of individual charisma: Parliament, the Supreme Court and even the Congress party carried some of the aura of grand and majestic things. In those days, when people came from the provinces to the capital, many went to visit Parliament, as people do when they go to places of pilgrimage. Who would go in a spirit of pilgrimage to the houses of Parliament today?

It is said that Nehru used his enormous personal influence to keep his party, his cabinet and even Parliament in thrall. But it is one thing for a leader to impose his will on Parliament, and quite another to tolerate or even encourage the violation of its dignity by all and sundry. The English political theorist Walter Bagehot distinguished between the 'efficient' and the 'dignified' parts of a constitution, and every major political institution must have something of both, though not in the same proportions. I will say nothing of the lack of efficiency in our Parliament; what is equally if not more worrying is the erosion of its dignity. In our kind of democracy, all legitimate authority flows from Parliament. If the very fountainhead of legitimate authority is exposed to contumely and ridicule, then no individual leader, however exceptional his qualities, can save democracy from corruption and ruin.

The decline of intense and concentrated personal

charisma is not necessarily harmful for the life of democracy. It is in any case highly volatile, and it is difficult to see how anyone can work towards the emergence of a charismatic leader. Institutional charisma is a different matter. The protection and preservation of the dignity and majesty of Parliament, the Supreme Court and other significant institutions is a collective task that requires conscious and earnest attention. In the last two decades, it is Parliament that has suffered the most from thoughtless assaults on its dignity from within and outside. A new Parliament is soon to be constituted. One can only hope that its members will set about their tasks not only with efficiency but also with some sense of their own dignity.

29 April 1996

Continuity of Institutions

I ndividual and collective life depends to a large extent on the institutions of society. By an institution I mean a social arrangement that has a distinct identity, specific rules of operation and a defined sphere of activity, for instance a school, a bank or a monastery. Every institution provides certain facilities, but it also imposes certain constraints. An individual would not be able to do many of the things he needs or desires to do in the absence of such institutions. At the same time, an institution obliges its members to act in certain ways and to refrain from acting in other ways.

The major institutions of society, such as universities, temples or political parties, have lifespans that extend beyond the lives of their individual members. We cannot appreciate how an institution works without understanding how it maintains its continuity. The continuity of an institution is not a static continuity like that of a building or a piece of furniture, but a dynamic continuity like that of a living organism.

Neither the replacement of ordinary members nor the succession to positions of influence and authority takes place automatically in institutions. They are governed by rules and conventions that may be explicit or implicit. In some cases the rules and conventions are so well established that replacement and succession seem to work automatically. In others, there is disagreement and confusion over what the rules are and what they ought to be.

The arrangements for replacement and succession vary from one society to another and, within the same society, from one type of institution to another. The oldest recognized principle, which is still widely acknowledged, is the one based on genealogy, i.e. family and kinship. In India, such very important associations as lineage, clan and caste recruit members entirely on that basis. Succession to office in many if not most traditional institutions is based on birth in a particular family or kin group. The basic idea, which is deeply ingrained and widely shared, is that family and kinship are the best guarantors of the qualities required for both membership and leadership in such institutions.

Not all institutions can ensure continuity by depending on family and kinship for replacement and succession. Modern institutions recruit new members at all levels through impersonal rules which stress ability and performance as against birth. It will be absurd to propose that the head of the University of Delhi, or the Reserve Bank of India, or the National Physical Laboratory be succeeded by his son, his nephew or his son-in-law. Howsoever grudgingly, many Indians have come to realize that ability and performance, and not just, birth, must count if continuity is to be maintained in at least some of the key institutions of society.

Where does the political party stand in the spectrum of institutions between those which regulate succession solely by the rules of kinship and those which regulate it solely by impersonal rules? The Congress party provides an object lesson in the tangled issues involved in institutional succession in a complex and changing society. Nehru was replaced, after a brief interregnum, by his daughter as the supreme leader of the Congress. At that time, some felt uneasy about what looked like the beginnings of dynastic succession, but her supporters argued that birth should not be a disqualification.

As Indira Gandhi began to do well in office, opinion turned, and many began to wonder if birth in a premier political family did not after all give one a decisive advantage in politics. When she was assassinated, it appeared natural for the President of India to invite her son to head the caretaker government, although for most of his life he had shown little aptitude and, indeed, little inclination for politics. The tragic circumstance of the succession created a wave of goodwill for Rajiv Gandhi throughout the country, and nothing is more valuable in a democracy than the goodwill of the people. Rajiv Gandhi's performance in office was indifferent and erratic, but his own life too was tragically cut short, this time at a very young age.

With the assassination of Rajiv Gandhi, the political primacy of the Nehru-Gandhi family became an established fact among the leaders, ordinary members and supporters of the Congress party. Soon it became apparent that no major decision could be taken without the approval, or at least the concurrence, of his widow, even though she did not hold any office in either party or government. When at last Sonia Gandhi agreed to lead the Congress party in the 1999 elections, it was counted as a blessing by millions of its members and supporters throughout the country. Now there is speculation as to whether her daughter or her son will stand from Amethi when she vacates her seat; whichever way it happens, that too will be counted as a blessing by many a seasoned Congressman.

By linking its fortunes indissolubly with the fortunes of

a single family, the Congress party has done irreparable harm to itself and to the cause of Indian democracy. Other parties are bound to follow its example as is indeed happening in several Indian states. The natural tendency in a traditional society is for succession to office to follow the lines of a genealogy. The Congress party, with its great tradition of public service, could have set a good example by turning its back on this tendency. It is, instead, setting the worst possible example.

The abject surrender to the real or imagined wishes of the head of a single family has steadily robbed the Congress leadership of all initiative and all self-respect. The press and the public describe this as sycophancy. The sycophancy continues because it offers certain immediate and tangible political returns. Large sections of the Indian population, particularly in the countryside, from Amethi to Bellary, genuinely believe in the magic of genealogy, just as they believe in other forms of magic. The ageing and crafty leaders of the Congress know this well, and hope that they will benefit by playing on these beliefs. Those who gather votes by invoking family and kinship do no less harm to liberal democracy than their adversaries who mobilize political support by appealing to religion. Family, kinship and religion, each supremely important in its own sphere, poison the wells of public life when they seep into institutions that were designed to remain insulated from them.

28 October 1999

VIII
Tradition and Modernity

The Indian tradition is both rich and diverse, and it is difficult to speak of it as one single and unitary tradition. It has accommodated many new elements in the course of the centuries, and it has undergone many changes. Today, Indian society and culture are exposed to influences from outside to an extent that has no parallels in the past. I believe that Indian civilization is sufficiently resilient to be able to benefit from these influences without losing its own identity.

The attitudes of the Indian intelligentsia towards tradition and modernity are fluid and ambivalent. Respect for tradition does not call for an uncritical appreciation of every aspect of it, as I try to show in the essay 'Sense and Shastras' with reference to Bankimchandra, the great nineteenth century writer. Every tradition accumulates elements which succeeding generations find more or less unacceptable and in need of replacement by new elements. A tradition has a life of its own, although growth and decay do not follow the same temporal rhythm in it that they do in the life of an individual.

There are certain historical epochs in which people feel a strong urge to change the existing tradition root and branch in order to infuse new life into a stagnant social order. Something of this kind was felt in India around the time of Independence when many of the leaders of the nation wanted the rigid and hierarchical traditions of social life to be replaced by something more open and more flexible. It is in this context that we have to see the general and widespread critique of caste, and also Dr Ambedkar's celebrated attack on the village community in the Constituent Assembly.

In the early decades of independence, there was a certain public enthusiasm for the modernization of

Indian society. That enthusiasm began to cool down in later decades, and particularly after 1977, as the social costs of modernization began to be increasingly apparent. Today, modernization has come under attack from two sides, the traditionalist and the post-modernist. Traditionalists and post-modernists make strange bedfellows, but they are united by their common antipathy to modernity. To be sure, modernization has social costs, but the costs of shutting the door on modernization are much larger.

How Modern Are We?

How modern are we? This, I believe, is a question which preoccupies a large number of educated Indians. I am not thinking now merely of certain economic arrangements, but of a whole conception of social and cultural life whose connections with the former are at best only vaguely understood.

The concern for the kinds of programmes and policies which are likely to lead to greater economic prosperity is entirely commendable. Again, if in order to attain this prosperity we have to discard certain social habits and institutions which are dispensable, it would be well worth our while to know what the latter are. But very little will be gained by pretending that these habits and institutions do not exist, or that they have already become so attenuated that they will disappear in their natural course while we attend to the more urgent tasks of economic and political development.

Much as we may like to think otherwise, it will be hard to deny that many spheres of social life in India are still governed by traditional norms and values. Even the most modern among Indians marry in the traditional way, have deep and widespread attachments to their family and kin group, and at times display a concern for status and hierarchy which might shame an orthodox Brahmin. Yet there are remarkable inhibitions on their part to talk or even think of their own personal lives in terms of these institutions and values. Undoubtedly the inhibitions derive from the fact that they are still too closely involved in a pattern of social life whose existence they would like to wish away.

It is often said that Indian intellectuals, or more generally, the Indian middle classes, are cut off from the people at large. I think the situation is a little more complex. It is not that there are no links between the two but the attitude of the former towards these links is highly ambivalent. Most Indians, intellectuals or otherwise, have in fact close links with their society through the ties of kinship, caste and community. But this is often accompanied by an uneasy feeling that to recognize this fact would be to admit that one is traditional or even backward.

This probably is the reason why so many educated Indians suffer from a peculiar form of myopia when it comes to an understanding of their own society. They will assert that caste has become obsolete when even a casual examination of their own social circles should convince them of the rarity of inter-caste marriage. They will argue that urban Indians are becoming increasingly secular when there are many indications to the contrary. It is amazing how many educated Indians are convinced that the 'joint family system' is breaking down in spite of an almost complete absence of any firm evidence that this is indeed what is happening.

Any proper understanding of the problems of contemporary India will have to come to terms with the fact that India is still largely a traditional society. To take one example, the relations between the sexes (or between the generations) are very different here from what we consider such relations to be in the advanced industrial societies of the West. It is possible that when economic change comes, these also will change in India. But this is at best a piece of speculation. In the meantime we look at the statistical tables which tell us how many women are studying in universities or working in offices, and feel that a completely new pattern of relations is just round the corner.

Educated Indians are very sensitive on the question of caste, particularly when it is discussed in the presence of foreigners. Most of them believe, understandably, that caste is an unmixed evil (I am, of course, not suggesting that it is good). Many of them would like to think that it has ceased to exist at least as far as they themselves are concerned. Any discussion of caste with educated Indians is likely to reveal a certain amount of embarrassment and a great deal of ignorance. For most of them caste is something that belongs to India's shameful and backward past and to be preoccupied with it today is perhaps to indicate a morbid or obscurantist temperament.

Very recently a certain interest has been created in caste because of its widely-reported role in politics. This role again is evaluated in different ways. For one thing it is viewed as representing only one aspect of Indian society, its more traditional and backward aspect. For another it is believed to be something purely transitional, to be replaced by a more 'rational' pattern of politics.

But caste plays a part in many spheres of Indian life, and not just in politics or in the rural areas. It still restricts marriage and other forms of social interchange. More important, the conceptions of hierarchy, on which the traditional caste system was based, are carried over into many areas of modern social life. The real significance of caste in modern India may well be that it provides a model for hierarchy in terms of which many of the newly emerging relations are ordered.

India is not only a traditional society, it is one in which more than 20 per cent of the population is officially classified as backward (If we include the other backward classes the proportion will be considerably higher). There is a widespread tendency to simplify the problem of the Harijans (and also of the Adivasis) and to view it in direct economic terms. Actually their position in Indian society owes as much to the ritual values of purity and pollution as to economic factors. Economic disparities in India are tied to religious values as both cause and consequence.

Kinship, caste and religion—these are among the major areas of life studied by sociologists in India. They are problems which directly concern the vast body of Indians who live in some 550,000 villages spread throughout the country. They concern particularly the scheduled castes the scheduled tribes and the other backward classes who together constitute about half of the total population. They concern also, though perhaps less manifestly, the urban middle classes including the top sections among them whose members are responsible for shaping the country's policies.

Much of the conventional wisdom about Indian society derives from the experiences and above all, the aspirations of its middle class. The Indian middle class has long been under the spell of western civilization not only in its technically efficient aspects, but also in other regards. It is natural that under western influence, educated Indians should have developed a critical attitude towards their traditional culture. But they generally go beyond that; they often become self-consciously virtuous about their own emancipation from tradition and develop psychological blocks towards those aspects of their culture which are likely to appear backward or ridiculous in western eyes.

The image of Indian society that has emerged from this naturally suffers from a number of distortions. But which aspects of this society should be accorded priority in discussion and analysis will itself depend upon the image of it. I have noticed that educated Indians often regard the sociologist's preoccupation with kinship, caste and ritual as obscurantist or even reactionary. Perhaps they feel a little of the same moral indignation with which a Nayar informant told a British anthropologist: 'We have no customs.' After all it is only too human to feel that if we do have customs which appear odd in relation to our explicit ideals, it is best not to talk too much about them.

The task of the sociologist is to study values and institutions of every kind, including the ones which appear odd by certain standards. In any society, sociologists may play a conservative or a radical role. In India they are usually viewed as playing a conservative part. This is largely because of their preoccupation with problems which are considered remote and therefore trivial from the viewpoint of upper-middle class aspirations. People who study kinship, caste and ritual are regarded as backward-looking, as being obsessed with institutions which have become or are becoming defunct. But a wider perspective may well show that these are the institutions of the great majority of Indians and that they probably have far greater staying power than is commonly believed.

There is a good deal of mystification in the conventional wisdom purveyed by middle-class intellectuals in India. This mystification is so deep and far reaching that one often fails to notice it. One of its principal sources seems to be the urge to appear modern and consequently to shy away from anything that might appear as a reminder of the essentially traditional and backward nature of one's own society. It is in this context that the sociologist should strive for the 'demystification' of widely held notions regarding what is basic and what is superficial in our contemporary society.

4 July 1968

Sense and Shastras

Bankimchandra's essay on polygamy is not widely known among those who are unfamiliar with Bengali, even though it has been available in an English translation for some time. It is remarkable for its exposure of the pitfalls of using intellectual sophistry in the cause of social reform. It also throws an interesting light on our present predicament over a uniform civil code.

The essay was a polemic against the redoubtable social reformer, Ishwarchandra Vidyasagar, who was regarded by many, including Bankim, as the greatest Sanskrit pundit of his time. Vidyasagar had taken up cudgels against the practice of polygamy and argued, firstly, that it was against the shastras, and hence, secondly, that it should be prohibited by law. Bankim took issue with him on both counts.

It should be said at the outset that Bankim himself was against polygamy. But he was opposed to it because he found it to be against reason and good sense, and not because it was contrary to the shastras. The past history of polygamy was not an important consideration in determining how we should deal with it in the present. Displaying a parade of learning to confound the defenders of polygamy did little good to the cause of either social reform or learning. This argument has some relevance for the present-day champions of secularism who take great pains to establish by historical research that several kings and emperors of the past, both Muslim and Hindu, were of a very secular disposition. They were probably nothing of the kind, but that cannot go against the case for a secular state today.

Vidyasagar's appeal to the shastras to establish the case against polygamy was demolished with some relish. Bankim first pointed out that pundits had invoked the authority of the shastras on both sides of the case. Being a man of limited learning, he could not decide which was the correct interpretation of the shastras. He was prepared to accept the authority of Vidyasagar since he was the most learned among the pundits, but he was at the same time worried by the thought that an even more learned pundit might emerge in the future and declare that polygamy was in conformity with the shastras and not against them as Vidyasagar maintained. What would one do in that event?

Bankim then went on to say that for all his great learning, Vidyasagar did not in fact reveal all that had been written in the shastras on the subject of marriage. There seemed to be no end to the conditions listed in them under which a man was permitted to discard an unsatisfactory wife and secure a fresh one. If one went by the shastras, one could suit one's convenience and select one or another rule from any number of those that were available. The urge to find a prescription in the shastras for every contemporary problem was irksome to Bankim. It is worth quoting him on the subject: 'Indeed, it is not possible for any society to be fully regulated by all the prescriptions to be found in the shastras of Manu and the others. It is doubtful if ever, at any time, those prescriptions were fully operative in any society. Many of them are inoperable. Many, though operable, involve such hardships to man that they would drop out on their own. Many are mutually contradictory. If any society is ever destined to keep all these prescriptions in operation, such a society must indeed have an evil destiny.' He used the same vitriol in attacking punditry of the Arabic as well as the Sanskritic variety. In the matter of social reform, appealing to reason was far better than appealing to the shastras.

Bankim was against polygamy, but he did not favour using the strong arm of the government to put it down. He argued that polygamy was already declining, that public opinion was turning against it, and that it should be allowed to die a natural death. Nothing much was to be gained by working up a frenzy against something that not many persons were any longer prepared to defend on grounds of principle.

It would be particularly inappropriate, Bankim maintained, to ask an alien government to enact a law against polygamy on the ground that it was contrary to the Hindu shastras. He pointed out that half the inhabitants of Bengal were Hindus and half were Muslims. 'If there is to be a law for the prohibition of polygamy, that law ought to be for both Hindus and Muslims. But how can polygamy be prohibited and made a punishable offence for the Muslims on the ground that it is against the Hindu Shastras?' He drew attention sharply to the dilemma the state would have to face in having to legislate social reform involving religious sentiment and at the same time remain impartial towards all its subjects.

It would of course be absurd to argue in principle against legislating for social reform. Indeed, the state has a duty to use its legislative powers to eliminate social evils and create conditions for better social practices. But

Bankim was writing about the state under a colonial regime and not a sovereign democratic regime. In today's context, the state should be able to act with much greater confidence in its capacity to carry public opinion with it and even to shape it through legislative action. The abolition of untouchability is a case in point. What the colonial state was unable or unwilling to do was done firmly and decisively by the Constitution of India.

Even in a democratic regime there are limits to which social reform can be driven through legislation. Societies change through the operation of many different currents among which legislation is not always or necessarily the decisive one. Where the deeper currents operating in a society are not clearly understood or wished out of existence, the actual consequences of an act of legislation may be the opposite of its intention. These sensible, though conservative, arguments were presented by Bankim with remarkable force and clarity. The present turmoil over a uniform civil code is something that he would have easily understood. His recommendations on it would no doubt have been different from ours. But we may still benefit from his penetrating insight into the problems to be faced by sweeping attempts at social engineering.

Legislation has an important role in giving direction to social reform, but society has a way of extracting its price when the limits of that role are ignored. As I have said, it can be effective only when legislators are able to carry public opinion with them and give it a focus. It is true that the scope of legislation is larger in a democratic regime than in a colonial one. But it is not unlimited. Democratic leaders have much to gain from the support of the people, but they also have much to lose from their opposition. In the mid-fifties, when the Hindu Code Bill was being enacted, our legislators had confidence in their own integrity and in the support of the people. That confidence has largely evaporated, and now they can only flounder around, making more and more laws that are less and less effective.

3 February 1996

Assault on Secularism

Indians who have set their hearts and minds against secularism will not fail to take note of the adoption of the Shariat Bill by the National Assembly of Pakistan. Some of them may envy the direct and forthright manner in which Nawaz Sharif has sought to replace secular by religious principles in the governance of his country. Support for such a measure is easier to secure in Pakistan than in India, for in these matters both history and demography give a clear advantage to our neighbours over us. It will require less exertion to base the Constitution of Pakistan on the sharia than to base the Indian Constitution on the *Dharmashastra*. But should we regard this as a matter for regret and set Pakistan up as the guide to our future?

India is larger and socially more diverse than Pakistan, and it has gone further along the road to modernity. Turning back will be much more difficult for India than for Pakistan. Our secular legal and constitutional order has not done all the work it was expected to do. But undoing the work that has already been done will exact incalculable social and political costs.

We should not underestimate the hostility to secularism in India, and the many sources from which it draws its sustenance. There is antipathy to secular ways of life and to secular principles of governance, but the two kinds of antipathy do not necessarily spring from the same source. Much of the hostility to secularism is derived from our lack of ease with modernity and the modern world which is dominated economically, politically and culturally by the West. It is understandable that secularism should be viewed with mistrust by the masses of Indians who have made very little progress along the path of modernization. But it has also come under attack from an unexpected quarter: from cosmopolitan and well-travelled intellectuals who have tasted of the bitter fruit of what they call 'post-Enlightenment modernity'. The opposition to secularism is creating some very strange bedfellows in this country.

The secularization that is characteristic of our times is a diffuse and pervasive process whose consequences are always far-reaching though often unanticipated. It is not necessarily destructive of religion in the true sense of the term, although it is easy to represent it as such. What it does is to bring about a change in the place of religion in the social order, particularly in the public domain. The opponents of secularism, both traditional and post-modern, argue on the other hand that there can be only a religious morality and no secular morality, and that secularization is destructive of both religion and morality.

What needs to be stressed is that the opposition to secularism does not arise solely from feelings of religious piety. Some of the leading intellectual opponents of secularism are in their own lives remarkably free from any kind of religious encumbrance. Their opposition has less to do with religion than with politics and culture. At the same time, their arguments serve to fuel the passions of those who do adhere to established religious beliefs and practices. In a country like India—or Pakistan—it does not take much to convince the masses of impoverished, undernourished and uneducated people that whatever is modern or of western provenance is godless, immoral and socially disruptive.

What appears as disingenuous in the intellectual stance described above is not so much the critique of secularism as the promise of an alternative social order packaged along with the critique. Over the last fifty years there has been growing disenchantment, particularly among the intelligentsia, over the poor performance of our secular Constitution, our secular legal system and our secular public institutions. None can deny the yawning gap here between expectation and attainment. But to be disenchanted with all of this is one thing and to put the responsibility for communalism, casteism and social violence on the advance of secular ideas and institutions is quite another. If we have failed to keep religion and politics apart, surely this has happened despite our secular Constitution and not because of it.

Disenchantment with the present should not lead to the construction of an imaginary past and a programme for the future modelled on that past. It is increasingly argued that our present form of secularism, based on western ideas of modernity and progress, is a sham, and that true secularism, based on the tolerance of diversity, is what prevailed in our own society before modernization began its disruptive work. The latter is at best a half-truth. The tolerance of the past included the tolerance of a great deal that ought not to be tolerated in a democratic society based on the rule of law: the indignity, oppression and violence inflicted on women, Harijans, Adivasis and many others. The challenge before secularism today is to create tolerance among communities on the basis of equality and not on the basis of hierarchy as in the old social order.

There is no denying the violence and disorder associated with our modern secular legal and political order. Communal riots and caste pogroms have become the staple of the print as well as the electronic media. The forms of violence have changed with changes in the technology of violence. But we should not delude ourselves into believing that there was little or no violence in pre-modern India. Violence inevitably takes a different form in a democratic as against a hierarchical society. We will never be able to reckon the scope and extent of the violence inflicted on disadvantaged members of society and tolerated by them in their everyday life in the past. The daily violence that people inflict upon their acknowledged inferiors has a less dramatic appearance than the outbursts of violence that they practise against their equals, their near equals and their would-be equals.

Nawaz Sharif has said that laws based on the sharia will act as a bulwark against terrorism, gang rape and other forms of social and political disorder. He has also said that those laws will give the fullest protection to women and to the minorities. Anti-secularist intellectuals will decide for themselves what they will make of such declarations. The rest of us can only hope that it will not be argued in our Parliament that recasting the Constitution of India along the lines of the *Dharmashastra* will ensure a better future for women, Harijans and Adivasis.

29 October 1998

Fear of Modernity

What should be the attitude to tradition of the reasonable man? There are those who demand adherence to tradition at any cost and ask that it be made the measure of all things. There are others for whom tradition is merely an encumbrance to be disposed of as unceremoniously as possible. The two attitudes are equally untenable, and, unfortunately, the prejudices of the diehard traditionalist and those of the unthinking modernist reinforce each other.

For the sociologist it is a truism that no society can move into the future without some attention to what it has inherited from the past. Just as each generation does not create the language that it speaks, so also does it not create on its own its everyday beliefs and practices. The significance of tradition is easily recognized in the domains of music, painting and the arts. But tradition is indispensable also for science which could hardly advance unless each generation of scientists built on the work of the preceding generation. In science as in the arts, a tradition is kept alive by being subjected to continual scrutiny and renewal. There is all the difference in the world between a tradition that is alive and hence forward-looking and one that is lifeless and backward-looking.

The problem in contemporary India is that 'tradition' is coming to be increasingly used as a weapon of offence and defence in the culture wars among politicians and politically-minded members of the intelligentsia. This is altogether different from the way in which tradition enters the life and work of the craftsman, the painter, the musician, the scholar or even the scientist. One can work within a certain tradition and build one's work on it without being an advocate of tradition as such. One can, on the other hand, champion the cause of tradition in public without engaging actively in any tradition in either one's life or one's work. What has become a source of anxiety is that the champions of tradition in the political arena are backward- rather than forward-looking, and that tradition is increasingly becoming an alibi for backwardness.

There are three points that must be kept in mind if we are to proceed with a serious discussion of tradition. Firstly, when we speak of India as a whole, we have to speak of tradition in the plural and not just in the singular. Secondly, tradition should not be equated with sheer antiquity; it is less a matter of old age than of filiation and continuity. Thirdly, some traditions decay and die while others are born and grow to maturity; there is no point of time at which society declares a moratorium on the birth of new traditions.

It is natural that a country with such a large and diverse population as ours and with such a long history should have a plurality of traditions. India is the home of more than a dozen important languages, each with its own literary traditions as well as of some of the major religions of the world, each with its own traditions of piety and observance. It has in the course of a very long history incorporated into its stream of life beliefs and practices from many different parts of the world, and has been remarkable in the extent of its tolerance of diversity.

Many will say that it is not enough to point to the plurality of traditions in India. One has also to ask if these diverse traditions, some very particular and local and others of wider scope, are not related to one another and to something larger than each or any one of them. No doubt the different parts are connected, but they are connected as in a kaleidoscope in which the pattern changes with every change in the angle of vision. The unity of the national tradition in a country such as ours can at best be a loose one, and that unity cannot in any case be imposed or sustained by state power.

National traditions are not only loosely integrated, but the boundaries between them are always porous, enabling more or less easy and continuous interchange of elements among them. The receptivity of a tradition to new elements from outside is an index of its health. Traditions prosper and flourish when they are forward-looking and keep their frontiers open; they become atrophied and moribund when they close their boundaries and become backward-looking.

Today, new elements of belief and practice travel with unprecedented speed from one end of the world to the other. Is the Indian tradition, or, rather, are the various traditions that have grown in India receptive and resilient enough to cope with the challenges and opportunities of a rapidly changing world? Modernization is by no means a painless process, and it does not spread its costs evenly among societies, or among the different classes and communities within the same society. But society as a whole pays a higher price in the end by turning its back on the changes emanating from the outside world in order to safeguard all its ingrained beliefs and practices.

Classes, communities and parties that are unable or unwilling to cope with the strains of modernization invoke the sanctity and the inviolability of the national tradition in order to resist it. They use tradition as a shield to protect themselves from many things that cannot and should not be resisted. Their passions are fuelled not by the love of tradition but by the fear of modernity.

For those who use it as a political weapon, tradition is one single thing and not a multiplicity of things, and it is something that prevailed in the remote and mythical past rather than in recent and historical times. The traditions in science, pedagogy or even politics that have grown in the last hundred and fifty years have little meaning or value for them. They wish to do away with all modern institutions which they label as western or alien, but they cannot live without the fruits of those institutions; and they lack the imagination and the ability to construct effective alternatives to them. They create fantasies of the distant past in order to set at rest their anxieties about the present and the future. Nobody who seeks to cancel out a society's immediate and recent past and to do away with all the resources created during it can be said to take tradition seriously.

14 December 1998

Trials of Indian Democracy

Indian democracy has been sailing through troubled waters in the last couple of decades. It is not that there were no problems in the first quarter century after Independence. But these problems began to show an increasingly acute form with the Emergency and its aftermath. Within a short span of five years, the people of India experienced the two most fundamental threats to the democratic form of governance: authoritarianism and its twin, anarchy.

The success of democracy depends upon a number of different factors among which good laws are of great significance. The Constitution of India provides a very comprehensive framework for such laws. No Constitution, no matter how carefully designed, can be perfect or can anticipate every exigency that is likely to arise in the life of a nation. Our Constitution has had to accommodate some eighty amendments in the course of less than fifty years. In addition, there has been a plethora of legislation to facilitate the smooth and efficient working of democracy.

However suitable each of these laws might be in its own context, the increasing volume of legislation has not led to any marked improvement in the working of democracy. Some have begun to feel that creating laws piecemeal to meet every passing exigency can only deepen the crisis of governance. What is required, they believe, is a comprehensive review of the Constitution which alone can show a way out of the crisis. It is said in particular that the parliamentary system of government, well suited though it might be to a small and homogeneous country like Britain, cannot work smoothly in a large, complex and highly differentiated society such as ours. Hence, for democracy to work well in India, new laws will have to be created that will change the very structure of governance.

The success of democracy or, indeed, of any social institution, depends not only on good laws but also on favourable customs. It is these customs that give expression to the habits of the heart, so to say, and if only the laws change, leaving the customs as they were, no new form of governance can be expected to achieve its objectives. At the time of Independence all the effort was concentrated on the creation of a good Constitution and good laws, and it was hoped that these would set the pace for the required changes in established attitudes and sentiments. Not enough thought was given to the inertia and the obduracy of custom. Legislators, judges and lawyers all spoke boldly and clearly in favour of new and progressive laws. The sociologists who knew something of the obduracy of custom had but a small voice in the affairs of the nation; and they held their peace for fear of being labelled as conservative and backward-looking.

Today, the gap between law and custom remains as wide as it was fifty years ago, and its implications are still not taken seriously by the intelligentsia. Nowhere is the gap between the two more glaring than in the context of equality. This is of some significance here since equality is inseparably linked to the very idea of democracy. While all democratic systems make some concessions to various forms of inequality, no democracy can function effectively without a certain basic equality in human relations. In India, the laws are all on the side of equality, but custom puts almost its entire weight on the opposite side.

It has been said that the guarantees of equality in the Constitution of India add up to more than the guarantees in the British and the US Constitutions taken together. Yet everyday social life is still governed substantially by the hierarchical attitudes and sentiments carried over from the past. The awe for those who are superior by birth or social position and the contempt towards social inferiors are equally widespread in the rural and the urban areas, and among the educated and the uneducated. In politics in particular, the relations between leader and follower are marked by deference and submissiveness to an unusual degree, and this makes the free and open exchange of ideas and opinions impossible. Here, as in many other matters, the Congress party is the best exemplar of our political culture. For this the blame cannot lie alone with any single individual or family; it lies with leaders and followers alike.

These habits of deference and submissiveness must not be confused with civility which is a very different thing and an invaluable asset for democracy. Deference and submissiveness towards the leaders of one's party, faction or group are usually accompanied by rude, intemperate and abusive conduct towards political adversaries. Both types of conduct are now on regular display on our various television channels.

The success of democracy requires a certain commitment to impersonal rules and a certain willingness to be governed by them, irrespective of immediate consequences. Our customs give greater weight to persons than to rules: personal attachments, loyalties, grievances and animosities often become decisive. Explaining her vote in the no-confidence motion on 17 April, the leader of the Bahujan Samaj Party said that, although she did not reveal her mind during the debate, she had decided well in advance to vote against Vajpayee in order to give a fitting reply to the BJP for what it had done to her and her party in Uttar Pradesh. Her conduct was in line with the age-old customs of village politics; it is doubtful that those customs are conducive to the working of a modern democracy.

More than a hundred and fifty years ago, Alexis de Tocqueville had pointed out in his great work, *Democracy in America*, that good customs contribute even more to the success of democracy than good laws. He had compared the Americans favourably with his own countrymen, the French. He had said that the French were adept at making laws but that their customs were not as beneficial as those of the Americans, which was why democracy was more vigorous in America than in France. We are, if anything, even more adept than the French at making laws, but our customs hold us back even more strongly. Good laws are indeed indispensable, but the mere multiplication of laws without any thought for the inertia and obduracy of custom is not likely to lead us out of the troubled waters in which we find ourselves today.

29 April 1999

20X1373 $\frac{1}{2}$
366